Exploring English Language Teaching

D0220229

Routledge Introductions to Applied Linguistics is a series of introductory level textbooks covering the core topics in Applied Linguistics, primarily designed for those entering postgraduate studies and language professionals returning to academic study. The books take an innovative 'practice to theory' approach, with a 'back-to-front' structure. This leads the reader from real-world problems and issues, through a discussion of intervention and how to engage with these concerns, before finally relating these practical issues to theoretical foundations.

Exploring English Language Teaching provides a single volume introduction to the field of ELT from an applied linguistics perspective. The book addresses four central themes within English language teaching: 'Classroom interaction and management'; 'Method, Postmethod and methodology'; 'Learners'; and the 'Institutional frameworks and social contexts' of ELT. For each, the book identifies key dilemmas and practices, examines how teachers and other language teaching professionals might intervene and deal with these concerns, and explores how such issues link to and inform applied linguistic theory.

This second edition has been extensively revised and updated to explore the latest practical developments and theoretical insights in the field of ELT. With new material, including expanded discussions of CLIL, the role of new technologies in ELT, and the teaching of large classes in difficult circumstances, and with an updated glossary and suggestions for additional reading, this is an indispensable textbook for language teachers and students studying in the areas of Applied Linguistics, Language Teacher Education, and ELT/TESOL.

Graham Hall is Associate Professor of Applied Linguistics/TESOL at Northumbria University, UK. He is the editor of *The Routledge Handbook of English Language Teaching* (Routledge, 2016).

Routledge Introductions to Applied Linguistics

Series editors:

Ronald Carter, *Professor of Modern English Language, University of Nottingham, UK*

Guy Cook, *Professor of Language and Education King's College London, UK*

Routledge Introductions to Applied Linguistics is a series of introductory level textbooks covering the core topics in Applied Linguistics, primarily designed for those entering postgraduate studies and language professionals returning to academic study. The books take an innovative 'practice to theory' approach, with a 'back-to-front' structure. This leads the reader from real-world problems and issues, through a discussion of intervention and how to engage with these concerns, before finally relating these practical issues to theoretical foundations. Additional features include tasks with commentaries, a glossary of key terms and an annotated further reading section.

Exploring Language Assessment and Testing
Language in Action
Anthony Green

Exploring Digital Communication
Language in Action
Caroline Tagg

'The innovative approach devised by the series' editors will make this series very attractive to students, teacher educators, and even to a general readership, wanting to explore and understand the field of applied linguistics. The volumes in this series take as their starting point the everyday professional problems and issues that applied linguists seek to illuminate. The volumes are authoritatively written, using an engaging "back-to-front" structure that moves from practical interests to the conceptual bases and theories that underpin applications of practice.'

Anne Burns, Aston University, UK

For more information on any of these and other titles, or to order, please go to www.routledge.com/Routledge-Introductions-to-Applied-Linguistics/book-series/RIAL

Additional resources for Language and Communication are available on the Routledge Language and Communication Portal: http://dev.routledgetextbooks.uk.corplan.net/textbooks/languageandcommunication

Exploring English Language Teaching

Language in Action

Second Edition

Graham Hall

Routledge
Taylor & Francis Group

LONDON AND NEW YORK

Second edition published 2018
by Routledge
2 Park Square, Milton Park, Abingdon, Oxon, OX14 4RN

and by Routledge
711 Third Avenue, New York, NY 10017

Routledge is an imprint of the Taylor & Francis Group, an informa business

© 2018 Graham Hall

The right of Graham Hall to be identified as author of this work
has been asserted by him in accordance with sections 77 and 78
of the Copyright, Designs and Patents Act 1988.

First edition published by Routledge 2011

British Library Cataloguing-in-Publication Data
A catalogue record for this book is available from the British Library

Library of Congress Cataloging-in-Publication Data
Names: Hall, Graham, 1969– author.
Title: Exploring English language teaching / by Graham Hall.
Description: Second edition. | Milton Park, Abingdon, Oxon ;
New York, NY : Routledge, [2017] | Series: Routledge Introductions
to Applied Linguistics | Includes bibliographical references and index.
Identifiers: LCCN 2017014260| ISBN 9781138722781 (hardback) |
ISBN 9781138722811 (pbk.) | ISBN 9781315193380 (ebook)
Subjects: LCSH: English language—Study and teaching—Foreign
speakers. | English teachers—Training of.
Classification: LCC PE1128.A2 H285 2017 | DDC 428.0071—dc23
LC record available at https://lccn.loc.gov/2017014260

ISBN: 978-1-138-72278-1 (hbk)
ISBN: 978-1-138-72281-1 (pbk)
ISBN: 978-1-3151-9338-0 (ebk)

Typeset in Sabon and Helvetica Neue by
Florence Production Ltd, Stoodleigh, Devon

Visit the companion website: http://routledgetextbooks.com/
textbooks/_author/rial/

To Keith and Audrey;

to Helen;

and to Georgia and Rosa.

Contents

Tables and figures

Tables

Figures

Acknowledgements

Many people have contributed to this second edition of *Exploring English Language Teaching*. Once again, many thanks to the series editors, Guy Cook and Ronald Carter, who have provided generous encouragement throughout the development of the book, both as I have been writing it and between editions. Thanks also to Louisa Semlyen and Laura Sandford at Routledge for giving me the opportunity to revise and update the book to reflect developments both in ELT and in my understanding of the field between editions. I hope I manage to convey these changes – some notable, some more nuanced – to readers.

Like all books, this edition draws upon the work of others. Paul Booth, Deborah Cole and Diane Slaouti provided invaluable comment on the first edition and suggested possible ways forward; further feedback from teachers, teacher educators, other ELT professionals and applied linguists who have encountered *Exploring English Language Teaching* has been incredibly helpful. Additionally, any text which tries to bring together the diverse and complex undertaking that is ELT owes an enormous debt to all the teachers, researchers, thinkers and writers who have shaped the field, many of whom are referred to throughout this book. Among them, the teaching and research of Dick Allwright have particularly shaped my ideas about ELT. All errors, misrepresentations and omissions in the text are, of course, my responsibility.

Finally, to my family. Thanks to my parents and brother for their love and support as I have explored ELT over the years. And thanks, as ever, to Helen and our girls, Georgia and Rosa, not only for their love, care, and cups of tea, but also for their questions, comments and clarity about this book. This edition is dedicated to my parents and to them.

Permissions

The publishers would like to thank the following copyright holders for permission to reprint material:

Extract from Corbridge-Pataniowska, M. (1992) *Teach yourself Polish*, John Murray Press, an imprint of Hodder & Stoughton.

Extract from the Cambridge and Nottingham Corpus of Discourse in English (CANCODE) "In the hair salon" in Ronald Carter, Michael McCarthy, Exploring Spoken English, 1997, Copyright Cambridge University Press, reprinted with permission.

Every effort has been made to contact copyright-holders. Please advise the publisher of any errors or omissions, and these will be corrected in subsequent editions.

Series editors' introduction

The *Introducing Applied Linguistics* series

This series provides clear, authoritative, up-to-date overviews of the major areas of applied linguistics. The books are designed particularly for students embarking on masters-level or teacher-education courses, as well as students in the closing stages of undergraduate study. The practical focus will make the books particularly useful and relevant to those returning to academic study after a period of professional practice, and also to those about to leave the academic world for the challenges of language-related work. For students who have not previously studied applied linguistics, including those who are unfamiliar with current academic study in English-speaking universities, the books can act as one-step introductions. For those with more academic experience, they can also provide a way of surveying, updating and organizing existing knowledge.

The view of applied linguistics in this series follows a famous definition of the field by Christopher Brumfit as:

> The theoretical and empirical investigation of real-world problems in which language is a central issue.
>
> (Brumfit, 1995: 27)

In keeping with this broad problem-oriented view, the series will cover a range of topics of relevance to a variety of language-related professions. While language teaching and learning rightly remain prominent and will be the central preoccupation of many readers, our conception of the discipline is by no means limited to these areas. Our view is that while each reader of the series will have their own needs, specialities and interests, there is also much to be gained from a broader view of the discipline as a whole. We believe there is much in common between all enquiries into language-related problems in the real world, and much to be gained from a comparison of the insights from one area of applied linguistics with another. Our hope therefore is that readers and course designers will not choose only those volumes relating to their own particular interests, but use this series to construct a wider knowledge and understanding of the field, and the many crossovers and resonances between its various areas. Thus the topics to be covered are wide in range, embracing an exciting mixture of established and new areas of applied linguistic enquiry.

The perspective on applied linguistics in this series

In line with this problem-oriented definition of the field, and to address the concerns of readers who are interested in how academic study can inform their own professional practice, each book follows a structure in marked contrast to the usual movement *from* theory *to* practice. In this series, this usual progression is presented back to front. The argument moves *from* Problems, *through* Intervention, and *only* finally to Theory. Thus each topic begins with a survey of everyday professional problems in the area under consideration, ones that the reader is likely to have encountered. From there it proceeds to a discussion of intervention and engagement with these problems. Only in a final section (either of the chapter or the book as a whole) does the author reflect upon the implications of this engagement for a general understanding of language, drawing out the theoretical implications. We believe this to be a truly *applied* linguistics perspective, in line with the definition given above, and one in which engagement with real-world problems is the distinctive feature, and in which professional practice can both inform and draw upon academic understanding.

Support to the reader

Although it is not the intention that the text should be in any way activity-driven, the pedagogic process is supported by measured guidance to the reader in the form of suggested activities and tasks that raise questions, prompt reflection and seek to integrate theory and practice. Each book also contains a helpful glossary of key terms.

The series complements and reflects the *Routledge Handbook of Applied Linguistics*, edited by James Simpson, which conceives and categorizes the scope of applied linguistics in a broadly similar way.

Ronald Carter
Guy Cook

Reference

Brumfit, C. J. (1995) 'Teacher Professionalism and Research', in G. Cook and B. Seidlhofer (eds) *Principle and Practice in Applied Linguistics*. Oxford: Oxford University Press, 27–42.

Note

There is a section of commentaries on a number of the tasks, at the back of the book from p. 257. The (TC) symbol in the margin indicates that there is a commentary on that task.

Part I

Classroom interaction and management

1 The language classroom

Roles, relationships and interactions

the classroom is the true centre of the educational experience, and ... it is here, through the teaching-and-learning process, that education 'happens'.

(Wright, 2005: 1)

This chapter will:

- consider the social as well as pedagogic character of English language teaching classrooms;
- explore how teachers assume a variety of roles in class, and investigate how these roles may affect language learning and 'classroom life';
- investigate how patterns of classroom interaction, including teacher and learner talk, error and corrective feedback and teachers' questions, may affect opportunities for language learning;
- encourage readers to reflect on their own beliefs and classroom practices, while acknowledging possible alternatives.

Introduction: thinking about the 'ELT classroom'

English language classrooms are complicated places. Common sense tells us that classrooms are places where 'people, typically one teacher and a number of learners, come together for a pedagogical purpose' (Allwright, 1992: 267). However, in addition to their physical (or virtual) location and pedagogic function, classrooms are also *social* environments, that is, language lessons can be understood as social events based upon social relationships and social interaction (Erikson, 1986; Breen, 2001a; Tudor, 2001), where 'events interweave, as participants experience them' (Wright, 2012: 61). The beliefs and expectations of parents, institutional managers and governmental agencies *beyond* the classroom and the relationships between the participants *in* the classroom (i.e., teachers and learners) affect classroom practices and behaviour. Thus:

> The classroom is not a world unto itself. The participants . . . arrive at the event with certain ideas as to what is a 'proper' lesson, and in their actions and interaction they will strive to implement these ideas. In addition the society at large and the institution the classroom is part of have certain expectations and demands which exert influence on the way the classrooms turn out.
>
> (van Lier, 1988a: 179)

Clearly, therefore, *diversity* and *complexity* are fundamental elements of language teaching and learning, and of language classrooms (Tudor, 2001; Williams *et al.*, 2015). Given the number of participants who in some way affect what happens in a language classroom, and the varied local contexts in which English language teaching (ELT) takes place, each classroom is unique; and it is this human and contextual complexity (Tudor, 2001) that makes classroom language teaching 'messy' (Freeman, 1996). What goes on in a classroom is inevitably much more than the logical and tidy application of theories and principle; it is localized, situation-specific, and, therefore, diverse. Indeed, using the metaphor of 'coral gardens' to convey their socially complex and diverse nature, Breen (2001a) has suggested that individual language classrooms develop their own specific character and culture. (As we shall see in Chapter 3, where we shall examine the image of 'coral gardens' in more detail, metaphor has proved a particularly useful way in which teachers and applied linguists have characterized and explained language classrooms and language teaching.) Recognizing the complex and diverse nature of ELT classrooms around the world, and the social as well as pedagogical aspects of classroom life, is the starting point of our exploration of roles, relationships and interactions in second language (L2) classrooms. How might teachers organize and manage their classrooms and learners, and what practical dilemmas do they face when doing so?

Before we proceed: teacher beliefs and classroom practice

Much has been written about the links between teachers' beliefs (also sometimes labelled 'personal theories') and their classroom behaviour (e.g., Crookes, 2003; S. Borg, 2006). M. Borg (2001: 186) summarizes a belief as:

> A proposition which may be consciously or unconsciously held, is evaluative in that it is accepted as true by the individual . . . [and] serves as a guide to thought and behaviour.

Although terms such as 'rules of thumb' or 'teacher lore' (Crookes, 2003) may appear to downplay their importance, as Crookes remarks (47), 'it is impossible to act, as a teacher, without having theories (including values) that inform teaching actions, at least to some degree'.

Equally notable is that teachers' beliefs are derived from and influenced by a range of sources including the perspectives of others (e.g., colleagues, teacher-trainers and educators, and academic research and researchers) and their own practical experience of what is and is not successful. This suggests that a two-way relationship exists between beliefs and practice, with beliefs informing (but not determining) practice and, vice versa, practice informing what an individual may believe.

However, even establishing what teachers (indeed, anyone) actually believe is extremely challenging, involving, as it does, issues of consciousness (e.g., have I ever consciously thought about a topic before? do I really know what I think about it?), the ways in which peoples' ideas change over time, how articulate a person is at expressing their beliefs, and social pressures and expectations on speakers that cause them to modify what they may reveal. Several researchers have also found mismatches between what teachers say they believe and what their classroom practices actually seem to demonstrate (e.g., Phipps and S. Borg, 2009). The potential role contextual and institutional factors might have in affecting and constraining teachers' behaviour should also be acknowledged (as we shall see in later chapters).

That said, at some level, teachers' classroom practices are informed by their personal theories in areas as broad as 'what is teaching?' and 'what role should the teacher and learners take in the classroom?', through to the more specific 'how should learners be organized and seated in classroom activities?' and 'how should language be elicited . . . and corrected?'. Sometimes, this is through deliberate and explicit thought and reflection; sometimes, however, it is through implicit, taken-for-granted assumptions, or beliefs that were previously learned or instilled on teacher training programmes and which are now realized through routine (and routinized) teaching practices.

Thus, teachers should not be viewed as 'skilled technicians who dutifully realize a given set of teaching procedures in accordance with the directives of a more or less distant authority' (Tudor, 2001: 17). Instead:

> Teachers are active participants in the creation of classroom realities, and they act in the light of their own beliefs, attitudes, and perceptions of the relevant teaching situation . . . we need to be aware of 'the unique contribution which each individual brings to the learning situation' (Williams and Burden, 1997: 95).
>
> (Tudor, 2001: 17–18)

Task 1.1 Thinking through 'beliefs'

- What are your beliefs about the ideas that 'errors in the language classroom should be corrected as soon as they are made' and 'getting learners to work in pairs or groups is the most effective way of promoting learning in the ELT classroom'?

- What other beliefs do you have about how English is taught? For example:

  - What is/are the most appropriate role(s) for the teacher and learners in the L2 classroom?

  - How much should teachers and learners talk in class?

  - Should the learners' first language (ever) be used in class? If so, when and by whom, how and how much? If not, why not?

  - What is the most effective way of arranging the desks and seats in an L2 classroom?

- Have your ideas and beliefs about how to teach English changed over time? How? Why?

- Can you think of an example where what you do in class seems clearly related to what you think you believe about how to teach English?

- Can you think of another example, this time where what you do in class seems to contradict what you think you believe about English language teaching? Why do you think this is?

Thinking about classrooms: exploring teacher roles

We can see, therefore, that how teachers manage classrooms, and the roles that they and learners enact in class, will vary according to their beliefs and their teaching context. However, although teachers (and learners) may be more comfortable with one particular way of organizing teaching and learning compared to another (e.g., 'teaching from the front' compared to group-based discovery activities), they are likely, of course, to take on more than one role in the classroom, switching between them as required. Additionally, how teaching is conceptualized – as the transmission of knowledge from teachers to learners, or as the provision of opportunities for learners to discover and construct knowledge for themselves – will also affect the role teachers assume in the classroom. We shall discuss differing approaches to teaching in more detail in the next chapter, examining broader philosophies of education in Chapter 12; now, however, we shall turn to examine the practical implications of 'role' in the L2 classroom.

First thoughts: teachers and students . . . teachers and learners

Observing that *role* can be defined in a variety of ways, Wright (1987: 7) suggests that it is 'a complex grouping of factors which combine to produce certain types of social behaviour', while Widdowson (1987) emphasizes the importance of social expectations and norms in prescribing (or constraining) the personas and behaviour (i.e., the role) of teachers and learners. Widdowson characterizes the classroom as a 'social space', and both he and Wright recognize that teachers need to balance both social and pedagogic purposes within their classroom behaviour (as we have seen).

Thus, Wright highlights the job or *task-related* (i.e., pedagogic) elements and the *interpersonal* (i.e., social) elements of the teacher's role. Likewise, Widdowson suggests that teachers are obliged to function as representatives of institutions and society, leading to clear, fixed and hierarchical relationships in the classroom between teachers and *students*; but teachers also engage in more pedagogically oriented relationships with *learners*.

By using different terms for the same group of classroom participants, Widdowson highlights the dual nature of the teacher's role and teacher-student/learner relationships. Teacher authority is derived from social and institutional position (*'do this because I tell you and I am the teacher'* (1987: 86)) and from pedagogical knowledge and expertise (*'do this because I am the teacher and I know what's best for you'* (ibid.)), and teachers can be as authoritative when guiding a learner-centred activity as when 'teaching from the front', albeit in a different way. However, teachers may face difficulties if pedagogical practice and development runs counter to social norms and expectations (e.g., the introduction of 'learner-centred' or 'humanistic' pedagogy in more deferential and hierarchical social and institutional contexts, or vice versa).

Teachers in the classroom: a range of roles

Harmer (2015: 116–117) lists the key classroom roles of the L2 teacher as *controller*; *monitor and evidence gatherer*; *prompter and editor*; *resource and tutor*; and *organizer/task-setter*. Similar frameworks are outlined by other applied linguists (Wright (1987), for example, lists *instructor*, *organizer*, *evaluator*, *guide*, *resource* and *manager*). Harmer (2015) observes that the role teachers take depends on what they wish learners to achieve at a particular point in a class, or, as Richards and Rodgers (2014: 33) put it, 'the type of function they are expected to fulfill, whether that of practice director, counselor, or model, for example'. This will also depend on the learners' attitudes to teacher/ learner roles and relationships (see van Lier's view quoted in the introduction to this chapter). Richards and Rodgers (2014) also note that teacher role affects the interactional patterns that develop between teacher and learners (we shall examine classroom interaction more closely later in this chapter and in Chapter 2.)

Ultimately, Harmer (2015) suggests, teachers are *facilitators*, helping their students to achieve their goals whatever teacher role or roles predominate in the classroom, and the notion of 'facilitation' retains a key place in many ELT training courses and reference books (Thornbury, 2006: *xi*, 79), as it recognizes that teachers do not cause learning *directly*; instead they provide the conditions for learning to take place. As Thornbury comments, 'the learner should not be seen as the object of the verb *to teach*, but the subject of the verb *to learn*' (ibid.: 79). Thus, teachers who facilitate learning may be required to act as a prompt for learners, take account of interpersonal relationships within the classroom, and provide language resources when appropriate; the ways in which teachers achieve this will depend, of course, on factors such as the learners' age, L2 level and motivation, which we shall examine in more detail in Part III. (The idea that teachers do not 'directly cause' learning has major implications for classroom language learning and teaching, of course, summarized by two questions, both of which acted as titles for two articles published in the 1980s – 'Does second language instruction make a difference?' and 'Why don't learners learn what teachers teach?' (Long (1983a) and Allwright (1984) respectively.) We shall return to these questions in later chapters.

Task 1.2 Teacher and learner roles in the ELT classroom

Think of your own English language teaching context.

- What do learners expect of teachers? For example:

  - How are teachers expected to dress?

  - How do teachers refer to learners? e.g., given name, family name . . . and as students or as learners?

  - How do learners refer to their teachers? e.g., given name, sir, Mr/Miss/Ms . . .

  - Are teachers and learners socially 'distant' from each other?

- To what extent do learners expect teachers to be controllers and managers or prompters and guides? Why might this be so?

- To what extent do you as a teacher share learners' perceptions and beliefs about what are and are not appropriate teacher and learner roles in the ELT classroom?

- Have you ever experienced difficulties in the classroom or adjusted your teaching 'style' and the roles you enact to accommodate the beliefs of others (e.g., learners, managers, parents)?

From teacher role to teacher talk . . .

We have already noted the diversity and complexity of ELT classrooms around the world: cultural contexts, institutional curricula, teacher and teaching styles and beliefs, and learner needs and expectations differ from country to country (Mercer, 2001). Yet despite this variation, the way language is used in the classroom remains broadly similar because:

> Wherever they are and whatever they are teaching, teachers in schools and other educational facilities are likely to face some similar practical tasks. They have to organize activities to occupy classes of disparate individuals. . . . They have to control unruly behaviour. They are expected to teach a specific curriculum. . . . And they have to monitor and assess the educational progress the students make. All aspects of teachers' responsibilities are reflected in their use of language as the principal tool of their responsibilities.
>
> (Mercer, 2001: 243)

Thus how teachers talk and how they talk to learners are key elements in organizing and facilitating learning. This is particularly important in an L2 classroom where the medium of instruction is also the lesson content, that is, language is both 'the vehicle and object of instruction' (Long, 1983b: 9). This contrasts with other subjects such as physics or geography where the content (or message) is separate from the language (or medium). And, despite the emergence and theoretical dominance of Communicative Language Teaching, Task-based approaches and learner-centredness within ELT (outlined in Chapter 5), teacher talk still takes up a great deal of time in many classes (for example, Walsh (2011) suggests that 70–80 per cent of class time is typically given over to teacher talk).

Teacher talk, then, is the language teachers typically use in the L2 classroom. Teacher talk can be conceptualized in two ways – specific-ally as a modified form of language that is similar to the *foreigner talk* L1 speakers use when talking to L2 learners or the *caretaker talk* parents use with children – slower, louder and more deliberate, with greater use of pauses and emphasis, and often grammatically simplified (but not grammatically inaccurate); or as the general term for the way teachers interact with learners in the language classroom. As Lynch (1996) points out, attitudes to modified teacher talk vary widely – is it a valid concept, should it be used in the L2 classroom, and, if so, when? Although understandable and inevitable, especially with lower levels, many applied linguists and teachers suggest that teacher talk should not be over-simplified as learners require challenging language input for their language to develop (see Chapter 6 for further discussion of this issue).

The balance of teacher talk and student talk (or teacher talking time (TTT) and student talking time (STT) is also a matter of some debate. Typically, communicative and interaction-based approaches to ELT have suggested that teacher talk should be minimized in the classroom (as suggested above), thereby providing opportunities for learners to talk, and to practise and produce language. However, learners also require language *input* and opportunities for language *comprehension*, both of which teachers can provide (we shall return to these points in Part II). Clearly, the roles teachers adopt in the classroom, and their beliefs about how L2 learners learn, will affect the amount of teacher talk learners are exposed to. Equally, teachers need to consider not only the *quantity* of teacher and learner talk but also its *quality*. Thus, according to Walsh (2011: 35), successful teaching requires teacher (and learner) talk that is ' "fit for purpose", that enable[s] pedagogic goals and language use to coincide', and that is appropriate 'in relation to the "context of the moment" and task in hand'.

Task 1.3 Teacher talk in the L2 classroom

- 'Language is both the message and the medium'. In what ways might listening to teachers and the language they use help learners learn?

- When you talk to learners in class, do you modify the way you speak? If so, what do you do?

- What do you think are the benefits, and the potential dis-advantages, of modifying your speech to learners?

- Chaudron (1988),Tsui (1995) and Walsh (2011) suggest that teacher talk might account for around 60–80 per cent of L2 classroom talk. Do you recognize this from your own experience?

- What do you think is an appropriate balance of teacher talk and student talking time in the classroom, and why?

. . . and classroom interaction

It is evident that the roles teachers (and learners) take on in the language classroom also affect not only the amount and quality of teacher talk, but wider patterns of *classroom interaction*, 'the general term for what goes on in between the people in the classroom, particularly when it involves language' (Thornbury, 2006: 26), or, as Malamah-Thomas puts it, 'the social encounter of the classroom' where 'people/things have a reciprocal effect upon each other through their actions' (1987: 146).

What kind of questions might teachers ask?

Questions, particularly questions asked by teachers and answered by learners, tend to dominate L2 classroom interaction. Indeed, Chaudron (1988) suggests that questions constitute 20–40 per cent of classroom talk, while Tsui (1995) refers to a class in Hong Kong where almost 70 per cent of classroom interaction could be accounted for by the teacher asking a question, a learner or learners responding, and finally the teacher providing feedback to the response (i.e., the *Initiation-Response-Feedback* exchange (Sinclair and Coulthard (1975), discussed later in this chapter). Questions help teachers elicit information, check learners' understanding and keep learners' attention. They also provide learners with language practice opportunities when they answer. Teacher questions, therefore, fulfil a clear pedagogic purpose and also enable teachers to exert *control* over the patterns of class-room interaction and, therefore, over learners (an issue we shall return to shortly).

Apart from the generic functions of questions identified above, different types of questions generally lead to qualitatively and quan-titatively different responses from learners, some questions thus leading learners to 'work harder' with the language. Question types include:

- *Closed* and *open* questions, whereby questions with only one accept-able answer, usually factual, are 'closed', whereas questions with a range of possible answers, usually 'reasoning questions', are 'open'. Tsui (1995) suggests that closed questions are more restrictive (and less likely to encourage continuing interaction) than open questions.

- Display and referential questions refer respectively to those questions to which teachers already know the answer as they ask them and those to which they do not. Walsh and Li (2016) note that referential questions are more likely to promote discussion and debate, engage learners, and prompt learners to use more complex language as they convey meaning in their answers. Often beginning with a *wh-* question (e.g., *who, what, why* etc.), referential questions thus tend to lead to 'natural' responses by learners, and to genuine communication in the classroom. Display questions, meanwhile, are also very unusual in communication outside the classroom (Nunan and Lamb, 1996).

There are clearly good reasons to use all question types in the ELT classroom, Walsh and Li (2016: 491) suggesting that different question types will be more or less appropriate according to a teacher's immediate goal as 'the extent to which a question produces a communicative response is less important than the extent to which a question serves a purpose at a particular point in a lesson'. Thus, the use of appropriate questioning strategies depends on the *function* of a question in relation to what is being taught (Nunn, 1999).

We shall return to the possible linguistic and social effects of teacher questions as a potential classroom intervention in the next chapter.

Giving explanations . . . or causing confusion?

Tsui states that 'the role of the teacher is to make knowledge accessible to students' (1995: 30), that is, to provide explanations. There are of course a number of ways this might be achieved, from teacher-led *deductive* explanations, where learners might be given an explanation of a particular language feature and examples of its form, meaning and use (Ellis and Shintani, 2014), to guiding learners through a process of *inductive* discovery, where the teacher helps learners to find out about language and language rules for themselves (see Chapter 4 for further discussion). However, as Lynch (1996) suggests, from the learners' perspective, L2 classrooms can be confusing places and ' "explanations" are only explanations if they are recognized' (32); similarly, Martin points out that explanations are only explanations if they are understood (1970, in Tsui, 1995: 31). In terms of classroom interaction and teacher (and learner) talk, therefore, Tsui suggests that effective explanations require:

- the active engagement of learners in processing new information and linking it to old information;

- effective and linked stages which neither over-explain nor under-explain the issue.

A key issue for teachers, therefore, is establishing how detailed an explanation should be, with most teacher training and development texts suggesting that 'good' pedagogic explanations balance 'truth-fulness' with 'usefulness'; that is, they avoid overwhelming learners with detailed and all-encompassing descriptions of language items (e.g. the English language article system), but provide 'pedagogic rules' which 'should cover the great majority of instances learners are likely to encounter and some obvious exceptions, but avoid too much detail' (Ur, 1996, in Ellis and Shintani, 2014: 86). Thus, Thornbury (1999) draws on Swan (1994) to suggest a range of criteria that might underpin pedagogic explanations, including: *truth* (explanations should represent real world language use); *clarity* (ambiguous or difficult terminology should be avoided); *simplicity* (explanations should be simple enough for learners to understand); *demarcation* (make clear to learners the limits of the explanation); *conceptual parsimony* (draw on concepts which are familiar to learners); and *relevance* (explanations should only include those points learners need to know).

Teachers face the challenge of accommodating these concerns in practical ways that are appropriate for their own teaching context.

Errors in the classroom: dilemmas, possibilities and practices

According to van Lier, 'apart from questioning, the activity which most characterizes language classroom is correction of errors' (1988b: 276 in Walsh and Li, 2016: 492). Yet the issue of error and how errors are treated in the classroom often provokes strong opinions from teachers and learners alike, ranging from a little or even a 'no correction' stance to an ideal where all errors are corrected (unlikely in the real world!). Methodologically speaking, these positions can be associated with, for example, the Natural Approach (Krashen and Terrell, 1983), where error correction was avoided, and the Audiolingual approach to L2 teaching, in which correction was highly valued (see Chapters 5 and 6 for further discussion).

At present, however, most teachers seem to be positioned somewhere in the middle of these two extremes, for, as Edge (1989: 1) comments in a deceptively simple analysis of the dilemma teachers face:

Most people agree that making mistakes is a part of learning. Most people also agree that correction is part of teaching. If we agree so far, then we have a most interesting question to answer: if making mistakes is a part of learning and correction is a part of teaching, how do the two of them go together?

How might these questions be resolved in practice?

What is an error?

Errors are an inevitable part of L2 learning and L2 classrooms, but as Allwright and Bailey (1991: 83) suggest, this raises many further questions. Why do learners make errors? Are errors a problem or are they a natural and important part of L2 learning? How should teachers react to errors, and does correction actually affect the learners' progress?

Corder (1967) differentiated between errors and mistakes, a distinction that has been subsequently maintained by many applied linguists. If learners get something wrong because their developing internal second language system (i.e., their *interlanguage*) is not yet complete or 'fully *competent*', this is a *developmental error*. Errors may also be caused by *interference*, that is, the influence of the learners' L1 on their L2, which is said to affect the L2 in a range of ways, including grammar, lexis and phonology. Grammatically, for example, the English system of prepositions presents particular challenges for learners whose L1 expresses similar concepts in different ways (e.g., speakers of German, Russian and Arabic); L1 speakers of several East Asian languages experience difficulty with English articles as reference is realized differently in, for example, Japanese, Korean and Mandarin. Likewise, lexical errors may occur where similar sounding words carry different meanings in a learner's L1 and the target L2 – in Spanish, for example, *sensible* means 'sensitive' rather than the English 'to have good sense'. Finally, *unique errors* are neither developmental nor interference-based, but may be 'induced' (Ellis and Shintani, 2014) by other processes, for example, due to simplifications, overgeneralizations or misunderstandings during instruction. We shall examine how applied linguists have conceptualized developmental errors in more detail in Chapter 9.

Errors, therefore, are systematic representations of a learner's L2 development and can thus help teachers (and learners) discover how far the learner's knowledge of the L2 has progressed. In contrast, *mistakes* are the result of slips of the tongue (where learners actually know the right language but fail to produce it). Mistakes are said to occur when learners 'fail to perform to their competence' (Ellis, 1985 in Johnson, 2008: 335) and, in theory, can be self-corrected by learners.

Corder (1967) suggests that mistakes 'are of no significance to the process of language learning', but acknowledges that determining the difference between an error and a mistake is extremely difficult. Indeed, Bartram and Walton (1991) go as far as to categorize the error/mistake distinction as 'purely academic' and not relevant for teachers, a point also made by Mackey *et al.* (2016: 500), who argue that the difference between errors and mistakes is 'most likely imperceptible in an authentic classroom setting'. Allwright and Bailey (1991), meanwhile, suggest that errors are identified in comparison to native speaker standard language norms, which fails to recognize the sociolinguistic reality of learners' exposure to other varieties of English, a point we shall return to in Chapter 12.

Treating error: dilemmas and concerns

Hendrickson (1978) offers five key questions for teachers dealing with errors:

- Should learner errors be corrected?
- If so, when?
- Which errors should be corrected?
- How?
- And by whom?

Whether an error should be treated depends, of course, on the teacher first noticing it, and the kind of error that is made. Learners may make errors of linguistic form, for example, lexical (i.e., incorrect word use), grammatical (i.e., morphosyntax or word order difficulties), or phonological (i.e., pronunciation problems). Meanwhile, pragmatic errors may break typical meaning conventions, even when linguistic forms are correct (Mackey *et al.*, 2016). Subsequently, Johnson (2008) suggests, teachers may evaluate the seriousness or *gravity* of the error, Hendrickson (1978) prioritizing those errors that affect communication and meaning (i.e., *global* errors rather than *local* errors); those that stigmatize learners, for example, by not attending to politeness and appropriacy in interaction; and those that are particularly frequent.

Whether and when to treat an error also depends upon the context in which the error is made. Regarding spoken errors, most teacher training and development texts suggest a difference between accuracy and fluency-focused classroom activities (see also later chapters' discussion of a focus on form and/or meaning). Typical concerns include, for example, whether to interrupt learner talk in fluency-focused activities or whether to delay treatment (which is assumed to be more immediate in accuracy-focused activities); how to show that an error has been made (e.g., by asking learners to repeat themselves or via a gesture); how to guide learners to the correct language (e.g., through learner self-correction, help from classmates, teacher explanation, or teacher reformulation (repeating back the correct form); and how to avoid learner embarrassment and maintain classroom rapport. The treatment of written errors similarly depends on the purpose of the writing and the teacher's aims when providing feedback, for example, to provide correct forms for learners, or to prompt the learners to self-correct.

Providing 'corrective feedback': a range of possibilities

As the above discussion illustrates, error and its treatment is far from straightforward, to the extent that, when describing possible responses to errors and mistakes, the notion of 'correction' by the teacher is perhaps too narrow, and we can use the term *corrective feedback*. This refers to 'teacher (or peer/interlocutor) responses to learner utterances that contain errors, actual or perceived' (Mackey *et al.*, 2016: 500).

Oral corrective feedback provides a way of repairing classroom interaction when something goes wrong, and, importantly, is 'a tool to turn errors into opportunities for L2 development' (ibid.), as it indicates to learners what their errors are. Thus, it provides 'negative evidence' about their language use and, dependent on the feedback provided, might provide them with the correct form (i.e., 'positive evidence'). Drawing on Lyster and Ranta (1997), possible ways for teachers to provide oral corrective feedback include:

- *clarification requests*: asking the learner to clarify their meaning, without indicating the error or breaking the overall flow of the interaction;

- *elicitation*: prompting the learner to reformulate their speech;

- *explicit correction*: telling the learner they have made a mistake and providing the correct language;

- *metalinguistic feedback*: commenting on or questioning the well-formedness of a learner's utterance without explicitly providing the correct form;

- *recasts*: rephrasing the learner's utterance, correcting the error while retaining the meaning;

- *repetition*: repeating the learner's utterance, including their error(s).

It is worth noting some key differences between these possibilities. When engaging in explicit correction and recasts, teachers provide input and information to learners, while clarification requests, elicitation, meta-linguistic feedback and repetition provide learners with the opportunity to self-correct. Meanwhile, clarification requests, recasts and repetition provide more implicit corrective feedback to learners than elicitation, explicit correction and metalinguistic feedback, all of which highlight errors and correct language forms more overtly.

Similar patterns emerge when considering possible ways of providing learners with corrective feedback in response to their written errors. *Direct correction* involves the teacher crossing out the error and writing the correct form nearby; for *indirect correction*, teachers highlight the learner error (e.g. by underlining), but do not provide the correct form; or teachers may use marking code, i.e., a form of *metalinguistic feedback*, to indicate the type of error (e.g. tense, vocabulary, punctuation). Other approaches include *reformulation*, whereby teachers provide a correct model by rewriting the learner's whole text, rather than identifying specific errors, while attempting to preserve their original meanings (Johnson, 2008). Meanwhile, Ellis and Shintani (2014) suggest providing learners with detailed metalinguistic explanations of a particular type of error (e.g. article use) while not correcting these errors in their writing. They argue that all learners in a group can receive the same explanation, therefore making this approach time-effective for teachers and requiring learners to make the corrections themselves. As with the provision of oral corrective feedback, therefore, we can see differences between these approaches in terms of who provides the correct form for learners, although all written corrective feedback is, by its very nature, explicit (ibid.).

So, why treat error?

The theoretical debates that underpin corrective feedback and the repair of classroom interaction are examined in more detail in Part II, where we investigate the importance (or otherwise!) of explicitly *focusing on language forms*, whether learners can and should *notice the gap* between their own language and the target language, and how learners' *struggle for meaning* (i.e., self-repair) might assist L2 development. However, in the context of this chapter's more practical focus, what is the significance of corrective feedback? Why treat error?

Walsh (2006a: 10) suggests that corrective feedback, 'like other practices which prevail in language classrooms, is a ritual, something [teachers] "do to learners" without really questioning their actions'. Noting that this is understandable (and therefore not a criticism), Walsh argues that the consequences of how, when and, implicitly, which errors are repaired are 'crucial to learning'. This suggests that corrective feedback *is* (or can be) effective, in that it does benefit learners' L2 development; a range of evidence from both experimental and classroom-based studies supports this conclusion. However, the claims made for corrective feedback are generally quite cautious, noting, for example, that it can be 'moderately beneficial'; that it needs to be intensive (i.e., a single instance of corrective feedback is generally ineffective); that context matters; and that no single corrective feedback technique has yet been found to be significantly more effective than others – thus, teachers should implement a range of feedback strategies with their learners (see, for example, Mitchell *et al.*, 2013; Ellis and Shintani, 2014; and Mackey *et al.*, 2016 for more detailed discussion).

Furthermore, looking at corrective feedback from a more social perspective, although we have observed that avoiding embarrassment and maintaining learners' face is an important consideration for teachers, learners generally believe that error correction is a key part of the language teacher's role. As Seedhouse states:

> Learners appear to have grasped better than teachers and methodologists that, within the interactional organisation of the L2 classroom, making linguistic errors and having them corrected directly and overtly is not an embarrassing matter.

> (1997: 571)

We have already recognized that learners and teachers bring with them to class a set of beliefs and expectations, and in Chapter 7 we shall investigate the role of beliefs, and the implications of teachers and learners holding different beliefs, in more detail. Thus, regardless of its pedagogic role, the provision of corrective feedback also fulfils the more 'social' function of meeting most learners' expectations of the teacher's classroom role.

Task 1.4 In your context: making sense of error and corrective feedback

- We have noted the suggested difference between an 'error' and a 'mistake'. Do you recognize this difference from your own experience (as a teacher or as a language learner), and how relevant is this concept to your own classroom practice?

- How do *you* define error, and how do you identify errors in your classroom?

- English language teachers vary in their attitude to error and corrective feedback, from providing little or no correction to providing and encouraging a great deal of systematic repair. What is your opinion? Which kind of teacher are you and how do you compare to other teachers you know and work with?

- To what extent do you consider corrective feedback to be a useful classroom activity? How might it lead to L2 learning?

- Do you notice more errors than you highlight or correct in class, or in learners' writing? If so, what kind of errors do you focus on? If 'it depends', what does it depend on? How do you select which errors to focus on?

- How are errors treated in your classroom, and when you read learners' written work? What strategies and techniques do you use/are used?

- As a teacher, have you ever been in a situation where your beliefs about corrective feedback did not correspond to the learners' beliefs? If so, was the situation resolved (and how)? Consider:

  - the amount of correction and the gravity of errors.

  - mechanisms for repair (e.g., teacher-centred, peer-assisted, and self-correction; clarification requests, explicit correction, recasts, elicitation and so forth).

Classroom interaction – a final consideration: 'control'

As we have seen, classroom interaction is shaped by teachers' decisions. For example, learners will reply in different ways using different language when teachers ask open referential questions rather than closed display questions. In general, teachers also direct turn-taking and topic selection in the classroom. Thus, due to their 'special status', teachers orchestrate and control classroom interaction and communication (Breen, 1998; Walsh, 2011; Walsh and Li, 2016). (Of course, most teachers deal with issues of disruption and discipline which are also issues of 'control'; for a review of these and other issues of classroom management, see Harmer, 2015; Wright, 2005.)

The *Initiation-Response-Feedback* (IRF) exchange is one of the most typical interactions in L2 classrooms. Here, the teacher initiates an exchange and requires a learner response. Subsequently, the teacher provides evaluative feedback on that response (Sinclair and Coulthard, 1975). For example:

Teacher: *Now, who wrote a play called Romeo and Juliet?*
Learner: *William Shakespeare.*
Teacher: *Shakespeare. Yes, that's right. Does anyone know any other plays that Shakespeare wrote?*

Here, the teacher leads the interaction, confirming and positively evaluating the learner's response before moving on to the next stage of the interaction.

Walsh (2011) summarizes the reasons for the prevalence of IRF in the L2 classroom – it matches teacher and learner expectations of what classrooms should be like; teachers often want to provide reassuring and positive feedback to learners; asymmetrical power relations in the classroom ensure that teachers 'hold the floor' more often than learners; and it is a time-efficient way of moving classroom interaction forward, albeit via a somewhat limited exchange.

However, in an IRF sequence, the teacher makes two 'moves' for every one made by a learner, thereby contributing to the high level of teacher talk found by Chaudron, Tsui, and Walsh that we noted earlier. IRF sequences have also been criticized for limiting learners' opportunities for interaction, in terms of both quantity and quality, and can be seen as a way in which both turn-taking and topic are nominated and/or dominated by teachers. Thus while potentially meeting both teachers' and learners' social expectations of role and classroom behaviour, IRF sequences reduce learners' opportunities to lead and participate in classroom interaction.

Similarly, the ways in which teachers manage questioning, explanations and corrective feedback raise similar issues concerning the relationship between patterns of interaction, language use and control within the L2 classroom. These issues are not solely 'pedagogic' but also concern the nature and distribution of power in the classroom and education more generally, for, as Allwright and Hanks (2009: 65) suggest:

> Attractive to most people . . . control can certainly make life easier for the controllers, but it can create problems for the controlled, and for the health of the system as a whole.

We shall explore these issues in more detail in the next chapter, in which we shall also revisit the IRF sequence, examining how teachers might intervene and adapt their approach to classroom interaction.

Task 1.5 Interaction, control and class size

English language classes vary considerably in size, from one-to-one teaching and small group classes to classes that contain fifty (and more) learners.

- In what ways might teacher and learner roles, classroom interaction and issues of control vary and differ according to class size?

- Although class size is often linked to other contextual factors such as availability of resources and local educational traditions (see Chapter 2 for further discussion), do you think there are any aspects of role, interaction and control which might not alter according to the size of class?

Summary . . . and moving on

At the end of this, the first chapter, it is necessary to both draw together its key themes and to map their place in the wider debates of English language teaching (and the other themes and parts of this book).

The chapter has both investigated some of the key practices and dilemmas teachers experience in the L2 classroom and touched on a wide range of issues that will require further exploration. First, the discussion highlighted the diverse, complex and essentially pedagogic and *social* nature of ELT classrooms. Fundamentally:

A popular notion is that education is something carried out by one person, a teacher, standing in front of a class and transmitting information to a group of learners who are all willing and able to absorb it. This view, however, simplifies what is a highly complex process involving an intricate interplay between the learning process itself, the teacher's intentions and actions, the individual personalities of the learners, their culture and background, the learning environment and a host of other variables.

(Williams and Burden, 1997: 5)

The chapter then explored teacher roles and classroom interaction, and it is worth emphasizing that the focus was explicitly on how teacher behaviour may affect classroom discourse, control and, in due course, L2 learning. In later chapters, we will attend to the management of the social dimensions of learning such as motivation and group dynamics.

But, as we have seen, teacher decision-making and behaviour is constrained by personal philosophy, space, time and available resources, interpersonal and institutional factors, community considerations, syllabus and assessment, and classroom routine (Lynch, 1996). Thus finding potential 'interventions' to the classroom dilemmas outlined here is not straightforward, and it is to possible ways ahead that we now turn.

2 Intervening in the language classroom

Classroom management, interaction and learning opportunities

Since teachers' lives are different one from another, so their expertise will differ, with no model emerging as an obvious template. What is right is what works in a given context in terms of all the various cultures which operate there.

(Sowden, 2007: 309–10)

This chapter will:

- problematize notions of 'the good language teacher';
- examine differing patterns of classroom management and control, and the possible implications of these teacher interventions for classroom interaction and L2 learning;
- consider the impact and role of new computer and online technologies in (and beyond) the ELT classroom;
- consider the management of 'large classes' in 'difficult circumstances';
- relate these discussions to an 'ecological' perspective on language teaching.

Introduction: the good teacher?

Almost everyone has an opinion as to what makes a 'good' teacher. In most countries, we spend thousands of hours as schoolchildren experiencing and evaluating teachers in action (M. Borg, 2004). Although these experiences of teaching are necessarily partial as learners do not see what goes on 'behind the scenes' in terms of, for example, pre-class preparation and decision-making or post-class analyses and marking, they inform our beliefs as adults about what a 'good teacher' does and what 'good teaching' is (Lortie, 1975; M. Borg,

2004). Indeed, one of the aims of teacher training and education is to challenge teachers to move beyond the limited and unanalysed understandings of teaching that this *apprenticeship of observation* provides (Lortie, 1975).

Moving beyond these partial understandings, several surveys have attempted to collate the characteristics and actions of teachers that are most likely to lead to effective teaching (Williams and Burden, 1997). Sometimes termed *process-product* studies (i.e., they aim to identify what teaching processes lead to satisfactory products, outcomes and results), they tend to outline the personal characteristics of 'good' teachers or list desirable teacher behaviour. For example:

> An outstanding teacher should be an inspiring instructor who is concerned about students, an active scholar who is respected by discipline peers, and an efficient organised professional who is accessible to students and colleagues.
>
> (Ericksen, 1984: 3, in Williams and
> Burden, 1997: 47)

And

> Nine key factors contributing to effective teaching:
>
> - clarity of presentation;
> - teacher enthusiasm;
> - variety of activities during lessons;
> - achievement-oriented behaviour in classrooms;
> - opportunity to learn criterion material;
> - acknowledgement and stimulation of student ideas;
> - (lack of) criticism;
> - use of structuring comments at the beginning and during lessons;
> - guiding of student answers.
>
> (Rosenshine and Furst, 1973, in
> Williams and Burden, 1997: 47)

While it might seem difficult to disagree with these findings, they are problematic in a number of ways. They offer less than expected in terms of actual classroom practice as they are open to a variety of interpretations; for example, *how* should learner answers be 'guided' in practice? How much 'variety' should a lesson include? What is 'enthusiasm'? Additionally, we noted in the previous chapter that each classroom is unique and complex. Thus what 'good' teachers do will vary according to their personality and beliefs, cultural and contextual background, and the aims and needs of learners (discussed further in later chapters); searching for a generalizable model of 'good teaching' is unrealistic in a profession that is so diverse. Finally, it is worth noting that teachers, already busy with their daily professional and home lives, can find models such as Ericksen's outline of an 'outstanding teacher' (p. 23) overwhelming and potentially demoralizing. Whether such models are helpful or in fact encourage teacher 'burnout' is open to question.

Thus, modelling and characterizing a 'good teacher' is problematic. And yet, for teachers hoping to develop their professional practice, exploration of and reflection upon classroom life and their role within it *is* necessary.

As we observed in Chapter 1, teachers provide or contribute to the conditions for L2 learning to take place, which includes, among other things, organizing, motivating and guiding learners. Thus, noting that there is more than one 'right' way to teach and that 'language teaching can be seen as a principled problem solving activity: a kind of operational research which works out solutions to its own local problems' (Widdowson, 1990: 7), in the rest of this chapter, we will investigate further how teachers might intervene in and manage classroom life and classroom interaction, and explore how this can affect opportunities for L2 learning.

In the ELT classroom: classroom management, control and interaction

Classroom management, that is, how teachers organize and direct learners and learning to make the most effective use of available time and resources (Thornbury, 2006), is 'the central element of every teacher's daily professional experience' (Wright, 2005: 1). However, Wright (2012) also suggests that discussions often reduce classroom management to a series of techniques for controlling classes, through the organization of seating, grouping of learners, and dealing with misbehaviour and discipline issues. Wright (ibid.: 61) argues that this idea of classroom management as a set of control strategies is 'outmoded and unhelpful'. Given that classrooms are complex environments in which events and learners' (and teachers') experiences inter-relate and interweave (see Chapter 1), then managing classrooms should be seen as a set of unfolding and responsive pedagogic practices that affect opportunities for L2 learning. Wright (2005; 2012) therefore suggests that, in addition to managing the two institutional 'givens' of *time* and *space* (the time learners spend together is limited and clearly delineated; 'space' is the location of teaching learning, i.e., the allocated classroom, which again imposes limitations), classroom management also entails managing *engagement* and *participation*. Given its social as well as pedagogic character, emotions and mood (i.e., engagement) inevitably permeate classroom life, while making good use of learning opportunities by managing participation, usually through classroom talk and interaction, is central to language teaching and learning. As Wright notes (2012), the inter-relationships between these four elements are complex, and, as teachers manage them, classroom life unfolds.

Order, opportunity and high and low structure classrooms

It is unrealistic to think that what learners do and say in the classroom can be completely planned and controlled by the teacher. Unplanned and uncontrolled learner discourse is an inevitable element of most L2 classrooms and actually contributes to language learning (we shall examine how language teaching methodologies take account of this and how applied linguists conceptualize this learning in Chapters 5 and 6). Thus, as Wright (2005) observes, any action in the classroom, by teachers or learners, can elicit a variety of possible responses, ranging from the expected to the unexpected, and these elements of classroom interaction provide *learning opportunities* that teachers and learners can exploit. Learning opportunities are those occasions, from brief moments to longer-term opportunities, when learners *may* learn. They may result from conscious and imposed encounters with language, or they may be an unconscious consequence of 'natural' language use. Encountering an opportunity to learn does not mean that learning necessarily takes place (Allwright, 2005; Wright, 2005). However, given that language is the medium and the message of an L2 classroom (see Chapter 1), it is possible to regard all elements of L2 language use in class as a learning opportunity.

Wright (2005) suggests that teachers who acknowledge the complexity inherent in classrooms and hold an *opportunity view* of classroom management may seek to create uncertain conditions that can be exploited as learning opportunities. This contrasts with an *order view* that claims learning to be a consequence of teacher control and the simplification of classroom complexity. According to order perspectives, teachers instruct while learners successfully follow teachers' instructions and do as they are told. However, according to Wright, teachers and learners 'intuitively know that this is not true' (123).

Within an opportunity perspective of classroom management, therefore, learners may be encouraged to take 'risks' with language and to *negotiate meanings* in classroom discourse (see Part II). More broadly, as we shall explore in subsequent chapters, we may see links with *Communicative Language Teaching* and *Task-based Language Teaching*, with *Dogme approaches to ELT*, and with moves towards *learner autonomy*.

Management decisions	High structure	Low structure
PLANNING	Teacher-centred and teacher-controlled	Grouping around activities and learner choice
CLASSROOM PROCEDURES	Imposed routines	Participative decision-making and consultation
QUESTIONING	Display, closed, assertive, IRF exchanges	Referential, open, i.e., 'authentic'
REWARD/PUNISHMENT	To modify behaviour	To encourage pupil self-discipline

Table 2.1 High and low structure in classroom decision-making
Source: After Briggs and Moore, 1993: 496–7; adapted from Wright, 2005: 125.

Briggs and Moore (1993, in Wright, 2005) frame this discussion in terms of 'high' and 'low' structure classrooms. As Wright (ibid.) summarizes, *high structure* classrooms, which draw upon the order view of classroom management, emphasize the teacher's role in organizing learning with little learner involvement in decision-making about lessons. Meanwhile, more opportunity-based *low structure* approaches to classroom management encourage learner involvement in decisions about what and how to learn as they adopt a more autonomous approach to their own learning. High and low structure approaches are summarized in Table 2.1.

Thus, high and low structure approaches to classroom management differ in the amount of control teachers and learners have over classroom practices. Where management focuses on high structure and order, classrooms and classroom discourse are more likely to be teacher-centred, thereby affecting the way teachers ask questions, give explanations, correct errors and control topics. Low structure classrooms provide more opportunities for learner participation and interaction, inevitably making classrooms more unpredictable places. High and low structure approaches to classroom management are not only issues of control and power, therefore; they affect the quantity and quality of classroom interaction and, hence, opportunities for L2 learning. We shall now explore the relationship between interaction and learning opportunities in more detail.

Task 2.1 Managing your classroom

- To what extent are your lessons a combination of planned and unplanned activities and opportunities for L2 learning?

- How often do you 'abandon' *your* plans in class and provide opportunities for the *learners* to shape the lesson(s)?
- How is 'control' maintained in your classroom? Consider:
  - explicit rewards and discipline;
  - patterns of classroom interaction, questioning techniques, the IRF exchange and topic control;
  - other classroom routines and behaviour of both teachers and learners.

The interaction continuum

As we shall see in later chapters, much applied linguistics research now places interaction of one sort or another at the centre of language teaching and learning, interaction being:

> The social behaviour that occurs when one person communicates with another. Interaction in this sense is *interpersonal*. It can occur face-to-face, in which case it usually takes place through the oral medium, or it can occur as displaced activity, in which case it generally involves the written medium.
>
> (Ellis, 1999: 1; original emphasis)

We should also note that the rapid technological developments of recent years mean that both oral and written interaction can also now take place online (see later in this chapter).

Rivers (1987: 4–5) observes that interaction is the key to teaching language for communication, noting that, through interaction:

> . . . students can increase their language store as they listen or read authentic linguistic material, or even the output of their fellow students . . . In interaction, students can use all they possess of the language – all they have learned or casually absorbed – in real-life exchanges where expressing their real meaning is important to them. . . The brain is *dynamic*, constantly interrelating what we have learned with what we are learning, and the give-and-take of message exchanges enables students to retrieve and interrelate a great deal of what they have encountered – material that . . . might otherwise lie dormant until the teacher thought to reintroduce it.
>
> (original emphasis)

We shall return to examine how these key learning processes might operate in Chapter 6; for now, however, let us return to the relationship between classroom management and interaction.

The 'interaction continuum' characterizes the tension already noted between teacher-controlled and learner-managed classrooms (Kramsch, 1987). At one end of the continuum, teacher control is maintained via 'instructional discourse', where teacher and learner roles and statuses are fixed and predictable; tasks are teacher-focused and involve the conveying and receiving of information; and linguistic accuracy is important. At the other end of the continuum, 'natural discourse' is sustained through flexible and negotiated teacher and learner roles; tasks are group-oriented and meaning-focused; and the interaction itself is the focus of learning (i.e., the learning opportunity). Kramsch's model suggests that 'natural discourse' creates or allows for more uncertainty in all aspects of classroom practice. Thus, classroom discourse and interaction is less predictable in more learner-centred and meaning-focused L2 classrooms, as summarized in Table 2.2.

Of course, while specific classrooms might draw upon one discourse more than another, most L2 teaching and learning draws upon *both* as teachers and learners establish 'convivial discourse' somewhere in the middle of the continuum (Kramsch, 1987). Indeed, instructional and natural discourse are 'neither mutually dependent nor mutually exclusive, though they interrelate and interact in complex ways to provide organizational structure [to the lesson]' (van Lier, 1988a: 155), with the balance of classroom discourses, interaction and control changing between and within lessons according to the particular aims and needs of the class at that time. However, we should remember, as noted in Chapter 1 (and explored further in the final part of this book), that teachers are rarely 'free agents' in guiding this process, constrained as they are by social and institutional factors.

	Instructional discourse	'Convivial discourse'	Natural discourse
	◀——————————————————————▶		
Roles	Fixed statuses		Negotiated roles
Tasks	Teacher-oriented		Group-oriented
Types of knowledge	Focus on accuracy		Focus on meaning and fluency of interaction

Table 2.2 The interaction continuum

Source: Adapted from Kramsch, 1987: 18.

Summarizing classroom interaction: the story so far

Inside two language classrooms

Task 2.2 Classroom roles, interactions and interventions in practice

Look at the extracts from two different English language classrooms below, and consider the differences between the two sequences.

- What role(s) does the teacher take in each, for example instructor, evaluator, guide, resource? (More than one role may be possible in each case.)

- How much does the teacher talk? How much do the learners talk?

- What classroom interaction features can you identify in terms of:

  - IRF exchanges.

  - Giving instructions and explanations.

  - Eliciting learner language.

  - Question types.

  - Repair.

- Where would you position the two extracts on the interaction continuum?

- How would you assess them in terms of 'control'?

- Do they focus on language forms or meaning?

- What L2 learning opportunities arise during each exchange?

Extract 1: from a Norwegian primary school, focusing on the language point 'have got':

1.	**T:**	Now I want everybody to listen to me, and when I say 'you are going to say after me', you are going to say what I say. We can try . . .
2.	**T:**	I've got a lamp – a lamp. Say after me 'I've got a lamp'
3.	**LL:**	I've got a lamp
4.	**T:**	I've got a glass, a glass. Say after me 'I've got a glass'
5.	**LL:**	I've got a glass
6.	**T:**	I've got a vase, a vase. Say after me 'I've got a vase'
7.	**LL:**	I've got a vase
		. . .

8.	T:	I've got a hammer. What have you got, Tjartan?
9.	L1:	I have a hammer
10.	T:	Can everybody say 'I've got'?
11.	L1:	I've got
12.	T:	Fine. I've got a belt. What have you got? Kjersti?
13.	L2:	Hmm – I've got a telephone
		. . .
14.	T:	And listen to me again – and look what I've written. I've got a hammer – just listen now – have you got a hammer?
15.	L:	Yes
16.	T:	Raise your hand up now Bjorn
17.	L3:	Yes
18.	T:	I've . . .
19.	L3:	I've got a hammer
20.	T:	You've got a hammer and then you answer 'yes, I have' – 'Yes, I have'. I've got a belt. Have you got a belt, Vegard?
21.	L4:	Er . . . no
22.	T:	You only answer with 'yes'
23.	L4:	Yes
24.	T:	Yes . . .
25.	L4:	I . . . have
26.	T:	I have . . . fine . . . I've got a trumpet. Have you got a trumpet, Anna?
27.	L5:	Ah . . . er . . . erm . . . yes, I have

(adapted from Seedhouse, 2004: 102–3)

Extract 2: *From a primary school in Abu Dhabi, in which a learner comes to the front of the class to share his experiences with the rest of the class:*

1.	L1:	Before on Wednesday I went to a trip in Dubai because my father's work they gave him a paper that we could go to a free trip to Dubai
2.	T:	Ah . . .
3.	L1:	Ya, and on the paper it said we could stay in a hotel for any days you want so I said to my father for two days and when I was going to Dubai Mark called me
4.	T:	He called you?
5.	L1:	Ya, and we were talking and then when we finished talking . . . er . . . on Thursday my father took me to Burjuman, ya, there was something like this big just twenty dirhams, ya, I bought it and it . . .

6.	**T:**	. . . What is this . . . something like this . . . it's big?
7.	**L1:**	It's like a penguin but not a penguin. It's a bear, ya, not very big like this
8.	**T:**	Uhu . . .
9.	**L1:**	Like me, ya. I press a button, it moves like this, and it carries me up like this and puts me down
10.	**T:**	Are you serious?
11.	**L1:**	And also in the hotel I saw the tallest man in the world and the shortest man in the world
12.	**T:**	Really? Ha! Where do they come from?
13.	**L1:**	Er . . . I don't know. One is from China, I don't know, Japan and one is from here. The tall man, he's like this [extending his right hand up] bigger than the short man
14.	**T:**	Is he the same one that came to school?
15.	**L1:**	No, bigger than that one
16.	**T:**	Oh really? Even taller?
17.	**L1:**	[nods]
18.	**T:**	Jeez! OK, thank you Arash for sharing

(Yazigi, 2001: 42, in Seedhouse, 2004: 115–16)

The transcripts in Task 2.2 illustrate two very different types of classroom interaction. In Extract 1, the focus is clearly on a specific form (i.e., 'have got') with an emphasis on linguistic accuracy rather than the communication of real-world meanings, and there is no real 'topic' or content focus within the interaction. The teacher controls and, indeed, dominates turn-taking through the use of closed display questions and, on occasion, IRF exchanges (e.g., lines 10–12, with the teacher feedback 'fine'). Often, however, positive teacher feedback is more implicit, the learners presumably understanding they have completed the exchange appropriately if the teacher moves straight on to the next example as illustrated by the adjacency pairs in lines 2–3, 4–5 and 6–7. Additionally, when learners deviate from the language outputs the teacher expects, corrective feedback is provided. For example, in a scenario familiar to most classrooms, the teacher feedback on line 18 acts as a prompt when the learner hesitates. In contrast, however, the feedback on line 10 'corrects' a learner who has produced a linguistically accurate form, which also communicates the appropriate meaning (i.e., 'I have a hammer'). Again, this kind of exchange takes place in many L2 classrooms, although teachers might be less aware of it.

In Extract 2, however, meaning is paramount. Although any use of language, of course, employs linguistic forms, the focus of the exchange is a real-world topic that carries personal relevance for the classroom participants. Fluency, rather than accuracy, is encouraged. In this particular exchange, although the majority of the classroom talk is undertaken by the learner, the teacher has a clear role in setting up the activity, prompting further talk and clarifying meanings for other listeners. Thus questions are generally more open and referential, and corrective feedback is provided (e.g., through the use of 'taller' in line 16). However, although meaningful interaction is central, as Meerholz-Härle and Tschirner observe, the exact relationship between learner interaction and actual language acquisition remains unclear (2004: 111). We shall focus on this relationship in more detail in Part II, Chapter 6.

Teacher decision-making: 'making the right choice at the right time'?

Clearly, when deciding how to facilitate the construction of learning opportunities, teachers aspire to 'make the right choice at the right time' (van Lier, 2000), the 'right choice' being one which 'promote[s] learning and learning opportunities and which reflect[s] the pedagogic goals of the teacher, the goals of the learners, and the opportunities or constraints imposed by the context' (Walsh and Li, 2016: 487). However, clarifying what this might mean in terms of actual classroom decision-making and practice across the range of complex and diverse ELT learning environments is more difficult.

For example, we have already seen that error treatment is a complex process and that the provision of corrective feedback can be approached in a variety of ways. Thus although Lynch (1997) recommends that teacher intervention and corrective feedback (as opposed to learner self- and peer-repair) should be left 'as late as possible' (324), Ellis and Shintani (2014: 280) conclude that both immediate and delayed feedback may be beneficial, and that, although many teacher training and development texts recommend self-correction followed by teacher correction, applied linguistic research suggests that there is no 'best way' of conducting oral corrective feedback in the classroom (as was also suggested in Chapter 1).

There is similar ambiguity as to how teachers might approach 'teacher talk' in the L2 classroom. Leo van Lier (2001: 92) observes that:

> Teacher talk has been lauded for being comprehensible and criticized for being authentic and not attuned to student needs. Learner talk has been lauded for providing opportunities for negotiating

meaning and criticized for being a defective model, riddled with inaccuracies.

Hence, although research generally suggests that learner talk facilitates L2 learning more effectively than teacher talk, the extent to which the *type* of interaction matters is unclear; maybe it is enough that learners simply talk (van Lier, 2001). Teachers may be able to gain their own localized insights into these dilemmas by understanding and rational-izing the interactional decisions they take in the classroom (Walsh, 2006b: 139), but their insights as to what kind of talk is both appro-priate and best facilitates L2 learning will vary according to their context.

Cullen (2002) suggests teachers may also wish to re-evaluate the IRF exchange, which, as we have seen, is generally associated with teacher control and teacher-centred interaction. Cullen notes that teachers use the IRF exchange as a 'powerful pedagogic device' in the interaction-based and communicative L2 classroom if the third part of the exchange, 'F', includes *discoursal follow-up* as well as evaluative feedback. Learners' meanings can be clarified and contribute to emerg-ing class discussion and discourse through follow-up mechanisms such as repetition, elaboration, comment, or responding meaningfully to learner responses (Cullen, 2002) as shown, for example, in Figure 2.1. Li (2011), meanwhile, notes that IRF exchanges can 'spiral' construc-tively and creatively if the discoursal follow-up takes up, builds upon and then invites further learner responses, thereby creating a cumulative dialogue as part of the same pedagogic sequence. Thus, even in a com-municative or meaning-focused setting, IRF exchanges can be employed to intervene in and facilitate meaning-based learning opportunities when appropriate.

I	T:	What would you do if you saw a robbery?
R	L:	I'd shout
F	T:	You'd shout . . . Aaargh! . . . *Laughter* . . . I don't know if the police would hear you . . . *laughter* . . .

Analysis of F-move

You'd shout	Repetition
Aaargh!	Elaboration
I don't know if the police would hear you	Comment

Figure 2.1 The IRF exchange revisited: initiation – response – follow-up
Source: Adapted from Cullen, 2002: 123.

To summarize, there is an array of possible interaction-focused interventions open to teachers who have to make immediate decisions about what is appropriate when responding to individual learners' contributions, and balance competing forms of intervention in almost every lesson they teach (Cullen, 2002). Making 'the right choice at the right time' therefore depends on the teacher's understanding of the relationship between classroom interaction and learning opportunities in their own classroom context, and will most likely be the result of both planning and, in particular, a degree of improvisation and inter-active, 'online' decision-making on their part (Walsh and Li, 2016).

Task 2.3 The L2 classroom in practice: thinking about your context

What elements of classroom management and interaction that we have examined do you recognize from your own teaching? For example:

- What features of teacher and learner talk, interaction and control typify 'convivial discourse' in your professional context? How far do your classes draw upon 'natural discourse' or 'instructional discourse'?

- Can you think of occasions when interaction in your classroom has resembled Extract 1 in Task 2.2? When and why might you (as a teacher with your learners) manage interaction in this way?

- Similarly, can you think of occasions when interaction in your classroom has resembled Extract 2? When and why might you (as a teacher with your learners) manage interaction in this way?

Routine in the L2 classroom

Louden writes that 'teaching is a struggle to discover and maintain a settled practice, a set of routines and patterns of action which resolve the problems posed by particular subjects and groups of [learners]' (1991: *xi* in Williams and Burden, 1997: 52) while Appel (1995: 124) supports van Lier's (1988a: 227) assertion that:

There may be several valid arguments for the maintenance of a ritual element in the language classroom, quite apart from any direct language-learning benefits . . . Throwing out chorus work, display questions, repetition, and so on, since they are not 'authentic' communication . . . may constitute premature surgery.

Yet as we have seen, teachers may try to create uncertain conditions in the L2 classroom to facilitate learning opportunities (Wright, 2005).

- How far do you identify with each perspective? How far is routine desirable in the L2 classroom? And uncertainty?

- Is it possible for an L2 classroom to accommodate both routine and uncertain conditions? If so, how?

- What would happen if you were to change or challenge established patterns of interaction in your classroom? How would your learners, colleagues, school managers, and, if appropriate, parents react? How would you feel teaching in a different way?

Contexts for teacher decision-making: from new technologies to large classes

The spread of English and of English language teaching and learning around the world (see Part IV for further discussion) means that ELT is conducted in a diverse variety of contexts ranging from well-equipped, small-class private language schools to low-resource, large-class environments. How, then, might the management of classroom interaction, and the associated decisions and interventions teachers may make, differ from context to context? We will focus on the potential implications of these two apparently contrasting situations in ELT – where new technologies are common, and where English is taught to large classes in 'difficult circumstances' (West, 1960) – as both 'are part of the landscape of language teaching worldwide, and both therefore need to be accommodated inclusively in our understanding of what language teaching is and how it is lived out' (Tudor, 2001: 136).

New technologies in ELT: managing learning in the classroom . . . and beyond

This chapter has so far focused on an arguably 'traditional' view of classroom life – typically, the teacher and learners are together in the same physical location, interacting with each other, usually through speech (though sometimes via written tasks) in 'real time', i.e., synchronously. In an increasing number of ELT contexts, however, the emergence of computer and internet-based technologies has led to the development of online (or virtual) teaching and learning environments. The use of technology in language teaching is not new; language laboratories based initially around audio and more recently around multimedia systems have been in use since the 1950s, for example, and audio and video resources are used in many classrooms. However, the potential physical (and temporal) separation of learners from each other and from the teacher via online technologies is a potentially significant addition to the discussion of class management, L2 interaction, and language learning. As Gruba *et al.* (2016) note, although new technologies offer new possibilities and opportunities for language teachers and learners, they also present challenges and may disrupt established teacher and learner routines.

New technologies in ELT: terms, practices and settings

An array of acronyms has been used to describe the application of new technologies in language teaching and learning (e.g., CAI – Computer Assisted Instruction; TELL – Technology Enhanced Language Learning; WELL – Web-Enhanced Language Learning). Gruba (2004) suggests that CALL (Computer Assisted Language Learning) is now the most established term, which Gruba *et al.* (2016: 136) define as 'the full integration of technology into language learning' via a 'dynamic complex in which technology, theory and pedagogy are inseparably interwoven' (Garrett, 2009: 719-720). CALL thus incorporates both earlier notions of computers as 'patient tutors', providing students with activities such as quizzes, grammar exercises and reading and listening tasks, and more contemporary uses of technology which foster *computer-mediated communication* (CMC) through interactive forums, blogs, wikis and videoconferencing, both in writing and, increasingly, through speech (Gruba *et al.*, 2016).

However, as understandings of the role of technology in language education have changed, so has the vocabulary used to describe it (Dudeney and Hockly, 2012). Increasingly, for example, we might talk about specific aspects of CALL such as *mobile learning*, whereby learning experiences 'cross spatial and temporal borders' (Kukulska-Hulme *et al.*, 2009: 20) through the use of smartphones and other mobile devices; *game-based learning*, in which games and gaming techniques such as scoring systems, challenges and leaderboards are integrated into learning environments to deepen motivation and engagement (Gruba *et al.*, 2016); or language learning through *augmented reality* (AR), in which students carrying AR-enabled mobile devices can engage with virtual information superimposed on the real world landscape, such as information texts about physical landmarks which smartphone cameras 'read' (Dudeney and Hockly, 2012). Additionally, we might refer to *digital*, *online*, *Web 2.0*, or *information and communication technologies* (Gruba *et al.*, 2016).

Thus, in a rapidly developing field, it is perhaps easiest to follow Lewis (2009) and refer simply to *new technologies*, which can be broadly sub-divided into those that are *offline* or '*dedicated*' (Richmond, 1999, in Gruba, 2004), for example, stand-alone computer-based language exercises such as gap-fills and word-processing or writing development programmes; and those which are *online* or '*integrated*' (ibid.) via networked computers, enabling the development of, for example, blogs, the creation of virtual classrooms and online tutoring (often through customized web-platforms), and the use of email and social networking sites as teaching and learning tools. In 'technology rich' ELT environments, there has generally been a move towards integrated practices over the course of the last ten years.

Online technologies therefore have the potential to break down the language classroom as a stable, physical 'four-walled' environment, as learners and teachers are not limited to always attending lessons at specific times and locations (Gruba *et al.*, 2016: 143). In many contexts, therefore, computer and internet-based technologies have been *blended* with face-to-face classroom settings (Gruba *et al.*, 2016) in ways which allow for both in-class and out-of-class online activity and interaction, both synchronously and through delayed (i.e., asynchronous) communication. Furthermore, the emergence of new technologies has also led to the development of *fully online* teaching and learning environments (Hockly, 2015). As Hockly notes, these are sometimes 'formal' courses, combining asynchronous online study (e.g. reading or listening activities) with scheduled, real-time online interaction between teachers and learners, often via a video-conferencing platform. Alternatively, they may be online courses in which learners engage asynchronously with a series of pre-set online materials and tasks but without direct teacher intervention or interaction, as typified by Massive Open Online Courses – MOOCs. (Additionally, learners may access apps and other online resources even more flexibly, often through their own initiative. There are thus links between learning technologies and learner autonomy, which we will examine in more detail in Chapter 8.)

Computer-mediated communication (CMC): implications and interventions

Given these developments, it seems possible that, in some contexts at least, new technologies may 'disappear into' ELT courses and become a normalized and routine part of everyday language teaching and learning (Chappelle, 2010). And, in contexts where the use of new technologies is seen as an expected and necessary part of learning, there is an increasing recognition that technology should be subservient to the wider aims and contexts of language teachers and learners. Hence, Harmer (2015) notes similarities between online, blended and face-to-face learning environments, highlighting in each, for example, the need for teacher thought and planning, and issues such as learner motivation and engagement (we shall discuss learner motivation further in Chapter 7). Similarly, Lewis observes that 'technology is nothing without a teacher and a plan' (2009: 9). From this perspective, new technologies leave the various roles of teachers and learners relatively unaltered, although clearly *how* teachers perform these roles (e.g., resource, prompt and organizer) does potentially change. Kern (2006: 200–1) comments:

> Because the dynamics of interaction (and feedback-uptake relationships) in online environments differ from those in face-to-face interaction, teachers must be prepared for new ways of structuring tasks, establishing exchanges, guiding and monitoring interaction, and evaluating performance, not to mention mastering the relevant computer applications.

Clearly, however, control of some elements of the learning process does pass to learners. As CMC allows for synchronous or asynchronous communication, learners can participate in learning opportunities when and where they choose. Additionally, learners may be empowered to become independent decision-makers through the development of online English-using communities and use of apps that lie beyond their teachers' management and, sometimes, knowledge (Chapelle, 2001; Kern *et al.*, 2016).

Ultimately, however, decisions about the use of new technologies in L2 teaching and learning depend upon two fundamental issues: 'what kind of language does the learner engage in during a CALL activity?' and 'how good is the language experience in CALL for L2 learning?' (Chapelle, 1997: 22), i.e., what is the relationship between new technologies and L2 interaction, and how might this affect language learning? Kern *et al.* (2016: 549) observe that the nature and effectiveness of CMC will vary according to the medium (the language of blogs being different from, for example, text chat or video-conferencing), setting, task(s), and specificities of the learners. Drawing on Blake (2000), they note that while there are questions about the extent to which CMC fosters grammatical development among learners, the negotiation of meaning (see Chapter 6) that learners engage in during CMC means that they develop the ability 'to use their available linguistic, cognitive, social and material resources to deal with specific communicative situations' (Kern *et al.*, 2016: 549). For Kern *et al.*, the success or otherwise of new technologies in ELT thus depends on '*what* particular learners do with computers, *how* they do it, and what it *means* to them' (ibid.; original italics). As Lewis (2009) observes, therefore, while technology appears to offer attractive learning opportunities to teachers and learners, it is a means, not an end; thus teachers and learners should manage, not be managed by, technology (89).

Some final comments are necessary before we move on. First, of course, the current pace of technological development means that accounts of CALL tend to date quickly and the terms of reference surrounding new technologies in ELT are constantly evolving. Additionally, we should again acknowledge that a 'digital divide' exists within ELT and that for many English language teachers and learners, the management and nature of online interaction is not a practical concern. It is to these contexts that we now turn as we examine the management of L2 learning in large classes in difficult circumstances.

Task 2.4 New technologies and ELT

- What role do new technologies play in your teaching context? What is the balance of in-class and out-of-class technology use?

- In what ways do you feel new technologies facilitate L2 learning? Are there any ways in which the use of technology for language learning might be problematic?

- In what ways might computer-mediated interaction differ from face-to-face interaction? Consider both speaking and writing, the language that learners might use, and *how* they might use it.

  - Given that interaction has a central place in the creation of learning opportunities, what might these differences mean for language learning and the language that might be learned?

The dynamics of large classes in difficult circumstances

Although large classes have been common in many ELT contexts for a long time, they have been increasingly discussed in recent years (e.g., Hess, 2001; Shamim, 2012; Shamim and Kuchah, 2016). Yet it is difficult to define what is meant by a 'large class'. Hayes (1997) focuses on classes of fifty or more, while Coleman (2006) identifies classes in which the number of learners ranges from sixty to 300, 500 and even 5,000 (in an open-access university in Thailand). Additionally, as Coleman (2006) points out, not only does class size vary, so also do teachers' perceptions of the point at which a class becomes large. Moreover, large classes can be found in a wide range of ELT contexts, class size being just one of a range of contextual factors in any learning environment (Tudor, 2001). Clearly, 'large classes' are not a homogenous phenomenon (Coleman, 2006). They are, however, often seen as being difficult to teach.

Additionally, a substantial proportion of large classes are taught in 'difficult circumstances' (Shamim and Kuchah, 2016), which include: insufficient or outdated textbooks, limited space and crowded classrooms, and a lack of adequate resources for teaching and learning, including visual aids and new or online technologies. The perceived challenges surrounding the teaching of large classes are clearly compounded by these difficult circumstances. Yet as Shamim (2012) notes, the reduction of class sizes is an expensive reform and may be unlikely in many contexts. Thus, rather than arguing that 'smaller is better', Shamim (ibid.) argues that ELT professionals should focus on understanding and improving large-class teaching and learning.

Consequently, the teaching of large classes is given explicit attention in many teacher training and development texts (e.g., Brown, 2001; Johnson, 2008; Shamim 2012; Harmer 2015) which together identify a range of challenges for teachers including: classroom management, including organizing pair/group work and students' on-task behaviour; interactional and affective factors, such as getting to know students; assessment and feedback; and limited resources given the number of students in a class (Amnpalagan *et al.*, 2012). As Shamim and Kuchah (2016) note, some of these issues relate to physical aspects of the classroom and mixed ability classes, but others are linked to the teachers' wish to promote active learning in class. Some solutions are offered in the professional literature, for example, establishing clear classroom routines and engaging the learners themselves in classroom management tasks (Harmer, 2015), or individualizing learning through student selected materials (Ur, 2012); and, interestingly, these suggestions are not in theory so different from those facing all L2 teachers.

Shamim and Kuchah (2016: 530), however, suggest that these kind of ideas offer a problematic and superficial 'problems and solutions' approach to large-class teaching, providing 'teaching tips' which reflect 'best practice' in ELT more generally and which 'pose problems when applied in large classes in difficult circumstances'. They argue that, in practical terms, the physical constraints of large-class teaching, such as the difficulties teachers experience trying to move around overcrowded classrooms to promote learner interaction or provide learners with enough individual attention, do create specific challenges for establishing and maintaining L2 learning opportunities. Indeed, in a study of large classes in Pakistan, Shamin (1996) documents the emergence of two 'classes' or 'zones' within the same classroom, learners at the front participating in more 'learning-oriented' patterns of interaction, while those towards the back and out of the teacher's 'range' engage in nonproductive activities (such as chatting or doing other work). While a possible solution might be to devolve control and responsibility for interaction to learners at the back of the classroom (i.e., move towards low-structure classroom management), in the context that Shamin investigated, learners expected, and appeared to learn most effectively, within high-structure, teacher-centred classes.

Shamin's study suggests that a complex relationship exists between class size, classroom management and interaction, learner and teacher beliefs and behavioural norms, and the classroom's broader socio-cultural context. Shamim and Kuchah (2016: 531) thus suggest that the nature of 'classroom interaction needs to be redefined to take into account cognitively engaging activities which may not necessarily involve extended verbal exchanges'. For them, localized 'context-appropriate methodology' needs to be developed which might involve learners themselves reflecting on what they want to achieve, how they might do this, and where they might find appropriate resources to meet their learning objectives. Through sharing responsibility with learners, teachers might be able to facilitate learning in contextually appropriate ways which recognize the constraints of large classes and difficult circumstances. 'Good practice' thus develops from the 'bottom up' through local teacher and learner expertise, and encourages learners to take control of aspects of their learning in ways which match their expectations, beliefs and experiences, and learning goals, through a 'pedagogy of autonomy' (ibid.: 533) (see Chapter 8 for further discussion of learner autonomy).

Summary: classroom management and interaction . . . 'it depends'

This chapter has focused on the management of classroom interaction and learning opportunities in English language classrooms. While highlighting the role of interaction in L2 learning, the discussion has also emphasized the complexity and diversity of L2 classrooms, which, Tudor (2001) maintains, is an inherent, not incidental, feature of language teaching. As Tudor puts it, learners are not 'simply' learners, teachers are not 'simply' teachers, and language classrooms are not all the same. Rather, learning environments are complex systems built upon human relationships and located in specific, real-world contexts. Thus, 'in order to understand precisely what takes place in our classrooms, we have to look at these classrooms as entities in their own right and explore the meaning they have for those who are involved in them' (ibid.: 9).

This 'ecological perspective' (van Lier, 1997) suggests that what happens in the ELT classroom is not straightforward and predictable; instead, what happens in learning environments, and how teachers teach, in practice depends on:

> . . . who you are, what you know and believe, and what you want your students to be able to know and do. It depends on what you

are expected to teach, how you teach it, and what your students are
expected to do with what you have taught them . . . it depends on
how your students are viewed within the school where you teach
and within the community where your school is located. . . The list
goes on and on.

(Johnson, 1999: 1)

In terms of this chapter, although classroom management and interaction are key elements in the creation of L2 learning opportunities,
teacher and learners will approach them in different ways in different
classrooms and contexts.

In the next chapter, we will examine differing frameworks through
which applied linguists have theorized this complexity, investigating
in more detail conceptions of the L2 classroom and examining the
relationship between teachers' values and understandings of classroom
life and their teaching practices.

3 The language classroom in theory and practice

Complex, diverse and 'local'

> We live our lives in classrooms as much as outside classrooms; we bring our identities with us to our lives within the classroom, and construct new local identities; we have collective, communal classroom lives.
>
> (Gieve and Miller, 2006: 40)

This chapter will:

- investigate differing conceptualizations of the L2 classroom and explore the insights into classroom life which they provide;
- examine the ways in which language teaching is a 'local activity';
- consider how *values* and *power relationships* might affect classroom practices;
- encourage readers to reflect on whether and how these perspectives add to an understanding of their own English language teaching context.

Introduction: the classroom and 'the people in the room'

Experience tells us that no two classrooms are the same. As we have noted in Chapters 1 and 2, what happens in L2 classrooms in different parts of the world or in different social contexts is influenced by, for example, differing institutional policies, resource availability and societal goals and expectations. We shall examine these 'global' and contextual differences in more detail in later chapters. However, how might we account for variation between classes that take place in apparently similar contexts? If we were to walk into two classrooms in the same institution with apparently comparable groups of learners and with teachers seemingly following a similar classroom methodology and using the same textbook, why might the classes look or 'feel' different? Indeed, as most teachers have experienced within their own teaching, why does working with two apparently similar classes usually work out differently?

Clearly, there will be variation between even the most similar teachers and groups of learners, and we will examine, in later chapters, how individual teachers might interpret and employ language teaching methodologies, curricula and teaching materials in different ways. Similarly, in Part III, we shall explore how specific learner variables such as motivation, learning preferences and aptitude may affect how individuals learn. In this chapter, however, in keeping with our current focus on the management of classroom interaction and learning opportunities, we shall focus on the L2 classroom itself. How have applied linguists conceptualized the language classroom, and how might these ideas account for differences in how teachers and learners act and interact during lessons? The chapter will thus examine the L2 classroom as a *social* environment, the differing realities of classroom life depending on what people, both teachers and learners, 'bring to the room' (Gieve and Miller, 2006; see also Chapter 1).

Metaphors for language teachers and teaching

A *metaphor* is 'any comparison which cannot be taken literally' (Bartel, 1983: 3, in Oxford *et al.*, 1998: 4), or, as Holme puts it, 'a deviant or paradoxical use of language that is meaningful while being logically meaningless' (2004: 410–11); for example, 'learning is a journey', 'teachers are guides' or 'teaching is a two-way street'. Lakoff and Johnson (1980) suggest that metaphor is a fundamental way in which people reason about and conceptualize the world around them. Thus, when teachers and applied linguists draw upon these 'significant images' when talking about teaching, learning and language classrooms, they often reveal their beliefs about, and value-based perspectives on, classroom life (Thornbury, 1991: 193).

Thus, metaphors can provide insights into a range of issues within ELT. For example, discussions of the teacher's role in the classroom often move beyond the ideas of 'manager' or 'prompt', which we identified in Chapter 1, to more overtly metaphorical concepts such as teachers as *entertainers*, *gardeners*, or *jugglers*. Tudor (2001), for example, draws together Briggs and Moore's (1993) discussion of high- and low-order learning environments and van Lier's (1997) 'ecological' perspective on L2 classrooms through the music-based metaphors of the language lesson as a *classical symphony* in which all participants follow the composer through a pre-arranged plan (i.e., a high-order environment), or as an improvised *musical 'jam'* in which the musicians respond to one another's ideas to create new and unpredictable realities (i.e., a low-order and ecological perspective). Meanwhile, when examining metaphors for teacher control and the wider purposes of education, Oxford *et al.* (1998) identify *moulding*, *gate-keeping*, *gardening* and *democratizing* as key images representing education to maintain the existing social order, for cultural transmission, for learner-centred growth, and for social reform respectively. We shall explore the wider educational contexts for and potential purposes of ELT further in Part IV.

A further example of a particularly strong metaphor drawn upon by some English language teachers in recent years is the *Dogme* or *Teaching Unplugged* view of language teaching (Thornbury, 2000; Meddings and Thornbury, 2009). In the mid-1990s, the 'Dogme' group of Danish film-makers aimed to 'purify' film-making by eliminating all 'artificiality' from their productions via 'ten commandments'; for example, filming had to take place on location rather than on specially created sets, no artificial lighting was allowed, and music could not be used unless it occurred within the scene being filmed. Dogme approaches to ELT aim to similarly 'unplug' teachers and classrooms from a dependency on materials, teaching aids and technology, instead drawing upon 'raw materials' or content provided by the people in the room to produce learning opportunities via conversation-based interaction.

Dogme or *unplugged* teaching is interesting in a number of ways. As a metaphor, Dogme is both a way of teaching and an overt attitude *to* teaching; indeed, Meddings and Thornbury argue that it is a 'state of mind' (2009: 21). The beliefs and values that underpin Dogme teaching and its associated literature seem clear – teaching should be materials-light and conversation-driven, with language said to 'emerge' given the right classroom conditions. The Dogme metaphor offers a shortcut to this set of principles and practices.

Additionally, as this brief summary suggests, there are interesting parallels between Dogme in ELT and several of the issues that were explored in Chapters 1 and 2. Dogme teaching holds a particular perspective on classroom interaction, learning opportunities and the social character of the language classroom (as well as learner autonomy and, indeed, critical pedagogy, which we shall explore further in Chapters 8 and 12 respectively).

Thus, it is to images of the L2 classroom that we now turn in more detail. How have applied linguists and teachers conceptualized the language learning classroom; what metaphors have been suggested and what insights do they provide into classroom life?

Task 3.1 Metaphorically thinking

- What metaphors can you think of which describe language teachers or teaching? For example:

  - Language teaching is . . . *an art / a science*; . . . *exploration*; . . . *problem-solving* . . .

- Language teachers ... *transmit / build / share knowledge* ... *entertain / juggle / balance* ...

- Which metaphors best reflect your own professional experience?

Images of the language classroom

L2 classroom interaction and learning has been conceptualized through a variety of metaphors, for example, the classroom as control, as communication, as discourse, as socialization, as an 'ecological system', and as a 'complex system' (Breen, 2001a; Tudor, 2001; Wright, 2005; Larsen-Freeman and Cameron, 2008; Mercer, 2016). Each metaphor differs in the way it embodies and 'explains' the classroom. Thus, the 'classroom as socialization' implies that classrooms are places where learners learn the norms and values of society at large to which they then conform. Additionally, it suggests that classrooms develop their own social rules (Tudor, 2001). Meanwhile, the 'classroom as discourse' intimates that the surface 'text' of a class, what teachers and learners say and do during lessons, can provide insights into L2 teaching and learning as it reveals, for example, patterns of error treatment and repair, and patterns of classroom talk, interaction and control (Breen, 2001a). The 'classroom as an ecological system' (van Lier, 2000) and 'classroom as a complex system' (Larsen-Freeman and Cameron, 2008) perspectives, which are closely related, both remind us that classroom 'ecologies' (or systems) emerge from the dynamic inter-relationships between teachers and learners, and between the classroom and broader contextual factors (Mercer, 2016). Thus, Wright (2005) notes that a classroom system develops from the bottom up through the interactions of the teacher and learners, but is 'nested' in larger contextual systems, such as the school, wider educational policy and goals, and societal and national cultures, all of which intersect with and affect it. From an ecological or complexity perspective, each classroom is therefore part of a wide web of relations which makes it unique and unpredictable, its 'complexity' meaning that its character only emerges if examined holistically (Wright, 2005; Mercer, 2016).

As these brief summaries of the classroom as 'socialization', as 'discourse', and as an 'ecological' or 'complex system' suggest, different metaphors emphasize differing aspects of classroom life. Thus, *all* the examples above provide useful ways of thinking about language classrooms, and many teachers may readily accept all insights as valid and valuable.

Some metaphors, however, offer particularly contrasting visions of L2 classrooms. In this discussion, we shall focus on two very different images of the L2 classroom – the classroom as an 'experimental laboratory', and the classroom as 'culture' or 'coral gardens'. What insights might they offer English language teachers?

The experimental laboratory

Tudor (2001) suggests that the most traditional and perhaps widespread image of the L2 classroom is that of a 'controlled learning environment', or, as Breen (2001a) puts it, 'the classroom as an experimental laboratory'. This metaphor implies that learners follow a clear set of pedagogical procedures under the guidance of the teacher, and learning follows pre-set and expected patterns. Classrooms are high structure (see Chapter 2), and teaching and learning follows a curriculum which is, in effect, a 'statement of intent', that is, a plan of learning that leads directly to what is actually learned (Nunan, 1989a, in Tudor, 2001). According to Anderson (2015: 229), therefore, 'lessons are viewed as events in which teachers plan for and attempt to affect universal behavioural change in a group of learners by achieving their aims, objectives or learning outcomes'. The 'classroom as an experimental laboratory' thus reflects an outcomes-oriented approach to teaching and learning.

As we have seen, this somewhat mechanistic view of the L2 classroom has been criticized for being 'intuitively not true' and simplistic (Wright, 2005; also, Breen, 2001a; Tudor, 2001); in reality, what happens and what is learned in the classroom often differs from what is planned. Thus Breen argues that the 'experimental laboratory' metaphor characterizes learners as passive and learning as 'behavioural conditioning somehow independent of the learner's social reality' (2001a: 125). We shall discuss behavioural conditioning (and behaviourism) in more detail in Chapter 4.

However, while agreeing with Breen's overall analysis, Tudor (2001) points out that an element of planning, however loosely defined, is necessary in any classroom as it offers a starting point for the development of local classroom realities. He observes that most learners also expect a degree of teacher or institution-led control, although this is likely to vary from context to context. Meanwhile, Pang (2016: 446) argues that rejecting the role of planning for learning outcomes 'denies what a professional can shape in the learning process but also how a competent teacher can mediate learner needs in the process of instruction'. Consequently, the 'controlled learning environment' is an image of classrooms that 'few teachers will fail to meet in their working lives, even if the reality of this vision may be less obvious to them in the day-to-day experience of their own classrooms' (Tudor, 2001: 108).

The classroom as 'culture' and 'coral gardens'

Breen, rejecting the 'experimental laboratory' as an 'asocial' image of classroom life, contends that all classes develop complex social cultures, which he metaphorically compares to 'coral gardens' (an image Breen takes from the anthropological studies of Malinowski (1935/2002)). Breen maintains that this metaphor reflects 'the social reality of language learning as it is experienced and created by teachers and learners' (2001a: 127). In other words, it recognizes the complexity of the classroom setting itself, the complexity of interactions occurring within the classroom, and the connections between the classroom and its wider social context (Lima, 2010: 6). There are clear links, therefore, between the metaphor of the 'coral garden' and ideas surrounding the classroom as an ecological or complex system, noted earlier in the chapter.

Thus, the 'coral garden' suggests that teachers and learners both shape and are shaped by their classroom context (Wright, 2006), Breen noting that a language class:

> . . . is an arena of subjective and intersubjective realities which are worked out, changed and maintained. *And these realities are not trivial background to the tasks of teaching and learning a language.* They locate and define the new language itself as if it never existed before, and they continually specify and mould the activities of teaching and learning.
>
> (Breen, 2001a: 128; original emphasis)

In effect, lessons, classroom language and interaction, and any resulting learning opportunities are shaped by class participants in a dynamic process of personal engagement. The coral garden metaphor thus suggests that every class has its own culture that 'generates knowledge' (ibid.). The contrast with the predetermined uniformity implied by the 'experimental laboratory' is evident.

Breen identifies eight key features of the complex 'coral garden' culture of L2 classrooms. He contends that language classrooms are:

- *Interactive*: interaction ranges from the ritual and predictable to the dynamic, unpredictable and diverse.

- *Differentiated*: the classroom is experienced differently by each participant, and the culture of the classroom results from the meeting and mixing of these differing 'social realities'.

- *Collective*: classes have 'psychological realities' which result from the juxtaposition of personal learning experiences and communal teaching-learning activities.

- *Highly normative*: individuals conform to classroom norms and conventions to show they belong.

- *Asymmetrical*: the duties, rights and assumed knowledge of the teacher and learners are different. Asymmetries also exist between learners.

- *Conservative*: classroom groups seek social and emotional stability – perhaps even an equilibrium which does not necessarily assist learning. The conservative nature of classrooms makes innovation difficult.

- *Jointly constructed*: whether or not the teacher plans a lesson in advance, the actual working out of the lesson (and the language within it) is a joint endeavour.

- *Immediately significant*: what is done in the classroom, how and why are immediately psychologically significant to individuals, and the individual as a group member.

(from Breen, 2001a: 129–35)

From this perspective, classroom cultures are not seen as fixed and final but are dynamic and changing. They result from the relationship between social and psychological processes and between individuals and the wider group of learners in the classroom.

Several applied linguists, while acknowledging the value of the 'classroom as culture' metaphor, instead characterize classrooms as 'communities of practice' (E. Borg, 2003; Wright, 2005; Senior, 2006), emphasizing what teachers and learners *do* (or practise) to create and recreate (or maintain) their classroom community. Teachers and learners interact with one another 'to develop the unique cultural environment of each language class' (Senior, 2006: 199). Over time, a class establishes its ways of working and learning, newcomers to the class needing to learn about these practices in order to fit in successfully (Wright, 2005). Senior (2006) highlights tacit understandings over 'who sits where' and regular start-of-class routines (ranging from taking the register to pre-class chat) as examples of practices around which shared understandings develop and socialization into the classroom community takes place.

Although there are overlaps between the characterization of the 'classroom as culture' and as a 'community of practice', the latter's emphasis on *mutual engagement, joint enterprise* and *shared repertoire* (Wenger, 1998) stresses how teachers and learners work together through joint activities and shared practices to create each classroom's unique social and pedagogic environment (Williams *et al.*, 2015).

To summarize, therefore, in contrast to the 'experimental laboratory' metaphor, which emphasizes the pedagogical aspects of the L2 classroom (e.g., the methodology, curriculum, teaching materials and the teacher), the 'classroom as culture' and 'community of practice' conceptualizations emphasize that classroom language learning is not only a pedagogic experience, but also a social encounter. These contrasting perspectives are represented in Figure 3.1.

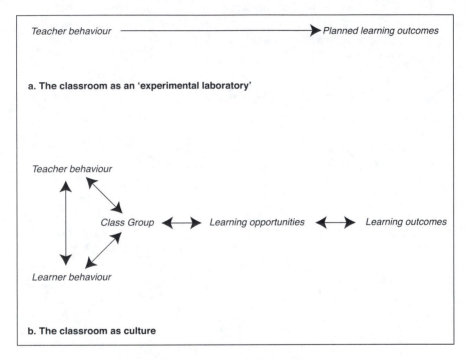

Figure 3.1 Metaphors and the teaching-learning relationship

Source: Both perspectives adapted from Senior, 2006: 278–9.

Task 3.2 Your context: laboratories, cultures and communities

- To what extent do you recognize the 'language laboratory' image of the L2 classroom in your own context?

- How far do you identify with the notion that each class has its own 'culture'?

- Have you ever noticed different learners seeming to experience the same lesson in very different ways (e.g., in terms of enjoyment, engagement or learning)? If so, what, if anything, did you, the teacher, try to do about it?

- Have you ever taught a group of learners who had already established classroom norms and a classroom culture before you met them (maybe they had been taught by another teacher before you)? How did you (both teacher and learners) negotiate this situation?

- Breen notes that, in addition to the asymmetrical relationship between teacher and learners, asymmetries exist between learners, and groups of learners, in a class. Can you think of any examples of this phenomenon?

- In your experience, what are the implicit 'rules of the game' or accepted classroom practices around which classes function? Can you think of any occasions where 'classroom harmony' has broken down? What happened and how was the situation resolved?

- Have you ever experienced difficulty with a class when introducing new types of material, tasks or classroom routines or procedures? If so, why do you think this was?

- What happens when a new learner joins an established class? What do they do to fit in? Do other learners help them? If so, how? How do you, the teacher, help them?

The ELT classroom revisited: social pressures and teaching locally

The 'classroom as culture' raises an interesting paradox for applied linguists and teachers alike. As we have seen, Breen proposes that classroom cultures are 'inherently conservative' and classes may seek a 'social and emotional equilibrium – even one which may seem to be antithetical to learning' (2001a: 132). Similarly, Allwright (1996: 210), noting the potential tension between social and pedagogic pressures within the L2 classroom, refers to:

> the possibility of a 'conspiracy' between teachers and their learners to give priority to social considerations, to pretend to each other 'all must be well pedagogically if all is apparently well socially'.

Senior (2006: 282) develops this point. She suggests that, in order to keep the class functioning, teachers constantly switch between pedagogically oriented and socially oriented behaviour as they try to meet the learning and social needs of individuals and the wider group. She contends that, as a consequence, teacher decision-making is 'impromptu' and 'often without prior deliberation or conscious thought'. Thus, teachers:

> may behave in ways in which they have behaved in the past, or they may make subtle adaptations to their tried-and-tested routines in response to new situations never previously encountered . . . [Thus] it is not surprising that the classroom behaviour of experienced language teachers is virtually impossible to predict.

Breen, Allwright and Senior's ideas, then, exemplify van Lier's 'ecological approach' to classroom life (see Chapter 2 and earlier in this chapter), and highlight the complex, diverse and socially specific nature of L2 learning, where no two classrooms are identical (although they may, of course, be similar!). In this holistic approach, teachers and learners interact with each other within the classroom and its (and their) wider social and institutional context. Consequently, language teaching and learning is a 'dynamic process whereby teachers and students attempt to negotiate their classroom behaviours' (Tudor, 2001: 207).

Yet, while language classrooms are complex and diverse, this is not to say that 'anything goes' (Mercer, 2016: 477). As already noted, the idea of classrooms as wholly independent entities is unrealistic; all L2 classrooms (and teachers and learners) are inevitably subject to external influences – indeed, ecological and complexity perspectives emphasize the dynamic inter-relationships between classrooms and the broader layers of their social context. Thus, the influence and implementation of classroom methodologies, curricula and broader educational policy and tradition may, in theory (although not necessarily in practice, as we shall see in later chapters), serve to 'regularize' classroom practice (ibid.). Hence, as well as being both social and pedagogic in nature, the L2 classroom also is a place where the 'local' and 'global' come together.

Nonetheless, it is at the local level that the management of classroom life and interaction is actually realized:

> [While] general principle can, of course, provide insights . . . effective teaching depends crucially on teachers' ability to understand and react to the particular group of students they have in front of them in a particular classroom (chalk-dust, broken chairs, and all). In other words, language teaching is a local activity.
>
> (Tudor, 2001: 207–8)

For example, classroom interaction and teacher and learner roles are significantly affected by class size; clearly, the extent to which learners might, for instance, work in groups or engage in rote learning strategies in a university class of 200 learners in China or a UK- or US-based language school seminar of twenty is likely to differ (see also Shamin and Kuchah (2016) in Chapter 2).

Thus, Tudor (2001) argues strongly in favour of locally based approaches to decision-making in language teaching and in the language classroom, suggesting that general principles within ELT need to be evaluated critically at the local level in terms of their 'local meaning and appropriacy' (ibid.: 211; see also, for example, Holliday, 1994 and 2005, and further discussion in Chapter 12 of this book). This should take into account a range of local factors ranging from levels of institutional support for language education through to 'a variety of social, economic or ideological factors and the way in which these impact on the attitudes and behaviours of students, teachers, or other participants' (Tudor, 2001: 211). Likewise, Mercer (2016: 477) suggests that teachers need 'to critically engage with and evaluate "global" or "public" principles and theories in relation to their own specific practice'.

These perspectives bring into sharp focus the links between context, complexity, beliefs and behaviours in English language teaching. In the next section, we shall investigate these links in more detail, examining how teachers' (and learners') values might affect and be revealed through classroom interaction.

Task 3.3 Social and pedagogic pressures: reflecting on practice

- How far do you agree with Allwright's proposition that 'getting along' socially sometimes seems more important than 'getting on' academically in the L2 classroom (Allwright and Hanks, 2009)? Can you think of any examples from your own experience? (A simple example, yet one which is familiar to most teachers, is when learners could respond to a teacher's question (i.e., they know the answer), yet choose not to do so. Why?)

Consider occasions when you have been a learner in a class.

- Have you ever experienced an instance when you were confused or wanted to know more about an issue, yet you did not ask the teacher for clarification? If so, why not? (Asking the teacher a question when you are confused would seem to be the logical 'pedagogic' response!)

- Have you ever disagreed with something the teacher said? Did you make your difference of opinion known? If so, how, and how was the situation resolved? If not, why not?

- Consider the issues we reviewed in Chapters 1 and 2 such as teacher questioning, turn-taking and error correction. In which ways might social pressures and the wish to 'get along' affect classroom management and interaction?

- If you have experience of CALL (as a teacher or as a learner), do you think the social pressures are the same in an online classroom or during online tasks and activities as in face-to-face teaching?

- Senior observes that experienced teachers make 'impromptu decisions' without 'conscious thought' (see above). What kind of decisions do you think she is referring to?

- She also argues that experienced teachers' behaviour is 'virtually impossible to predict'. How far do you agree with this suggestion? Do you recognize it in your own teaching or in any teaching you have observed?

Values in the ELT classroom

As a 'profoundly value-laden activity' (Johnston, 2003: 1), teaching English 'always involves values. Teachers make decisions based on values, and, during lessons, students and teachers express particular values' (Menard-Warwick *et al.*, 2016: 556). Johnston (2003: 6) defines values as 'that set of a person's beliefs which are evaluative in nature, that is, which concern what is good and what is bad, what is right and what is wrong'; Johnston also often refers to 'morality', which he regards as essentially synonymous with 'values'. Values are both individual and social in that all values are mediated through individuals who are subject to social forces. Thus, as Johnston (ibid.: 6) suggests, 'values only become interesting when they are played out in social settings – when our inner beliefs are converted into actions that affect others'.

Thus, for the purposes of this discussion, 'values' refers to that specific subset of a person's beliefs that focus on what is right and wrong, rather than broader teacher theories about, for example, how people learn languages (see Chapter 1 for further discussion of 'teacher theories'). Clearly, however, the concepts are closely related.

Values permeate all aspects of ELT including, for example, curriculum design and language testing; decisions about which variety of English might be taught (i.e., a native or a non-native speaker variety);

and the role of native speaker and non-native speaker teachers within the ELT profession as a whole. We shall return to these debates in later chapters. In this discussion, however, we shall focus on how values might be expressed during and through the management of classroom interaction in the L2 classroom.

Reflecting on classroom practices

Menard-Warwick *et al.* (2016: 557) distinguish between *values about* and *values within*, where 'values about' refers to the evaluation of particular topics in classroom discussions, and 'values within' refers to perspectives enacted through classroom interaction and pedagogical policies. For example, if students agree in a classroom discussion that men and women should have equal career opportunities, this is a value *about* gender; if women are encouraged to speak out in class, this demonstrates a value *within* the pedagogy of that classroom (ibid.).

Values 'about'

Talking *about* value-oriented topics is relatively common in ELT, due to the popularity of Communicative Language Teaching (CLT; see Chapter 5 for a summary of key principles, and Chapter 12 for a more critical perspective suggesting that CLT itself reflects a certain set of values – as Menard-Warwick *et al.* (2016) suggest, talking about values reflects a particular value-laden perspective on classroom life). CLT promotes communication, often through discussion, and talking about values can encourage learners to communicate more expansively than they otherwise might (Menard-Warwick *et al.*, 2016). This suggests that the actual values a learner expresses may not matter too much – the aim is simply 'to communicate'. Yet if this perspective – communication for communication's sake – is taken too far, it might trivialize learner contributions and convey a lack of seriousness about deep-seated values and concerns. Additionally, what might be considered as appropriate for discussion, for example politics, religion or sexuality, varies according to context, learners' age and so forth.

Value-oriented discussions are also complicated by the role and status of the teacher, who faces the dilemma of whether to state their own viewpoint. Doing so may silence those students who disagree, yet not doing so presents challenges to a teacher who disagrees significantly with the values a learner may convey (see the discussion of 'expressive morality', below, for further analysis). Although many English language teachers would not see their role as to teach values, they may 'hope that students will develop more "enlightened" attitudes through discussing controversial topics' (Menard-Warwick *et al.*, 2016: 556). However, what is meant by 'enlightened attitudes' is, of course, subjective.

Values 'within' classroom rules

Several researchers provide examples of the way values underpin and are reflected within classroom practices. Johnston *et al.* (1998) examine the explicit rules and regulations through which teachers (and institutions) control classes and learners, highlighting, for example, how some teachers might assign seats to particular learners, or deal with lateness and cheating. Hafernik *et al.* (2002) highlight the ethical dilemmas posed by poor attendance and poor study habits (including the non-completion of homework), both of which potentially challenge teacher and institutional authority and norms, but can also affect the learning opportunities of other learners in the class. Similarly, Hansen (1993) examines the values that underpin the apparently straightforward act of raising hands in class, suggesting that hand-raising establishes order and turn-taking, but also reinforces the values of learner patience and teacher authority.

Consequently, when summarizing the relationship between rules, power and values, Johnston *et al.* observe that 'matters of discipline and control are not merely technical, but also reflect trust or the lack of it, and constitute judgements on those who are being controlled' (1998: 170).

Value dilemmas 'within' classroom management and interaction

In addition to overt, rule-based structures of control, other aspects of classroom practice are also value-laden, for instance, the way teachers manage classroom talk, interaction and corrective feedback. For example, in most classrooms, it is usual that some learners will want to talk and contribute more than others, and will be more comfortable doing so. In such situations, teachers might face the dilemma of balancing the learners' right to speak (or not speak) with the principle of relatively equal learner turn-taking and participation in class, not only for reasons of having an equal 'voice' in class, but also because participation and language production is thought to develop learners' linguistic abilities (as we noted in Chapter 2 and shall return to in the chapters that follow). Johnston (2003) provides an example of an anxious 'silent' learner in class – should her right to be silent be 'protected' by the teacher (to reduce learner stress and also reinforce the learner's own right to make decisions about when to speak), or should she be encouraged to speak and, if so, how? There is no straightforward answer, as the teacher must consider the needs of the individual and of the other learners in the class, and also the values of 'voluntary silence' versus 'enforced speech' (ibid.: 35); values are realized through action as teachers and learners negotiate tensions between individuals and their social context, and between social and pedagogic pressures in the L2 classroom.

Similar dilemmas arise concerning the use of new technologies in L2 learning. For example, as Hafernik *et al.* (2002) ask, if some learners are more familiar with and can make more effective use of new technologies in the L2 classroom, what might this mean in terms of interaction and participation in learning activities, and for equitable access to language learning opportunities for all learners? How might or should teachers respond? Ultimately, teachers will need to make local and immediate decisions based upon beliefs about what is right for each learner, for the whole class and, indeed, for themselves (Johnston, 2003: 5).

'Expressive morality'

Johnston *et al.* (1998) propose that an *expressive morality*, which in part brings together 'values about' and 'values within', operates within ELT classrooms – the subtle acts, gestures and looks through which teachers send messages about their own values. For example, in a class discussion about working women (see Figure 3.2 below), although responsible for eliciting the information, the teacher in this example uses stress and intonation to comment ironically on, and show disagreement with, the learner's response (Johnston, 2003). Other learners laugh to show they understand the teacher's point. However, although gently revealing values that are at odds with those of the learner, the teacher does not make an explicit judgement and continues to attend to what the learners have to say, thus ensuring that the interaction continues. Johnston suggests that the teacher has resolved her own value-dilemma well in this interaction. The class can sense the teacher's own disagreement with the learner's perspective, but, in not explicitly judging his comments, she has also maintained a 'cornerstone of the ELT profession' (Edge, 1996, in Johnston, 2003: 32), that is, respect for learners and their views. Exchanges like this

Teacher:	Guys? Do you want your wife to work?
Learner:	If she wants a job, I'll allow her.
Teacher:	You'll *allow* her?
	. . . (General laughter) . . .
Teacher:	So how will you decide yes or no?
Learner:	[???]
Teacher:	Would you like her to work? What kind of job? Business jobs?
Learner:	No, business is too hard and she would have to work too many hours.

Figure 3.2 A classroom discussion about working women

Source: Johnston *et al.*, 1998: 176; Johnston, 2003: 31.

will be familiar to many teachers and, indeed, are unavoidable. As Johnston (ibid.) comments:

> While we cannot and should not avoid [expressive morality], I would argue that it is in our interest to become aware of the moral meaning our words and actions may convey and to sensitize ourselves to this usually invisible but always important dimension of classroom interaction.

Values in practice

Clearly, teachers are not the only source of values in the L2 classroom; learners' values also affect classroom life. Additionally, this chapter does not aim to guide readers towards one particular set of values or actions. As Johnston puts it, 'while there are better and worse courses of action teachers can take in particular circumstances – that is, their decisions matter – these decisions are always complex and polyvalent [i.e., multi-valued]' (2003: 23). Finally, as noted, although it may be possible for teachers to state what their values might be (Edge, 1996, for example, proposes *diversity*, *inquiry*, *cooperation*, and *respect*), it is only through their realization in practice that we can really establish how values inform the L2 classroom.

The values of teaching and teaching values

Although values inform classroom behaviour and may become evident during class discussions, as noted above, many English language teachers would not consider that they *explicitly* teach values or 'morality', nor, quite reasonably, would they see it as their role to do so. However:

> Even when morals are not being taught explicitly, schools and teachers are generally trying to do the right thing by their students, and thus they have (in a technical sense) a moral life, and may, like it or not, be seen as exemplifying one.
>
> (Crookes, 2003: 88)

In other words, teachers teach values as much by what they do as what they say (Dewey, 1909).

Furthermore, language teachers may be engaged in a potentially more complex value-based enterprise than teachers of other subjects, as L2 classrooms cut across linguistic and cultural boundaries with learners learning new ways of communicating with people from different backgrounds to their own (Crookes, 2003; Johnston, 2003). The subject matter, language, is a means by which people express their identity and culture. Thus, language teaching potentially provides learners with new ways of expressing who they are and, perhaps, even new identities (or new aspects of their identity). Additionally, Johnston argues that cultural values and related cultural practices may differ between native speaker teachers and English language learners, that native speaker teachers may become 'unwitting representatives' for their own 'national cultures' in the eyes of learners, and that non-native speaker teachers are often 'called on to act as representatives of the [language and cultures] they teach' (ibid.: 19).

In essence, therefore, teachers' (and learners') actions infuse classroom interaction and classroom cultures with values, that is, 'the values of teaching'. And, whether teachers intend it or not, learners identify the value-based messages that teachers impart (Johnston *et al.*, 1998) so that they are, in some way, 'teaching values' although this is 'usually unconscious and often ambiguous' (ibid.: 162). For this reason, teachers might wish to reflect on the potential conflicts between their own identities and values and their students' socio-historically situated experiences, beliefs and goals for learning English (Menard-Warwick *et al.*, 2016).

Values, power and society

Throughout these early chapters of the book, we have consistently returned to one particular issue within our discussion of classroom management and interaction – that of 'control'. For example, we have seen how issues of control are embedded in classroom talk and interaction (Chapter 1), examined the relationship between control and learning opportunities (Chapter 2) and, in this chapter, have acknowledged how control is embedded in, and results from, the values that inform classroom practices. Indeed, writing from a 'critical' perspective, Auerbach (1995: 12) places power at the centre of her analysis of classroom life:

> Once we begin looking at classrooms through an ideological lens, dynamics of power and inequality show up in every aspect of classroom life, from physical setting to needs assessment, participants structures, curriculum development, lesson content, materials, instructional processes, language use, and evaluation. We are forced to ask questions about the most natural-seeming practices: Where is the class located? Where does the teacher stand or sit? Who asks questions? What kinds of questions are asked? Who chooses the learning materials? How is progress evaluated? Who evaluates it?

Hence, critical approaches argue that power and politics are central and inescapable elements of ELT and, in later chapters, we will examine what critical writers have to say about the role of English and English language teaching in the world. However, within the context of

Task 3.4 Exploring values

- What 'norms, rules and regulations' are typical of classrooms in your teaching context? How do you deal with issues such as learner lateness, non-attendance, cheating, chatting or not paying attention and interrupting?

- Are the ways in which you might deal with these issues the same for every learner and for every class? If not, why not?

- What values underpin your classroom norms and rules? Are there any other ways the classroom could be organized and managed? How might the learners and your institution react?

- To what extent do you agree with Johnston *et al.*'s comment (1998: 170) that 'matters of discipline and control are not merely technical, but also reflect trust or the lack of it, and constitute judgements on those who are being controlled'?

- How far do you agree with the idea that 'teachers teach values as much by what they do as by what they say', i.e., that all classroom actions and activities are potentially value-laden? What are the implications of this statement for teachers and teaching?

- Do you think the age of the learners matters? Do teachers of adults face the same issues as those who teach children and younger learners?

- What values inform your teaching? What factors affect and inform your values? Consider, for example, your wider institutional, community and national context.

Pajares (1992) observes that the values individuals hold are often contradictory, partially clear, and even 'incoherent'. For example, we might value honesty, but also tact and diplomacy (i.e., not telling the whole truth); similarly, at what point does loyalty and consistency become inflexibility?

- Do you hold any values that are potentially contradictory?

- What value dilemmas have you faced in your teaching, where values that you hold have been in conflict?

- Did you manage to resolve the dilemmas satisfactorily? If so, how?

this chapter, critical perspectives on power and power relationships within L2 classrooms complement, and are perhaps not such a radical departure from, conceptions of 'classrooms as culture' and as value-laden environments.

Summary: negotiating the local – teachers as reflective practitioners

This chapter has investigated how applied linguists have conceptualized the ELT classroom as a pedagogic and *social* environment. L2 classes have been portrayed as complex local 'cultures' or 'communities', where behaviour is subject to competing classroom pressures and is informed by, and infused with, values (including power relationships). Thus as Holliday puts it, what happens in the L2 classroom is 'what happens between people: who we are and what we do' (2006a: 47).

For teachers aiming to understand this complex local reality, Schön (1983) contends that reflection-on-action is necessary, making implicit or practical knowledge explicit and considered. Williams and Burden (1997) similarly emphasize the need for teachers to become reflective practitioners, and draw upon Smyth's framework for critical reflection:

- What do my practices say about my assumptions, values and beliefs about teaching?
- Where did these ideas come from?
- What social practices are expressed in these ideas?
- What views of power do they embody?
- Whose interests seem to be served by my practices?
- What is it that acts to constrain my views of what is possible in teaching?

(Smyth, 1991: 116)

Smyth's questions offer a useful framework, not only for understanding the issues we have examined over the course of the last three chapters, that is, the management of classroom interaction and learning opportunities, but also for understanding English language teaching more generally. As we move on, to examine language teaching Method, Post-method and methodology, they remind us that teachers might want to 'think for themselves and never accept any idea on trust' (Hubbard *et al.*, 1983: 323, in Allwright and Hanks, 2009: 66).

Part II

Method, Postmethod and methodology

4 Language, language learning and Method

Dilemmas and practices

I cannot imagine how any teacher could operate without taking into [the ELT classroom] a set of understandings and beliefs not only about how languages can be and are learnt, but also about how and what teaching is all about.

(Harmer, 2003: 288)

This chapter will:

- examine the continuing relevance of the concept of Method for teachers in what is sometimes described as a 'Postmethod era';
- recognize that different classroom practices stem from differing beliefs about language and language learning;
- explore the practical dilemmas raised by these beliefs, and reflect upon how teachers may negotiate these dilemmas in the L2 classroom;
- encourage readers to reflect on their own beliefs and classroom practices, while acknowledging possible alternatives.

Introduction: why 'Method'?

For over a century, 'language educators sought to solve the problems of language teaching by focusing attention almost exclusively on *Method*' (Stern, 1983: 452), with methodologists asking which method or approach was the most effective for English language teaching – perhaps, for example, Audiolingualism, the Silent Way or maybe Communicative Language Teaching. (However, how far *teachers* followed or participated in these debates is more open to question, as is the degree to which such discussions were recognized globally or were essentially concerns of a largely UK- and USA-based methodological literature. We shall return to these points in later chapters.)

In recent years, however, the debate has developed in significant new directions. It has been argued that we are no longer asking the right question, that Method, traditionally seen as a theoretically consistent set of teaching principles that would lead to the most effective learning outcomes if followed correctly (Richards and Rodgers, 2014), is not, and cannot provide, 'the answer' to making English language teaching and learning more effective. Around twenty-five years ago, Prabhu (1990) proposed that any attempt to find a 'best' method was illogical given that teachers quite reasonably adapted and combined individual methods to accommodate contextual influences and their own personal beliefs. At the same time, applied linguists such as Pennycook (1989) argued that traditional views of Method frustrated teachers who, in the real world, were unable to implement them fully and consistently. Pennycook also argued that the idea of Method and the search for a best method maintained unequal power relationships within ELT between academics and researchers on the one hand, and teachers in language classrooms on the other.

As a result of this sustained criticism, the idea of 'Method' and the search for a 'best' method has receded in importance, at least in the thinking of many applied linguists. Indeed, researchers such as Kumaravadivelu (1994, 2003, 2006, 2012) have argued that we are now in a 'Postmethod era', to the extent that this idea is now regularly discussed and examined in teacher training and development texts (e.g., Thornbury, 2006; Harmer, 2015). Given these developments and the apparent move away from Method as a major focus within ELT, why does Method remain the focus of this and the following two chapters? As Allwright and Hanks (2009: 37) put it, 'why should we care about language teaching methods?'

Examining language teaching methods serves a clear purpose. If we are in a Postmethod era, methods can be studied 'not as prescriptions for best practice' but as both a source of 'personal practical knowledge' and 'for reflective review of the teacher's own core principles [and] theoretical understanding' (Richards and Rodgers, 2014: 358). For example, the development, drilling and practising of dialogues in the classroom defined the audiolingual era, yet drills are still used by many teachers today, whether or not they explicitly associate such techniques with Audiolingualism and know about the structuralist view of language and behaviourist theory of learning that underpin this method (see Chapter 5). Thus, Bell (2007), having asked whether teachers think that methods are 'dead', finds that they offer a source of options and practical classroom interventions, while Richards and Rodgers (2014: 16) suggest that knowing about methods 'introduces a variety of principles and procedures that teachers can review and evaluate in relation to their own knowledge, beliefs and practice'. Thus, even, perhaps especially, in a Postmethod world of methodological eclecticism, knowledge of methods is useful.

How theorists have conceptualized Method, individual methods and the Postmethod era will be further explored in Chapter 5, as will the distinction between Method and methodology. However, this chapter will continue by examining the key method-related practical dilemmas teachers face in the language classroom.

Thinking about language: *what* might teachers teach and learners learn?

I teach English, don't I?

Superficially, asking 'what do English language teachers teach and learners learn?' seems rather illogical. The question appears to answer itself; it seems self-evident to note that what teachers teach and learners learn in ELT classrooms is language, specifically the English language. However, if we start to 'unpack' this common-sense understanding of ELT, what initially seems clear is in fact revealed to be full of complexity, and raises a number of dilemmas that are embedded in the everyday practices of ELT teachers and their approach to teaching.

Just some of the issues our tautological question raises are:

- Is language in the classroom addressed primarily as a system of grammatical rules or patterns, or as a system for expressing meaning and communicating, perhaps communicating to solve tasks or for learners to express their own identity? Of course, it is possible, perhaps likely, that a combination of these perspectives may be part of teachers' understandings of language and apparent in their classroom teaching. If so, how can they be combined coherently?

- Similarly, which language skills are of primary importance (and of primary importance in the ELT classroom) – 'spoken skills' (i.e., listening and speaking) or 'written skills' (i.e., reading and writing)?

- Thus, what is meant by language knowledge (or knowledge of language)? Are learners learning *about language* so they are able to consciously and explicitly describe how language operates, or is the focus more on *how to use the language* via implicit knowledge below the level of consciousness, perhaps with little or no explicit attention to 'rules'? And how might teachers balance these perspectives in practice?

Linguistic and applied linguistic research has dealt with the issues raised above at length, as we shall see in Chapter 6. However, whether they draw upon 'academic' theories or not, the approach teachers pursue in their classes will be informed by their personal hypotheses and beliefs, whether these theories are explicit or remain unconscious.

There are many other classroom issues 'hidden' within our opening question, not least whether learners actually learn what teachers teach (as Allwright (1984) asks), or whether all learners pay equal attention and learn at the same rate (it seems reasonable to suggest that this is rarely the case!). Alternatively, touching on a very different issue, what, in fact, is meant by 'the English language'? Is it, among many possibilities, the English of people who, for example, live in Britain or the USA, and who speak English as their first language (in a high-status dialect and accent), or is it an English as spoken by people who have learned English as a second or additional language to communicate in international contexts? What, in fact, *is* the target language of the classroom? However, as these questions relate to themes other than our current focus of Method, we shall return to them in later chapters.

Understanding 'language': dilemmas for the ELT classroom

As Stern (1983: 119) notes, 'as soon as we try to learn [or teach] a language, we come up against the most fundamental questions about the nature of language'. One of the main problems is that 'language' has many ways of being understood, as does the term 'linguistic knowledge'. V. Cook (2016: 20), for example, identifies six major meanings of the term 'language' ranging from 'knowledge in the mind of an individual' to 'a set of sentences'; Hall (2013) identifies seven key elements within an understanding of language; and many other ELT and applied linguistics texts quite reasonably avoid defining language altogether!

However, how language is conceptualized is not just an issue for applied linguists and other theorists; it is also an issue with practical relevance in the ELT classroom. As Brown (2007: 7) observes, how teachers understand the components of a language influences how it is taught:

> If, for example, you believe that nonverbal communication is key to successful second language learning, you will devote some attention to nonverbal systems and cues. If you perceive language as a phenomenon that can be dismantled into thousands of discrete pieces and those pieces programmatically taught one by one, you will attend carefully to an understanding of the discrete forms of language. If you think language is essentially cultural and interactive, your classroom methodology will be imbued with sociolinguistic strategies and communicative tasks.

In effect, Brown is confirming that, at some level, teachers' conceptions of how language works, that is, what language is for and how language is used by people, affects what and how it is taught in the ELT classroom.

Task 4.1 Setting the scene: language and the English language classroom

Reflect upon your own experience as an English language teacher:

- What do learners need to *know about* language in your classroom? Why?

- What do learners need to *know how to do* with the target language? Why?

- Is one form of knowledge prioritized above the other? If so, why?

- To what extent do learners analyse grammatical rules and to what extent do they practise language skills?

- Which elements of language are of primary importance in your classroom, if any: for example vocabulary, grammar, speaking, listening, reading or writing? Why?

- To what extent do you analyse and present language rules to learners before they use the language in examples and through practice? To what extent do learners use language before looking for rules? What might this suggest about your view of language and how languages might be learned?

- What kind of learning activities and tasks do you think are most useful and effective in your classroom? How are they useful? Why might they be successful? Consider activities that might involve the whole class (including the teacher), those that learners work on in groups or pairs, and those that they undertake by themselves.

Thinking about second language learning: *how* might learners learn . . . and teachers teach?

Teachers' knowledge, beliefs and assumptions about how second languages are learned is a second area where differing conceptualizations might affect how teachers teach. These perspectives in part develop from, and overlap with, the ideas teachers might hold about language and knowledge of language that were introduced above; that is, a particular perspective on language may lead to a view of how languages are best learned. For example, if teachers feel it is possible to break language down into many discrete pieces as Brown observes they might (see above), then they may believe that language is best learned by analysing individual language items (with clear implications for classroom practice). If, however, teachers regard learners' linguistic knowledge as being primarily the ability to use language, with little need for conscious awareness of grammatical rules, then it is likely that their perspectives on how learners are thought to learn will differ, again with implications for how language is taught and learned in the language classroom.

Similarly, first language *acquisition* and second language *learning* are clearly very different, both in terms of the learner characteristics (e.g., the existence of another language in the learners' minds) and the environment in which they are learning (e.g., amount of time available for learning). Yet the fact that all children (unless they have a specific disability) acquire a language as they grow up has encouraged some applied linguists and theorists to speculate as to whether ELT classrooms can in some way recreate the conditions for learning that a child experiences when learning its first language, or the conditions under which someone may informally learn a language through *immersion*, without formal study, in a second-language environment. How far this is accepted as a reasonable foundation for classroom language learning clearly underpins how teachers might teach.

Task 4.2 First language acquisition and second language learning

- In what ways do you think first language acquisition and second language learning might be different? In what ways might they be similar? You may wish to think of specific second language learning contexts and groups of learners, for example, learning in a classroom or 'picking up' the language informally, and differences between young children, teenagers and adult learners of a second language.

- What might the implications of these similarities and differences be, if any, for second language teaching methodology?

Forming habits, engaging the mind, or working with others?

To what extent is language learning the formation of 'good' language habits, the result of learners using their minds' internal learning mechanisms, or the consequence of learners interacting with other people? While 'language learning as habit formation' is now no longer widely supported by theorists as a *comprehensive* account of how languages are learned (as we shall see), other approaches emphasize to varying degrees the innate properties of the human mind, or the cognitive processes learners' undertake when learning, or how learning may be a 'social activity' (and also a *consequence* of social activity).

Conceptions of learning therefore inform both approaches to how learners might engage with language generally, and also underpin many specific, well-used and familiar classroom activities.

Teaching 'good' habits in the language classroom: practices ... and limitations

Behaviourist approaches to learning suggest that learners can form 'good' habits and 'correct' patterns of language use by following a pattern of *stimulus*, *response* and *reinforcement*. In the classroom, then, *drilling* aims to encourage habit-formation through the accurate repetition of language forms. Language is developed in drills via *substitution* (and substitution tables) which reduce the likelihood of learner errors. Similarly, *presentation, practice and production (PPP)* approaches in the classroom look to develop learner language by establishing a context and clear model sentences (i.e., presentation) followed by choral drilling, individual repetition and teacher-led substitution (i.e., practice) before learners are given the opportunity to 'produce' language. Thus, error-free repetition and habit-formation precedes learners' own use of the language, reflecting the belief that 'practice makes perfect'.

However, while habit-forming activities may have a place in the ELT classroom, there have been numerous strong criticisms of the idea that habit-forming by itself offers a full explanation of how languages are learned – it fails to allow for the role of the human mind in learning, of consciousness, thought, and unconscious mental processes, and does not account for the creative use of language, whereby learners create new sentences which they have not previously heard or practised.

'If language is innate': the input issue

As we shall see in Chapter 6, some accounts of language learning suggest that humans are born with innate knowledge of a set of linguistic principles common to all languages, that is, a *Universal Grammar* (UG). Although first proposed by Chomsky as a mechanism explaining how children acquire their *first* language during the *critical period* of their development (i.e., pre-puberty), it has been suggested that UG may provide insights into second language learning (White, 2003).

The view that the ability to learn a language is innate (and hence second language learning may resemble first language acquisition) could lead teachers to suggest that exposure to language should be a primary concern in the L2 classroom, the implication being that exposure may lead to language being 'picked up' in a 'naturalistic' way. Indeed, Krashen (1982) developed the *Monitor Model*, in which he argued that, given *comprehensible input* (i.e., language just beyond what has already been acquired) and a relaxed state of mind that is ready to learn (conceptualized as a low *affective filter*), then learners would acquire language (see Chapter 6 for further discussion). Thus given appropriate input and a readiness to learn, learners would acquire language; language use follows, and is evidence of, acquisition. However, among many others, Long (1985) has further developed the input hypothesis, suggesting that *interaction* between language learners leads learners to adapt their speech to include comprehension checks, repetitions and recasts. He suggests that this acts as a mechanism for making input comprehensible for learners and thus introduces the concept of interaction to the process of learning English (we have already noted the central role of interaction in many approaches to language teaching and learning (Chapter 2), and will explore it further in the discussion below and in Chapter 6).

Krashen also proposed that language *acquisition* and *learning* are essentially different processes, acquisition being unconscious and 'natural' with no attention given to linguistic form, while learning involves conscious attention to language forms and rules. For Krashen, acquired language was more valuable as it, rather than learned language, was instantly retrievable for use; consciously learned language may only be a monitor or check on what is acquired.

The Monitor Model has been heavily criticized for offering an incomplete model of language learning (see Chapter 6 for further discussion), and a lot of applied linguists now consider Krashen's distinction between language acquisition and learning to be vague and unverifiable, leading many to treat these terms as synonyms. However, two of the Monitor Model's fundamental concepts, the importance of input (and how to provide or generate it in a comprehensible form) and the role of affect have remained key ideas within ELT, as has the debate surrounding whether or not it is useful to focus explicitly on language forms, leaving teachers with much to consider.

'More than just input': cognitive processes and classroom concerns

Cognitive perspectives on second language learning, although recognizing that Universal Grammar provides a valid explanation for first language acquisition, suggest that it does not fully explain second language learning. Drawing on the metaphor of computers processing data (Lightbown and Spada, 2013), cognitive approaches focus on the way our minds store information, process and make connections with it, and retrieve it at the right time. The theoretical elements of cognitive approaches will be explored further in Chapter 6.

In the classroom, however, teachers are faced with a number of dilemmas. First, should language features be brought to the attention of learners, and, if so, how might this be achieved? In contrast to

Krashen's ideas, teachers might hypothesize (as does Schmidt, 1990) that second language learners can only learn a specific language feature, or the narrow gap between their own performance and the target language, once they have paid conscious attention to it, that is, once they have *noticed* it. Classroom activities that might help learners notice include comparing their own recorded or written language against a model or example, or, indeed, drilling and repetition, where forms are highlighted, i.e., noticed. (It is interesting to note that the example of drilling demonstrates that, in the interrelationship between theory and practice, the same practices can sometimes be informed by different theoretical perspectives and beliefs, and unless one is particularly committed to a single approach, elements of different theories can inform, and be informed by, the ELT classroom.)

However, in order to use English effectively, learners need to be able to retrieve and use the right language at the right time quickly. Thus how can learners' use of 'noticed', conscious knowledge be made faster and, according to cognitive perspectives on language learning, be made automatic? How might knowledge about language be converted by learners into knowing how to use language? Or, in more practical terms, what is the role of *practice* and what forms might practice take? How much practice should learners engage in? Moreover, what is the role of learner pair and group work within the classroom? Is there a role for conversation and conversational interaction, and what purpose does it serve? As Ellis and Shintani (2014: 223) put it, 'are some kinds of interaction more likely to foster learning than others?'

Thornbury (2006: 173) identifies a number of different kinds of practice: *controlled* versus *free practice, mechanical* versus *meaning-ful/communicative practice*, and *receptive* versus *productive practice*, while Johnson (2008: 254) highlights the parallel between language learning and the development of other skills (such as learning a musical instrument) by suggesting that practice activities can range between 'scales' (i.e., controlled practice) and 'the real thing' (i.e., free production). Practice can therefore take many shapes and forms, from controlled drills and repetition, to pair and group information gaps, discussions, games and problem-solving activities (with either an explicit linguistic focus (i.e., noticing) or a focus on a 'real-world' context such as planning a journey or ranking information in order of importance). Clearly, in its more controlled forms, practice is associated with accuracy, while freer practice is said to develop learners' fluency. Teachers will direct practice, and intervene and correct (or not intervene and correct) in ways that they consider appropriate given their aims and the learners' needs, as learners develop their control of the language.

If controlled practice activities draw upon both theories of cognition (i.e., they help to automatize language) and, despite its evident weaknesses, behaviourism (i.e., drills help learners form good habits), learning through free practice and conversational interaction raises a more fundamental question about how English might be learned and taught. Allwright (1979) asks whether language learning can take care of itself while Grundy, paraphrasing Howatt (1984), asks whether learners might use language in order to learn it, rather than learn language in order to use it (1999: 54). Both are suggesting something fundamental about how languages might be learned in the ELT classroom, with implications for what teachers might consider practice to be and what it is for.

The input hypothesis, as we have seen, suggests that learners use language once it is learned, i.e., that practice and output is not part of learning but is a *consequence* of learning. Swain (1985), however, in her *output hypothesis*, suggests that learning takes place as learners produce language. She suggests that producing output is more challenging for learners than understanding input, that 'output pushes learners to process language more deeply (with more mental effort) than does input' (1995: 126). Thus in productive practice, learners are not just developing fluency, but are 'learning by doing'. From this perspective, practice is not a reflection and reinforcement of learning, but is part of the cognitive process of learning. We will examine how this may take place in Chapter 6. However, the implication of this idea for classroom practice is that free practice and conversational interaction really matter, with clear implications for the ELT classroom.

'Learning as a social activity': interaction and the 'co-construction of knowledge'

Although the behaviourist and cognitive perspectives on second language learning outlined above differ significantly, one characteristic they share is that they all focus on learning as a primarily individual activity, with individuals 'as the principal unit of analysis' (Williams *et al.*, 2015: 44). *Sociocultural* approaches to language learning, on the other hand, conceive of learning not as an individualistic, internal mental process but as an essentially social activity where learners are active and interactive, and where their social world impacts on their learning and language development (equally, individuals, through participation and engagement, influence their social worlds). From a sociocultural perspective, learning takes place through social interaction, with the learner being supported in and through talk and interaction by their teacher or peers in a process known as *scaffolding*. This scaffolded support enables learners to work at a level which would otherwise be beyond their reach, termed the *Zone of Proximal Development* or ZPD (Vygotsky, 1978). Language is seen as central to the development of knowledge as it *mediates* thinking, that is, it is a 'tool' which enables people to make sense of and understand the world (including what is said to them and what they say to others), and is used to organize and regulate mental processes. For example, we often use language for making lists (i.e., as a memory device), to talk through and solve problems, or to make decisions (Williams *et al.*, 2015).

According to sociocultural perspectives, therefore, all knowledge, including L2 knowledge, is developed, or co-constructed, in a collaborative manner with language and interaction being central to this process (see Chapter 6 for further discussion). Although we might see overlaps with some of the ideas outlined in previous sections, for example conversational interaction, or the resemblance of the ZPD to Krashen's comprehensible input, the ideas are not comparable due to their very different theoretical underpinnings. Long's interaction hypotheses and Krashen's Monitor Model (see above), for example, understand learning to be the result of the individual and internal cognitive 'processing' of language input; sociocultural approaches see learning as occurring *through* interaction (Lightbown and Spada, 2013). That said, classroom practices may look very similar to those described above as teachers face a number of questions including: how might classroom interaction, including teacher and learner talk, best scaffold learning? How might a classroom's culture effectively facilitate communication and the construction of knowledge? And how does the wider social context in which a classroom is located affect opportunities for interaction, collaboration and learning in class? These questions clearly link to many of the themes raised in Part I of this book.

The above discussion has briefly illustrated how classroom practice and theories of language learning may inform each other. The theoretical perspectives will be explored in more detail in the following two chapters; now, however, we will continue to explore further classroom dilemmas, possibilities and practices in more detail.

Matters arising: further possibilities, practices and pedagogical debates

Grammar dilemmas

Much of the above discussion hints at a key question that is a shared concern of both applied linguistic theory and ELT practice, that is, what is the place of grammar and grammar teaching in the ELT classroom? Ellis (1992: 191) has addressed the issue as follows:

Should teachers seek to intervene directly in the process of their students' L2 development (e.g. by teaching specific grammatical items) or should they intervene only indirectly (e.g. by providing opportunities for natural communication) and so allow learners to build their interlanguages [internal language systems] in their own way? . . . In what ways should direct intervention (e.g. grammar teaching) be carried out? . . . What types of classroom interaction are likely to prove optimal for L2 acquisition?

In the classroom, this debate realizes itself as whether learning takes place best when grammar features are examined explicitly and consciously (i.e., via instruction), or whether it is enough for learners to 'encounter' language and subsequently develop knowledge themselves, whether consciously or unconsciously (i.e., through exposure). As Thornbury (2006: 93) puts it, teachers and methods 'have positioned themselves along a scale from "zero grammar" to "total grammar"'.

There are several familiar arguments against the explicit teaching of grammar. For example, knowing a grammar rule is no guarantee that a learner can actually use the language spontaneously in and beyond the classroom. Additionally, it is claimed that the time spent explicitly engaging with grammatical rules could be better spent engaging in meaningful communication, and that grammar teaching therefore denies other learning opportunities. Thus, while Brown (2007) rightly says that teachers need to know grammar, V. Cook (2016: 49) comments, 'it is one thing to make teachers aware of grammar . . . it is something else to say that students themselves should be aware of grammar'.

In contrast, however, Ortega (2009: 139) provides a series of examples that strongly suggest both the rate of learning and linguistic accuracy increase when learners experience explicit grammatical instruction compared to 'uninstructed learners'. She does point out, however, that although rate and accuracy may increase, this is only when instruction works with the learners in terms of their readiness to learn specific grammatical features (we will examine the concept of learners' 'readiness' to learn in Part III).

Both teachers and researchers hold a range of perspectives on whether grammar should be addressed explicitly in the ELT classroom. Fundamentally, those who support an innatist, UG perspective on language learning doubt its value, while those who believe that there is a link between explicit, conscious knowledge of language and the ability to use it, a link created by the mind's cognitive processes, support it. In this latter perspective, focusing on just the meaning of language is insufficient.

What is notable, however, is that even if the suggestion that an explicit focus on language is advantageous for learners is accepted, it still leaves teachers with the dilemma of what forms such instruction might take and how such activities might be balanced with other elements of classroom life. Thus if 'there is a consensus that form-focused instruction is facilitative or even necessary . . . what remains controversial is the selection of structures, the timing and intensity and the choice of instructional options' (Pawlak, 2008: 193; also, Ellis and Shintani, 2014). It is to this issue that we now turn.

Focus on form or forms?

What form might grammar instruction take? Should the focus on grammar emerge from the language in the classroom, that is, around language features that occur naturally within the activities of the class; or should the class be structured around a form-based syllabus? In addition to 'grammar', instruction, of course, also attends to language features beyond, for example, tenses, articles and modality, and includes other areas such as discourse, pronunciation and vocabulary.

Attending to language items in the ELT classroom does not have to mean teachers and learners focus on explanations of individual grammar (and language) points in a predetermined sequence (known as *focus on forms*), although it could resemble this. Typically, *focus on forms* can be found in the predetermined grammar syllabuses or grammar strands that feature in many ELT coursebooks. In contrast, *focus on form* suggests that attention to language can happen at any point in a lesson or series of lessons, and it can be either teacher-led or occur through learner activity. The linguistic forms focused upon emerge as a consequence of the learners' engagement in meaningful communication and, as V. Cook (2016) suggests, there are several ways of drawing learners' attention to grammar without explaining it explicitly, such as using pauses in speech or italics in writing. In effect, this is Schmidt's concept of 'noticing' in practice (see p. 73).

However, we have already seen that explicit attention to grammar may only be effective if learners are ready to learn the particular feature, and thus focus on form 'is most successfully achieved by drawing attention to those specific features that the learner is attempting to use in meaningful communication, but is using incorrectly' (Ellis and Shintani, 2014: 144).

Supported by substantial applied linguistic research, ideas surrounding focus on form have considerable implications, not just for teachers, but also for ELT syllabus designers and textbook and materials writers, as they challenge still widespread focus on forms approaches to organizing language teaching and learning, in which language courses progress by teaching a pre-planned series of discrete language items. We shall return to these challenges in subsequent chapters.

Learning through deduction or induction?

The discussion so far suggests that some attention to grammar and other language points in the ELT classroom is likely, whether through a focus on form or a focus on forms. The degree to which attention to grammar takes place will also vary widely according to the beliefs, practices and norms of teachers and learners (which will, in turn, be influenced by the wider institutional and social context; see Part IV). Despite this variety, learners can be introduced to language rules through two very different routes.

In *deductive* approaches to learning, learners are first provided with the rules or generalizations about language, which are explained and demonstrated before being practised. Harmer (2015) makes the analogy that deductive learning is like a 'straight arrow', and highlights how PPP (see above) fits into this pattern, while Johnson (2008: 162) summarizes the move from rule to example as RULEG. On the other hand, teachers may pursue, and learners may prefer, *inductive approaches* to the presentation of language. Here, learners examine language examples, and work rules out for themselves (characterized as EGRUL by Johnson (ibid)). Inductive approaches characterize 'discovery' activities such as reading examples of contrasting grammar items, working out the difference in meaning and hence the rule. Figure 4.1 below provides an example of an inductive activity:

Look at the following pairs of sentences. What language form is used in each sentence and why? How do the simple and continuous aspects of the verb differ in meaning?

- He's broken his leg.

- I've been studying all day.

- The match has finished.

- She's been waiting here for half an hour.

Figure 4.1 An inductive learning task

Whether to follow an inductive or deductive approach may depend on several factors. Learning styles and learner preferences may underpin teachers' decisions – some learners may prefer the direct, teacher-led nature of deductive approaches, and most self-study grammar books follow this approach. However, inductive approaches, with the mental effort and processing required of learners, are thought to more accurately reflect the way the mind learns (see above; also Chapter 6). Clearly, some learners may prefer this latter style of learning, and it has been suggested that inductive approaches may develop *learner independence* and *autonomy* (concepts we shall investigate in Chapter 8).

How might teachers approach the issue of deductive or inductive approaches to learning? In practice, both deductive and inductive learning may take place in any one classroom, dependent upon the learners' preferences and learning styles, the teacher's view of effective learning, and the approach followed by materials and textbooks and institutional preferences. Teachers face the challenge of selecting and possibly combining the approaches effectively and coherently for learners, recognizing that learners' perspectives may change according to, for example, their age or L2 ability.

Teaching language skills: considerations and questions

Our review of pedagogical possibilities has so far been largely concerned with debates surrounding how L2 forms might be learned. The focus has in particular been on grammar, but debates surrounding noticing, focus on form(s) and even inductive/deductive approaches can also apply to the teaching and learning of vocabulary and pronunciation. Obviously, however, learners also need to develop their 'core' L2 skills (Burns and Richards, 2012: 195) of speaking, listening, reading and writing, which raises a range of issues for teachers and other ELT professionals, such as syllabus, curriculum and materials writers, to consider.

It is evident that the varying accounts of how learners learn which were reviewed earlier in the chapter emphasise some skills over others. For example, behaviourist perspectives stress accurate and controlled speaking; here, the role of listening is to provide models for speaking drills. Meanwhile, Krashen's Monitor Model accentuates the role of listening and reading as sources of comprehensible input, while Long's focus on the role of interaction in language learning highlights the skills of speaking and listening. And, as we shall see in Chapter 5, different language teaching methods draw upon these ideas, and consequently also emphasise some skills at the expense of others (Newton, 2016).

However, in a possible era of methodological eclecticism (see p. 66), in which the vast majority of English language learners will need and want to develop all four skills, what dilemmas do teachers face when teaching language skills? The discussion will focus on a number of issues common across the skills; for more detailed explorations of individual skills, see, for example, Field (2011) for listening; Nation (2009) for reading and writing; and Goh and Burns (2012) for speaking.

One central issue in the teaching of L2 skills is the extent to which they are taught and practised separately through, for example, a reading, a writing, a listening and a speaking class or activity; are in some way combined through integrated 'skills classes' or tasks; or are incorporated into other classroom activities. On the one hand, as Johnson

(2008) notes, the four skills might be treated separately as groups of learners may have different needs and abilities in each (they may be fluent speakers, for example, but less proficient readers and writers). Additionally, each skill presents different challenges to learners which might benefit from being addressed separately. On the other hand, it is evident that language skills are interconnected – conversation (and classroom interaction) requires both speaking and listening; learners studying English for Academic Purposes (EAP; see Chapter 10) might need to develop the skill of taking written notes while listening to lectures or to summarise books and articles that they have read. Furthermore, many classroom tasks will integrate two or more skills (e.g. a role play will involve both listening and speaking; dictation-based activities practice both listening and writing (and even speaking, if the learners also take on the role of text provider)); from this perspective, skills are inseparable from other aspects of classroom life.

Whether taught separately or through an integrated approach, L2 skills are developed through practice (Newton, 2016; see also p. 73 in this chapter), yet the form this might take can vary. If learners speak, listen, read or write during a task or activity, is this form of practice sufficient to support their L2 skill development? Or should learners first 'practice the performance' of an activity (i.e., the language skills that will be required) before actually engaging in the task itself (ibid.)? This raises key questions about whether learners 'learn as they use' language or 'learn to use' language which we will return to in Chapter 5 (and have noted previously).

In addition to the role of 'practice', a further consideration in the teaching of the receptive skills of listening and speaking is the extent to which learners should focus on *top-down* and *bottom-up* processes. In top-down processes, learners 'draw meaning from around or outside a text (e.g. from topic-related background knowledge or experience) to help make sense of it' (Newton, 2016: 430); that is, learners understand the context of the communication or text, and use this to understand its meaning. Top-down approaches to skill development in the classroom often involve predicting content, skimming and scanning (in reading), and global listening to understand the overall message of a text, with less attention given to the language and its specific features. In contrast, in bottom-up processes, learners 'extract information from the linguistic elements of a written or spoken text to construct meaning' (ibid.). This might involve decoding and interpreting language through word recognition, and parsing (i.e., analyzing and breaking down) sentences and sentence structures. For language learners, these processes are generally slower and require more conscious effort than top-down approaches. Although successful L2 reading and writing require both, Field (2011) argues that communicative language teaching materials often emphasise top-down skills at the expense of bottom-up approaches, and suggests that, while activities such as answering meaning-focused comprehension questions might provide some skills practice, they in fact tend to *test* existing skills, rather than actually *teaching* reading or listening.

For teachers and other ELT professionals, therefore, the challenge is to provide opportunities for the development and practice of both top-down *and* bottom-up processes. How this is achieved, however, is likely to depend on factors such as the learners' age or their learning goals. Equally, the teaching of writing and reading in particular are likely to be affected by the texts learners are likely to encounter or to produce. Reading a technical manual or writing an academic essay require different linguistic knowledge and skills to reading a newspaper or writing an email; consequently, teachers' awareness of learners' contexts and learning aims will affect the way language skills are taught.

Is there a place for the learners' first language in the classroom?

There is, or has until recently been, a widespread assumption that teachers and learners should use only the second language rather than the learners' first language in the ELT classroom (we shall encounter this belief again in subsequent chapters). Characterized by Hall and G. Cook (2012: 272) as the 'monolingual assumption', Kerr (2016: 514) notes that 'to many people, it is self-evident that the more a learner is surrounded by English, the more English they will learn . . . [From] this perspective, zero use of the learners' language is the ideal to be aspired to'.

There are of course good reasons for limiting L1 use and working as far as possible in the second language in the classroom. Learners will communicate more in English, which, according to Long (see above) means more input for others in the class. Using only English in the classroom also means that *all* language, whether the language used in learning activities or the *metalanguage* of the lesson (such as instructions and explanations), is potential input for learners. It also means that opportunities for English language practice and output will be maximized. On a practical note, of course, those teachers who either do not speak the first language of the learners, or who are teaching classes in which learners have differing first languages, have clear reasons for using only English in the classroom. Additionally, many teachers suggest that, in some contexts, if the learners' first language is used in class, then the learners may be more resistant to using English generally and employ their L1 more than perhaps teachers may wish.

In recent years, however, the monolingual assumption has increasingly been challenged. Writing from a socio-political perspective, Phillipson (1992) argues that the emphasis on second language only classrooms has been sustained by the socio-economic dominance of methods that have emerged in the UK and US, where classes are taught with mixed learner L1 backgrounds, and also by the teaching of English around the world by native-speaker English teachers who cannot speak the first language of the learners (see above, and also Chapter 12).

Meanwhile, focusing more on the nature of second language learning itself, Widdowson observes that language learning is 'in some degree, a compound bilingual experience' (2003: 152) and notes that learners keep their L1 and L2 in contact in their minds in the classroom. Similarly, the learners' L1 can be a resource in the development of their L2 – it offers a pre-existing cognitive framework of how language works and thus may enable speedier and more accessible explanations of language; it is, as Butzkamm (1989) suggests, a 'natural' reference system and a 'pathfinder'. In effect, the learners' L1 may enhance 'noticing' of features of English, perhaps by enabling learners to draw comparisons between the two languages.

In terms of classroom practices, therefore, G. Cook challenges the prevailing monolingual orthodoxy in ELT, noting that while there is a widespread assumption 'that students actually prefer monolingual teaching and learning . . . this is not based on any actual research findings' (2008: 80). Thus, Hall and G. Cook (2012; 2013) and Kerr (2016) summarize a range of possible classroom roles and functions for the learners' L1, including 'medium-oriented goals' (i.e., teaching or explaining the new language), 'framework goals' (i.e., organizing and managing the classroom itself), and 'social goals' (i.e., building rapport and managing personal and social relationships). Hence, using the learners' first language in the classroom may fulfil the 'functional' role of assisting explanations, enabling contrasts between languages and the 'noticing' of language to take place, and, in effect, incorporating those learning processes that the learners are already engaged in. However, it also serves a much broader purpose of recognizing the value of learners' first language identities, cultures and linguistic knowledge, i.e., it recognizes and values diversity both within the classroom and, implicitly, beyond.

The decision about whether, or how far, the use of learners' first languages is appropriate in the ELT classroom is complex. The case for excluding L1 has been strongly argued over a long period of time, creating a common-sense understanding that is sometimes difficult to see beyond (for learners as well as ELT professionals). However, there are several very valid arguments for drawing upon and using the learners' first language in the classroom (outlined in detail by, for example, G. Cook, 2010; Hall and G. Cook, 2012, 2013; Kerr, 2016; V. Cook, 2016).

Task 4.3 Reflecting on key dilemmas

- Thinking about your language teaching and learning experiences, which elements of these broad ideas about second language learning do you recognize from your own experience?

In your context:

- *Making language features explicit*: Are language features brought to the attention of learners? If so, how does this happen?

- *Language practice*: What is the role of 'practice'? How is language practised? What forms might practice take, and why is it organized in these ways?

- *Learner pair and group work*: What opportunities are there for conversational interaction? How is it organized, and why? What purpose does it serve? How might it link to some of the ideas discussed in this chapter?

- What are your perspectives on the following debates:

  - conscious and unconscious learning in the classroom?

  - focus on form . . . or on forms?

  - the place of L1 in the classroom?

How do you deal with these issues in your teaching, and why? Are there any alternatives to your current practices?

Summary: bringing the issues together

In this chapter, we have identified several interrelated questions and issues that ELT teachers face in the classroom. Richards and Rodgers (2014: 14) bring these problems and subsequent potential practices together in a series of key questions:

1. What should the goals of language teaching be? Should a language course try to teach conversational proficiency, reading, translation, or some other skill?

2. What is the basic nature of language, and how will this affect the way we teach it?

3. What are the principles for the selection of language content in language teaching?

4. What principles of organization, sequencing and presentation best facilitate learning?

5. What should the role of the first language or languages be?

6. What language acquisition processes do learners use in mastering a language, and can these be incorporated into a method?

7. What teaching techniques and activities work best and under what circumstances?

Differences in the way these concerns are addressed underpin the approaches of the various different named methods that have been practised in ELT over the last hundred years. To Richards and Rodgers' list of issues, Johnson (2008: 162) adds:

• How much 'engagement of the mind' does the method expect?

• Is the method deductive or inductive in approach?

• How much importance does the method give to 'authenticity of language'?

Additionally, Brown (2001: 34–5) considers the teachers' and learners' *roles* in the classroom when attempting to identify the key elements of methods. Meanwhile, Allwright and Hanks (2009) approach this issue from another angle, asking where the locus of 'control' is in the classroom and learning process.

All of which leads us to Chapter 5, where the concept of Method and methods, now made explicit, will be investigated in more detail as potential 'interventions' in the classroom dilemmas and practices that we have identified in this chapter.

5 Language teaching methods

Perspectives and possibilities

> What we have now is not answers or solutions but a rich array of realizations and perspectives.
>
> (Canagarajah, 2006: 29)

This chapter will:

- examine the differing ways in which the term 'Method' has been conceptualized, also distinguishing between 'Method' and 'methodology';
- explore how different language teaching methods can be seen as social 'products of their times';
- identify the key features of a range of methods, placing them within their wider social contexts and identifying them as potential sources of classroom intervention for teachers;
- consider ways in which the notion of Method has been critiqued and challenged;
- trace the possible emergence of a 'Postmethod era' and its potential implications for teachers.

Introduction: 'Method' – a range of terms

Terminology plays an essential role in the discourse of any profession, providing shared reference points and understandings of key concepts. Yet when applied linguists and teachers talk, read and write about *Method*, we find that the term is used in a variety of ways that, as Bell (2003: 326) notes, 'offers a challenge for anyone wishing to enter into the analysis or deconstruction of methods'.

Stern (1983: 452–3) suggests that:

> a method, however ill-defined it may be, is more than a single strategy or a particular technique; it is a 'theory' of language teaching ... which has resulted from practical and theoretical discussions in a given historical context. It usually implies and sometimes overtly

expresses certain objectives, and a particular view of language; it makes assumptions about the language learner; and underlying it are certain beliefs about the nature of the language learning process.

Similarly, Nunan (1991: 3) suggests that all methods:

> . . . assume that there is a single set of principles which will determine whether or not learning will take place. Thus they all propose a single set of precepts for teacher and learner classroom behaviour, and assert that if these principles are faithfully followed, they will result in learning for all.

Anthony (1963), however, puts forward two separate but related elements – method and *approach*. According to Anthony, method occupies a position between approach and *technique* within a three-tier hierarchy. 'Approach' is the set of assumptions about the nature of language and learning; 'method' is the plan of how to systematically present the language based on these higher-order assumptions; and 'techniques' are specific classroom activities utilized within a given method (e.g., translating sentences, memorizing dialogues, completing an information gap activity). Similarly, V. Cook identifies teaching techniques as 'the actual point of contact with the students' (2016: 258).

Richards and Rodgers (2014) provide a further analysis, proposing that the term 'method' comprises three elements. Their *approach* and *procedure* are broadly similar to Anthony's 'approach' and 'technique', while *design* includes the general and specific objectives of the method; the syllabus model (i.e., how language is selected and organized); learner roles (e.g., grouping patterns, whether learners influence the learning of others); teacher roles (e.g., teacher functions and influence over learning), and the role of any teaching materials in the method. However, as Brown (2001) points out, within ELT, 'design' is more often than not used to refer only to curriculum and syllabus design rather than the broader range of issues suggested by Richards and Rodgers. Most teacher training and development texts thus seem to highlight *approach*, *method* and *techniques* as key terms.

Finally, how has the difference between method and *methodology* been conceptualized? Brown (2001: 15) suggests that methodology refers to 'pedagogical practices in general' while Thornbury notes that methodology is 'a general word to describe classroom practices . . . irrespective of the particular method that a teacher is using' (2006: 131), i.e., it is 'the *how* of teaching' (Thornbury, 2011: 185). Kumaravadivelu (2006: 84) summarizes the difference as follows:

> Method [refers to] established methods constructed by experts in the field. . . Methodology [is] what practicing teachers actually do in the classroom to achieve their stated or unstated teaching objectives.

From this perspective, we might refer to the Grammar-translation Method or the Audiolingual Method, while focusing on the pedagogical (i.e., methodological) practices that these involve, for example, the translation of example sentences from first language to target language, or the use of oral drills.

In practice, however, the method/methodology distinction is not always clear (Thornbury, 2011: 186). Teachers' classroom practices (i.e., their methodology) may often follow a particular method, they may adopt and adapt a range of elements drawn from different methods which they find 'plausible' (Prabhu, 1990; see also discussion later in this chapter), or they may use textbooks which follow a particular method. Yet whatever the relationship between 'method' and teachers' classroom practices (to which we will return shortly; see also the introduction to Chapter 4), methodology remains an inescapable element of teachers' professional lives.

Methods, paradigms and change

Over the course of the twentieth century for ELT in particular, and long before for language teaching and learning in general, a variety of methods emerged. A number of differing accounts attempt to explain this 'profusion' of approaches (Allwright and Hanks, 2009: 8), each with its own particular perspective on the past. While most accounts suggest that it is possible to trace the emergence of methods in sequence over time (albeit offering differing reasons for *why* this happened), more recent and radical interpretations (e.g. Pennycook, 1989; Hunter and Smith, 2012) suggest that these narratives simplify and stereotype the past, and create a 'mythology' around methods. We shall return to these critiques later in the chapter. Firstly, however, we shall examine the more traditional characterizations of the emergence and development of methods over time – methods as 'progress', and methods as social 'products of their times'.

A profusion of methods

Task 5.1 Setting the scene: language teaching methods

- List the names of as many individual methods as you can.

- What do you know about the key characteristics of each method you have listed? What do teachers and learners do in the classroom, and why (i.e., what are the practices and theories for each)? At this point, do not worry if your knowledge of some of the details is a little hazy!

- When (approximately) did each of these methods emerge? Which ones came earlier, which came later?

- In which part(s) of the world have most methods originated? Why might this be?

- What reasons can you think of for the development or emergence of a new method – in general, and in relation to any of the methods you noted in answer to the first question?

- Why do you think there have been so many language teaching methods?

In their review of contemporary language teaching principles and techniques, Larsen-Freeman and Anderson (2011) discuss eleven methods: grammar-translation; the direct method; the audio-lingual method; the 'silent way': desuggestopedia; community language learning; total physical response (TPR); communicative language teaching (CLT); content-based instruction (CBI, the North American term, also known as content and language integrated learning (CLIL) in Europe); task-based language teaching (TBLT); and a politically-oriented participatory approach. Meanwhile, Richards and Rodgers (2014) outline sixteen approaches and methods, exploring grammar-translation and the direct method much more briefly than Larsen-Freeman and Andersen (ibid.), but also discussing the oral approach and situational language teaching; the whole language approach; competency-based teaching; text-based instruction; the lexical approach; and the natural approach. Both texts also reflect upon the role of methods within a possible postmethod era (we shall reflect further on 'postmethod' later in the chapter). You may have listed some of these possibilities in answer to the first question in Task 5.1.

Despite their similarities, the differences between these accounts indicate that no 'definitive list' of methods exists across the methodological literature of ELT (Hall, 2016), possibly because it is such a fast-moving and continually changing field (ibid.), or perhaps because there is a lack of agreement and theoretical consistency about Method and methods (Pennycook (1989), a point to which we shall return later in the chapter).

Histories of methods: from 'progress' to 'products of their times'

A traditional view of the development of methods over time is that 'there has been a series of language teaching methods over the years, each being succeeded by a better one until we reach the present' (Pennycook, 1989: 597). From this methods-as-progress perspective, method development has been cumulative, progressive, and relatively linear. However, long-term, historical perspectives imply that change and development in language teaching is cyclical and context-dependent. Kelly, in his history of 2,500 years of language teaching, suggests that the 'ideas accessible to language teachers have not changed' over this period (1969: 394), and states that 'nobody really knows what is new or what is old in present day language teaching procedures. There has been a vague feeling that modern experts have spent their time in discovering what other men [*sic*] have forgotten' (ibid.: *ix*; see also Pennycook, 2004: 278). Consequently, Adamson (2004) refers to 'fashions in language teaching methodology', and observes that 'no method is inherently superior to another; instead, some methods are more appropriate than others in a particular context' (605). Thus, the idea of language teaching methods as making 'continuous upwards progress through history' is 'dangerous' (Rowlinson, 1994: 7).

Paradigms and contexts

How, then, are particular methods said to emerge at particular times and in particular places? Given that 'there is nothing new under the sun' (Johnson, 2008: 161), methods are seen as reflecting *contemporary* (rather than 'best') theoretical ideas and practices in language teaching and learning (Adamson, 2004). Thus, with regard to ELT, G. Cook (2003: 30) notes that:

> Different approaches to teaching English did not occur by chance, but in response to changing geopolitical circumstances and social attitudes and values, as well as to shifts of fashion in linguistics.

Kuhn (1970/1996) suggests that academic fashions and philosophies might change over time through *paradigms* and the concept of *scientific revolutions*. Kuhn, who studied the limits of knowledge in science, defined a paradigm as:

> universally recognized achievements that for a time provide model problems and solutions to a community of practitioners.
>
> (Kuhn, 1970/1996: *x*)

Thus, they are the overarching and fundamental philosophies of what constitutes 'proper' or 'normal' thinking and behaviour (or theory and practice), determining and legitimizing what questions are asked and what answers are found. Once a paradigm has been established, it is difficult, impossible even, for those working within it to conceive of any other rationale until a 'crisis' prompts a 'scientific revolution'. Crises develop when tensions emerge within a paradigm caused by discoveries or inconsistencies that the paradigm cannot adequately explain. This leads to the eventual replacement of one paradigm by another.

Observing that 'the call for change is almost constant in education', Jacobs and Farrell (2003: 5) develop Kuhn's thesis within the context of English language teaching, suggesting that change within ELT does not occur in a step-by-step, evenly paced fashion, but instead occurs through 'revolutionary', 'tradition-shattering' transformation. Similarly, Brown (2001: 16) argues that, over the last century or so, new methods have broken with the old, while the emergence of Communicative Language Teaching in the mid-1970s has often been characterized as 'the communicative revolution' (e.g., Bolitho *et al.*, 1983; later in the chapter, however, we shall question use of the term 'revolution' in this context).

Additionally, links between method change in language teaching and changes in scientific and societal thinking more generally have been identified. Crookes (2009), for example, highlights moves towards the Direct Method and away from Grammar-translation in late nineteenth-century Europe. He argues that the Direct Method's emphasis on the use of L2 in the classroom and inductive learning (which we shall explore in more detail below) reflected wider societal interest in 'natural' learning, which, in turn, stemmed from ideas that emerged after the French Revolution. Consequently, previous 'authoritarian' or 'traditional' teacher-learner relationships thought to underpin Grammar-translation approaches to language teaching were questioned.

The Direct Method particularly flourished in the private language school sector in Europe where teachers could more easily focus on their relationships with learners (Crookes, 2009); meanwhile, in many 'mainstream' or state schools, with their differing priorities (and resources), Grammar-translation continued well into the mid-twentieth century. Elsewhere in the world, Grammar-translation also remained predominant, again as a consequence of wider societal trends. For example, Adamson (2004) notes that in China, Grammar-translation prospered until the 1960s as it both resembles traditional Chinese methods of learning and teaching, and met the need of post-revolution Communist China by developing learners' reading skills. In an era when English-speaking nations were anti-communist, this enabled China to access Western scientific and technical knowledge. Adamson argues that the subsequent adoption of teaching methods that focused on the development of oral skills (in the early 1960s) and communicative goals (in the 1980s) reflected the political context of 'modernization' and outward-looking economic development in China during these periods. Thus, as Adamson suggests, 'promoted methods are mirrors of the contemporary sociocultural climate' (615). And it is within this characterization, which links their development to broader social and intellectual trends, that we now turn to discuss specific methods.

'Methods in context': a review of recent history

Any review of methods involves an element of compromise for, as Johnson (2008: 163) remarks, the further back in time we start a review of methods, 'the more sense of direction it will give us', but 'the longer the journey will be'. Thus, with a few exceptions (e.g., Kelly, 1969; Crookes, 2009), most texts have focused on those methods developed, practised and popularized at differing times and in different contexts within the relatively brief era that spans from the late nineteenth century to the present day. Crookes notes, however, that 'our field has been bedeviled by ahistorical, decontextual presentations of "Methods"' (2009: 46) and comments that ELT professionals should aim to understand the 'complex, but not inherently progressive' nature of their development (ibid.).

Taking these points into account, we too will compromise. Focusing on methods which are central to the professional discourse of ELT, we start this review in the nineteenth century, a social context in which Grammar-translation was the traditional teaching method.

'Traditional' approaches and the Grammar-translation Method

The Grammar-translation Method within ELT (and as a method for teaching other modern languages) emerged from the teaching of classical languages such as Latin. Although, as Stern (1983) asserts, a focus on grammar and translation in language teaching has existed through the ages, the idea of Grammar-translation as a defined approach to language teaching only emerged in the late eighteenth century, and has subsequently also been referred to as 'the Prussian Method' (much of the original Grammar-translation literature emerged from Germany), the Grammar Method, the Classical Method, or the Traditional Method (Weihua, 2004a: 250).

Grammar-translation requires learners to focus on individual grammar points, which are taught deductively. Example sentences are then translated both from and to the L2, as illustrated in Figure 5.1. Grammar-translation thus focuses on accuracy and written rather than spoken language, with language being broken down and analysed at the level of words, phrases and individual sentences in the first instance; longer texts may be drawn upon dependent on the ability of the learners.

z okna z biurka z zebrania	*z* is pronounced as *z*	but: z pudełka z tego . . .	 (spud . . .) (stego)	*z* becomes *s*

Thus the final voiced consonant of a preposition remains voiced if the following word begins with a vowel or with a voiced consonant; but it changes into a corresponding breathed consonant (*d* into *t*, *z* into *s*) if the initial consonant of the following word is breathed. A monosyllabic preposition (*od*, *dla*, etc.) or a non-syllabic preposition (*z*) is pronounced together with the following word, so that there is no stop between the preposition and the following word.

LESSON 5

THE SECOND CONJUGATION

The second Polish conjugation comprises a very small number of verbs. These are conjugated as follows:

umieć, to know how to . . .	*rozumieć*, to understand
umiem, I know how to . . .	rozumiem, I understand
umiesz, thou knowest how to, etc.	rozumiesz, thou understandest, etc.
umie	rozumie
umiemy	rozumiemy
umiecie	rozumiecie
umieją	rozumieją

The two following verbs are conjugated much like *umieć*, but the third person plural takes the ending *-dzą*, not *-ją*:

wiedzieć, to know	*jeść*, to eat
wiem, I know	jem, I eat
wiesz, thou knowest, etc.	jesz, thou eatest, etc.
wie	je
wiemy	jemy
wiecie	jecie
wiedzą	jedzą

It will be noticed that *wiedzieć* is the third Polish correspondent for the English verb *to know*—the other two are *umieć*, in this lesson, and *znać*, in lesson four. *Wiedzieć* and *znać* are comparable to the French verbs *savoir* and *connaître*, or German *wissen* and *kennen*. *Wiedzieć* and *znać* are used as follows:

Wiem, że . . .	I know that . . .
Wiesz, kto . . .	You know who . . .
Wiesz, co . . .	You know what . . .
Wiesz, które . . .	You know which . . .
Wiesz, jakie . . .	You know what sort of . . .
Wiesz, czyje . . .	You know whose . . .
Wiesz, gdzie . . .	You know where . . .
Wiesz, kiedy . . .	You know when . . .
Wiesz, dlaczego . . .	You know why . . .
Znam to dziecko.	I know this child.
Znam to pismo.	I know this periodical.
Znam to słowo.	I know this word.
Znam to opowiadanie.	I know this tale.

Umieć expresses the knowledge of how to do a thing, a knowledge acquired by practice, training, study:

Umiem czytać.	I know how to read.*
Umiem pływać.	I know how to swim.*
Umiem śpiewać.	I know how to sing.*
Also:	
Nie umiem polskiego na dzisiaj.	I don't know my Polish (my Polish lesson) for to-day.

Translate into English:

1. Co je to dziecko? 2. Co jedzą te dzieci? 3. Ona to rozumie. 4. Ona to umie. 5. Wiem, że tego nie rozumiecie. 6. Nie rozumiesz tego słowa? 7. Czy pani wie, gdzie są dzieci? 8. Czy wy wiecie, co on czyta? Nie, nie wiemy, nie rozumiemy ani słowa. Może ty rozumiesz? Nie, ja także nie rozumiem. 9. Idę do biura. Wracam z biura. 10. Może pani wie, kiedy pan Rawicz wraca z

* Or, in English, simply: *I can read, swim, sing*. Note, however, that when *I can* implies ability based on former training, on having learned, or having been taught, *umiem* must be used in Polish; if it implies physical ability, *I can* would be rendered by *mogę*, a form of *móc*, to be able to (see p. 135), a direct English correspondent in this sense. Thus *umiem czytać* would be said by a small child, or a former illiterate, or by somebody referring to a special script, a foreign text, etc.; while *mogę czytać* would mean *I am able to read*, implying, for instance, because I feel strong enough to do so—an invalid speaking, or because I can see well enough to read, or because I am not forbidden to read, etc.

Figure 5.1 An example of grammar-translation materials

Source: Extract from *Teach Yourself Polish* (Corbridge-Pataniowska, 1992), first printed in 1948.

V. Cook (2016: 263) notes that Grammar-translation 'does not directly teach people to use the language for some external purpose outside the classroom'. Similarly, Richards and Rodgers (2014) suggest that languages are studied in order to develop the learners' intellectual abilities, and the study of grammar itself becomes the purpose of learning. Hence, many recent accounts suggest that Grammar-translation leaves learners unable to communicate in the L2. It would thus seem to stop some way short of current views of what language learning is for, leading Richards and Rodgers (2014: 7) to argue that:

> . . . it has no advocates . . . There is no literature that offers a rationale or justification for it or that attempts to relate it to issues in linguistics, psychology, or educational theory.

And yet, Grammar-translation has survived and is used in many parts of the world today, albeit in modified forms. V. Cook (2016), who refers to Grammar-translation as the *academic style*, observes that while many other methods do not focus on grammar explicitly (as we shall see), 'students continue to believe that this will help them' (264). He also proposes that Grammar-translation carries with it a 'seriousness of purpose' that may be lacking in other language teaching methods, seems appropriate in those societies that maintain a 'traditional' view of learner and teacher roles in the classroom, and holds that knowledge is something that teachers 'transmit' to learners (rather than learners discovering or constructing knowledge for themselves – we shall explore differing views of knowledge further in Chapter 12). Thornbury (2006) recognizes that the continued survival of Grammar-translation may be a consequence of its ease of implementation, especially with large classes. Thornbury (2006) also suggests that translation, which was rejected by other methods and approaches as we shall see, may be re-emerging within ELT (see also Chapter 4's discussion of L1 use in the classroom). G. Cook (2010), for example, draws upon a range of theoretical and pedagogical insights into the nature of language learning and its broader social purposes to re-interpret the role of translation in language teaching, and suggests a number of translation-based tasks for the ELT classroom including whole text translation, discussion of translation problems, and translation within a 'communicative framework' (ibid.) as can be seen, for example, in Figure 5.2 below.

Activity 53: Gist Translation

Aims
- To practise synthetic translation
- To make pragmatic decisions related to text type
- To practise pre-interpreting skills: memorisation, fast decision-making
- To learn to justify choices

Level
Beginners

Grouping
Pairs

Approximate timing
20 minutes

Steps
a. Student A reads a text, which is then left aside. The student then translates only what s/he remembers. Student B does the same with another text.
b. Students A and B exchange their translations and try to put the text which is new to each of them back into their source language.

Continued overleaf

c. Finally, they compare their rendering with the source text and comment on their translations and the similarities and differences at different levels between the source and the target texts. They also discuss the procedure.

Figure 5.2 A collaborative translation activity

Source: González Davies, 2004: 172–3.

Task 5.2 Thinking about Grammar-translation

How does the Grammar-translation Method approach the practical dilemmas of classroom teaching, which we explored in Chapter 4? Refer back to those debates and the ideas outlined above to answer the following questions:

- What goal of language teaching is envisaged by the Grammar-translation Method?

- How is 'language' conceptualized?

- How are languages learned?

- Who needs to be aware of grammar rules and structures?

- Is the focus on form or forms?

- What is the role of the learners' first language?

- How is language practised?

- Have you ever learned a language through Grammar-translation? What do you consider the main strengths and weaknesses of the experience?

- Do you ever practice Grammar-translation techniques in your own classes? When and why? How do learners react?

'The pendulum swings': the Direct Method

The Direct Method emerged in Europe at the end of the nineteenth century in reaction to Grammar-translation. We have already noted its philosophical links to the promotion of 'natural learning', the Direct Method also drawing on the belief that learning a foreign language is similar to acquiring a first language. Additionally, the late nineteenth century was an era in which the development of international business and travel required language learners to be able to use and communicate in the L2, an aim that Grammar-translation did not appear to fulfil. Consequently, the principles of the Direct Method have been characterized as follows:

1. Classroom interaction was conducted exclusively in the target language.

2. Only everyday vocabulary and sentences were taught.

3. Oral communication skills were built up in a carefully graded progression organized around question-and-answer exchanges between teachers and students in small, intensive classes.

4. Grammar was taught inductively.

5. New teaching points were introduced orally.

6. Concrete vocabulary was taught through demonstration, objects, and pictures; abstract vocabulary was taught by association of ideas.

7. Both speech and listening comprehension were taught.

8. Correct pronunciation and grammar were emphasized.
   (Richards and Rodgers, 2014: 12)

In practice, therefore, classes based upon the Direct Method tradition are small, use only the L2 as both a means of communication and instruction, are dominated by speaking and listening and involve little grammar analysis. Theoretically, the approach is also underpinned by a belief that language teaching should be based around phonetics and accurate pronunciation (Stern, 1983; Richards and Rodgers, 2014).

The Direct Method was popular (in some contexts!) in the first half of the twentieth century, and, although not widespread, it is still practised today, most notably by the Berlitz chain of language schools (who refer to it as the Berlitz Method). However, certain elements of the approach have been questioned. First, it is argued that, unlike Grammar-translation, the Direct Method can only be practised with relatively small classes, or rather, in contexts where classes can be divided into smaller groups (Weihua, 2004b). Brown observes that 'almost any "method" can succeed when clients are willing to pay high prices for small classes, individual attention, and intensive study' (2001: 22) and highlights the contrast between this context, stereotypically found in private language schools, and language teaching in public education contexts, where the Direct Method is less applicable. Additionally, the Direct Method places teachers at the centre of classroom activity, with critics arguing that learners, and the success of the method itself, are too dependent on a teacher's individual skill and ability (Brown, 2001). Finally, from a theoretical perspective, to what extent can the L2 classroom really recreate the ways in which children acquire their first language?

Despite these criticisms, the Direct Method has had a major impact on language teaching methods and methodology. Its core principle, the exclusive use of the L2 and avoidance of the learners' L1 in the classroom has, as Thornbury points out, survived 'as an article of faith amongst many teachers to this day' (2006: 67). And, logically, this principle has enabled language teachers to teach without knowing their learners' first language, hence paving the way for 'native speaker teachers' within ELT (an issue we shall return to in later chapters).

To some, the Direct Method was the product of 'enlightened amateurism' (Richards and Rodgers, 2014: 13), and theorists from the emerging field of Applied Linguistics argued that a much stronger theoretical basis was needed upon which to develop language teaching methods and practices. Ultimately, this would lead to Audiolingualism (or the Audiolingual Method) in the US and the *Oral Approach* in the UK. It is the former that was, and is, far more influential within ELT, which we shall explore below (for a thorough account of the Oral Approach, see Richards and Rodgers, 2014).

Task 5.3 How 'Direct' are you?

- Do you maintain (or try to maintain) an L2 only classroom? Why/why not?

- To what extent do you agree that language teachers do not need to know the learner's L1?

Language teaching as science: the Audiolingual Method

The Audiolingual Method perhaps most clearly exemplifies the suggested paradigmatic pattern of ELT methods and their links to the wider social context. As V. Cook (2016: 269) notes, it 'most blatantly reflects a particular set of beliefs about L2 learning' and, despite having been heavily critiqued and being apparently unfashionable, 'is still pervasive' within ELT (ibid.: 246). It is therefore very typical of a method that teachers can and do draw upon from time to time when developing an eclectic or Postmethod approach in the classroom.

The origins of the audiolingual approach lie in the conjunction of a number of contextual and theoretical factors. Towards the end of the

Second World War, the US armed forces needed to teach languages on a huge scale as US soldiers needed to communicate with both their allies and also in the countries where they were being deployed. The languages taught ranged from European languages such as French and German to East Asian languages such as Japanese and Korean and the 'Army Method', as it became known, focused on oral/aural work and pronunciation, realized through drills and conversation practice, with small groups of motivated learners and native speaker teachers (Richards and Rodgers, 2014).

This programme lasted only a couple of years and its success was based largely on the intensity of study and motivation of the learners (Byram, 2004a). Although it was not developed from a clear methodological basis, it provided a model for language teaching in subsequent years, with an emphasis on spoken rather than written language, and on 'mechanical' learning. Subsequently, when theorists combined a 'scientific' theory of language (i.e., structuralism) and a 'scientific' approach to learning (i.e., behaviourism), the Army Method offered an apparently successful early model from which a new method, the Audiolingual Method, was developed in the 1950s.

Within linguistics, structuralism holds that language can be broken into constituent parts such as phonemes, morphemes and words. These elements can then be analysed to discover the rules (structures) through which they combine to produce phrases, clauses and sentences. Structuralism thus theorizes language that can be observed (a central part of structuralism's claim to be 'scientific'), and analysis is based around examples of actual spoken language, i.e., structuralism prioritizes spoken language over writing. The combination of structuralism and behaviourist ideas of habit formation via stimulus-reinforcement-response (see Chapter 4) led Rivers (1964: 19–22) to outline the following assumptions of Audiolingualism:

1. Foreign language learning is basically a mechanical process of habit formation.

2. Language skills are learned more effectively if items of the foreign language are presented in spoken form before written form.

3. Analogy provides a better foundation for foreign language learning than analysis.

4. The meanings which the words of a language have for the native speaker can be learned only in a matrix of allusions to the culture of the people who speak that language.

What, therefore, might audiolingual classes look like in practice? Language is broken down into a series of patterns (i.e., structures), which are sequenced and taught to learners one by one. Following a clearly behaviourist approach to learning, 'good habits' are formed as new language is presented through set phrases and scripted dialogues that are repeated and drilled until memorized. In other words, learners are required to respond to a stimulus, with correct answers being reinforced. There is very little or no grammatical explanation in the audiolingual classroom – learning takes place inductively. The focus of classes is on accuracy and the avoidance of errors, learners having to master a structure before they can move on to the next one. Because the learners' L1 is regarded as a potential source of 'bad' habits (due to *interference*), the class takes place in the learners' L2 and typically makes use audio recordings, language labs and visual aids.

This technological aspect of the Audiolingual Method again links the approach to the broader social context in which it originally emerged, 1950s USA, where technology was seen to offer solutions to practical problems. Reflecting this, Audiolingualism regards learners as 'mechanistic, non-cognitive systems' (Crookes, 2009: 6), and 'demands students who do not expect to take the initiative' (V. Cook, 2016: 270). But how realistic is this?

Audiolingualism has been attacked on both theoretical and practical grounds. Theoretically, Chomsky (1966) argues that language is a property of the human mind, with sentences 'generated' from an innate knowledge of abstract grammar rules. Hence, speakers create their own sentences as a result of mental processes, not as a result of habit formation (we shall return to these debates in the next chapter). More pragmatically, the repetition and drilling inherent in audiolingual teaching can be boring and demotivating for learners, and, while it might appear to be successful with lower level learners, offers little to those who have progressed to a more advanced level.

As with the Direct Method, however, the legacy of Audiolingualism survives in ELT today in drill-based activities, dialogue-building and the emphasis on practice. Thus although rarely applied as a full and systematic method, it remains an approach that many teachers fall back on or dip into from time to time.

Beyond Applied Linguistics? Humanistic approaches to ELT

A number of language teaching methods emerged as confidence in the Audiolingual Method began to fade from the late 1960s onwards. Some had a firm basis within applied linguistics theory, developing from a theory of language and of language learning (e.g., Communicative Language Teaching, as we shall see). Others, however, emerged from educational theory and from psychology, having a strong view of learners and learning, but having less developed theories about language.

Grundy (2004) suggests that a paradigm shift towards humanistic (and 'more humane') teaching methods emerged partly as a reaction to the de-humanizing 'science' of Audiolingualism, but also as part of the late 1960s and early 1970s social unrest and student protests in Europe and the USA. Meanwhile, titles such as *Caring and Sharing in the Foreign Language Class* (Moskowitz, 1978) indicate the key concerns of these approaches, which, according to Grundy (2004) include:

- Respect for learners as people, including fostering the individual's self-esteem and the learners' respect for each other.

- Respect for the learners' knowledge and independence, that learners know best how and when to learn. Thus classroom activities should only be those the learners wish to engage in.

- Recognize the affective (i.e., emotional) as well as cognitive nature of the learning experience.

- Recognize the role of self-discovery, and of the individual learner's autonomy and independence.

- Teach in an enabling way, regarding teachers as enablers or facilitators who assist learners in their self-discovery rather than as instructors who 'transmit' knowledge to learners.

Humanistic language teaching therefore embodies a set of progressive educational values and beliefs about learners, learning, and the purpose of education more generally.

Four language teaching methods in particular are commonly termed 'humanistic' – *Community Language Learning* (CLL), *Suggestopedia, Total Physical Response* (TPR) and the *Silent Way*. What might they bring to the ELT classroom?

Community Language Learning: the teacher as 'consultant'

Drawing upon ideas behind counselling and therapy, Community Language Learning (or 'Counseling Learning' (Curran, 1972)) places the teacher in a 'consultant' role, with learners taking responsibility for lesson content. Generally, learners sit in a circle with the teacher outside it. Typically, learners might speak in their L1, with teachers translating and helping to formulate the utterance in English; their feelings are considered throughout. Language may be recorded to be analysed later, and the learners become progressively more independent as they progress. CLL is said to be too restrictive for exclusive use on institutional (and institutionalized) language programmes, but teachers often draw upon its principles of learner-centred participation and group-work, learner autonomy and, consequently, the teachers' facilitative (rather than directive) role in the classroom.

Total Physical Response: learning through physical action

Total Physical Response (TPR) links physical actions to learning. Developed by James Asher (1977), TPR theorizes that young children receive comprehensible input when acquiring their L1 largely in the form of commands or encouragement to act (e.g., 'sit down', 'come here'), and suggests that L2 learners can learn in a similar way, through commands that require a physical response. Central to TPR is the notion that almost all language can be presented through commands and physical actions, including complex grammar (Cain, 2004). Asher's ideas have much in common with Krashen's approach (see Chapters 4 and 6), highlighting the role of comprehensible input and the emergence of speech only after language has been acquired. Although TPR has not really had a role as a fully implemented method within ELT, teachers might draw on it from time to time, especially when teaching young learners (who might be less inhibited than adults when asked to move around the classroom). Its potential weaknesses (as a method) are whether it can offer a sustainable model of learning beyond beginner level, and how far it appeals to learners whose preferred approach to learning is more 'intellectual'.

Suggestopedia: removing the negatives

Developed by Georgi Lozanov (1978), our third humanistic method, Suggestopedia (or 'superlearning') proposes that learning can be accelerated via the processes of suggestion, relaxation and concentration, all of which can be enhanced by the physical environment in which learning takes place. Learners need to be relaxed and negative emotions should be removed. Hence, soothing background music is central in Suggestopedia and learners are 'infantilized' to create an atmosphere in which 'the self-confidence, spontaneity and receptivity of the child' can be regained (Bancroft, 1972: 19, in Richards and Rodgers, 2014: 320). To this end, teachers are quite clearly in control of the class, and learners may even adopt pseudonyms and imaginary personas. Perhaps unsurprisingly, Suggestopedia has been subject to criticism. It may not be practical where music and an especially comfortable learning environment is not available. Meanwhile, Scovel (1979) has accused Suggestopedia of being a 'pseudoscience', although he also acknowledges that it may provide a source of useful teaching techniques. Thus, it is perhaps Suggestopedia's emphasis on *affect* that is most relevant to the majority of teachers in their day-to-day teaching.

The Silent Way: letting the learners lead

The Silent Way is another humanistic method that is closely associated with a particular individual, Caleb Gattegno. Founded on the belief that language learning is a personal enterprise that is initiated and directed by individual learners themselves, its theory of learning is as follows:

1. Learning is facilitated if the learner discovers or creates rather than remembers and repeats what is to be learned.

2. Learning is facilitated by accompanying (mediating) physical objects.

3. Learning is facilitated by problem solving involving the material to be learned.

(Richards and Rodgers, 2014: 291)

In practice, the teacher keeps silent for much of the class, thereby requiring learners to create language rather than repeat it. Meanings are made clear through the use of two main aids – a phonemic chart to which teachers point to indicate the sounds that should be spoken, and Cuisenaire Rods, which can be used to illustrate sentence structures, to make shapes, and engage in any activity that helps learners work out meanings for themselves. Although teachers are silent (hence the method's name; the learners still speak!), they are still in control of the classroom as learners take responsibility for learning but teachers organize the learning opportunities (Harmer, 2015: 64). Although not widely practised, the influence of the Silent Way on ELT classrooms more generally is reflected in the development of discovery learning activities where learners work things out for themselves.

As this brief review has suggested, common to all humanistic methods is the centrality of learner-centredness, learner independence and autonomy, and affect (see later chapters).

However, why have these methods not taken more of a hold within ELT? Perhaps it is that many teachers do share these values but attempt to integrate them into other approaches rather than pursue something labelled explicitly 'humanistic'. Others have suggested that 'the underlying genuine and justified concern for socio-emotional growth . . . [has] been overtaken by an unhealthy desire to turn pedagogy into compulsory psychotherapy' (Allwright and Hanks, 2009: 44), while writers such as Brumfit (1982) argue that too much attention is given to the personal at the expense of analysis. Or perhaps it is, as Allwright and Hanks argue, that despite their apparent difference to other methods, they still perpetuate the notion of the method as a 'unique and highly specific package' (2009: 44), a view that teachers perhaps no longer subscribe to in an arguably Postmethod world in which teachers may adapt and implement practices from a variety of methods according to their own, and their learners', needs (see Chapter 4 and discussions later in this chapter).

Task 5.4 Humanistic approaches: exploring your context

- Not all applied linguists accept 'humanistic' as an appropriate label for the approaches outlined above, and they are also sometimes called 'alternative methods', 'designer methods', 'fringe methods', 'other styles' and, according to Stevick (1980), 'ways'. What is the connotation of each label? What view of the methods would a speaker who uses one or other of these labels hold? Do the possible differences between these names matter?

- To what extent do you think these methods are more 'humane' than other ELT methods outlined in the chapter or that you know about?

- To what extent do you think teaching should concern itself with learners' 'socio-emotional growth'?

- Which elements or practices from the humanistic approaches outlined above do you incorporate into your own classroom teaching, if any? If you do, when do you do so and why?

Changing aims within ELT: communication in the classroom

Communicative Language Teaching: strong or weak

Communicative Language Teaching (CLT), also known as the Communicative Approach, emerged in Europe and the USA in the 1970s. In the late twentieth century, it became the dominant approach within Western ELT and applied linguistics, so much so, in fact, that to admit to a disbelief in CLT would be regarded as 'heresy' (Brown, 2001). It has, as most readers will be aware, been 'exported' and promoted around the world in a variety of cultural and educational contexts, and with greater and lesser degrees of success (see Chapter 12 for further discussion).

The origins of CLT are generally traced to a changing view of language, away from language structures towards language functions and communication. This took place in an era when more people than ever were crossing international borders for work, and who thus had immediate functional language needs. Yet although the emergence of CLT is often portrayed as a 'revolution' (see earlier in the chapter), philosophically, the focus on learners and their needs reflects a view of learners as individuals, which we have seen previously within the Direct Method and in Humanistic language teaching (Crookes, 2009). Similarly, CLT's emphasis on meaning and communication was already part of the discourse of ELT, Savignon (2001: 18) noting that 'throughout the long history of language teaching, there have always been advocates of a focus on meaning . . . and of developing learner ability to *use* the language for communication'. (Consequently, as Hunter and Smith (2012) argue, methodological change is perhaps more evolutionary and less revolutionary than many narratives of methods suggest, a point we shall return to later in the chapter.)

Beyond this, discussing CLT is in some ways problematic as the term means different things to different people and everyday classroom practices can appear to be quite different when CLT principles are applied in differing social and educational contexts. Thus, CLT can be seen as an umbrella term that describes a change in thinking about the goals and processes of classroom language learning (Savignon, 2004), with a number of interpretations of how this might be realized in practice. Key to all strands of CLT, however, is the move from teaching language as individual linguistic structures to teaching people how to use language effectively when communicating, in effect a move from teaching linguistic competence to *communicative competence*.

Communicative competence essentially suggests that teaching learners to form grammatically correct sentences is not enough; learners also need to be able to use language appropriately in a variety of settings and situations, and with a variety of speakers (Hymes, 1972). Hence, in essence, the goal of CLT is to teach 'real-life' language.

In addition to this goal, CLT is especially concerned with *how* to teach language, V. Cook (2016: 274) observing that:

> The end dictates the means: a goal expressed in terms of communication means basing classroom teaching on communication and so leads to techniques that make the students communicate with each other.

Thus, CLT emphasizes meaning and 'genuine' communication in the classroom, communication itself being the central process and focus of the ELT classroom. Communicative syllabuses have thus evolved from their original *notional-functional* focus (see Chapter 11) to concentrate on what is done in the classroom, i.e., learning processes. Typical communicative activities are information-gap exercises (e.g., asking directions when only one learner can see the possible route), role-plays (e.g., a job interview), and problem-solving tasks (e.g., where learners might be asked to prioritize inventions or events in terms of their overall significance and justify their choices). Central to all these activities is the idea of communicative purpose, that learners need to communicate something based around content and meaning rather than specific linguistic forms. But how might language learning itself take place?

Most accounts of CLT now recognize 'strong' and 'weak' forms of the approach. As originally conceived in the 1970s, *strong forms* of CLT suggest that 'language is learned by using it' (see Chapter 6 for further discussion), i.e., 'by deploying their existing linguistic resources, at whatever level, to solve their immediate communication problems, learners would develop linguistically' (Allwright and Hanks, 2009: 46). V. Cook (2016) characterizes this as a *laissez-faire* attitude – that learners should be allowed to learn without interference from the teachers, and learn in ways that teachers cannot control. Meanwhile, *weak* CLT suggests that 'learners learn the language, then use it' (again, see Chapter 6). This might involve a return to more carefully organized syllabuses and using more controlled, 'pre-communicative' language-focused activities before learners move on to 'real' and meaningful communication.

It is the weak form of CLT that generally dominated, and perhaps still dominates, thinking within Western ELT. Allwright and Hanks (2009) acknowledge its very practical approach while also noting that it is more readily marketable within teaching materials than strong CLT. Indeed, Savignon (2004) maintains that CLT in its strong form cannot be adhered to via a single textbook, implicitly suggesting that ELT materials that are termed 'communicative' must be adhering to the weaker form. Indeed, it is perhaps the potential eclecticism of weak forms of CLT, mixing a planned and explicit focus on language and practice with communicative activities that has paved the way for ideas surrounding Postmethod eclecticism (see later in the chapter).

However, as we have seen throughout this chapter, all methods are subject to criticism, and CLT, in both its weak and strong forms, is no different. We have already noted V. Cook's concern that its approach to learning is laissez-faire, V. Cook himself suggesting that this can lead to the idea that all and any activity in the classroom is justifiable if it allows learners to communicate, i.e., talk. He asks whether learners are learning as much from an activity as they would from something else (2016: 277). This echoes common concerns that fluency might be over-emphasized at the expense of accuracy within CLT (Brumfit, 1984). Additionally, it has been suggested that many communicative activities are not, in fact, any more 'genuine' than activities put forward by other methods. For example, asking someone to give directions while working in a classroom pair-work activity does not serve any authentic communicative purpose; indeed, as soon as communicative activities and language are removed from their original context outside the classroom into a *learning* context, they may become inherently artificial (Widdowson, 1998) – we shall return to this point in Chapter 10. Similarly, an over-emphasis on the exchange of messages – any messages – within the classroom may lead to the trivialization of language teaching and learning, with all that this may entail for English language teachers' professional status (Pennycook, 1990; V. Cook, 2016; also discussed in Chapter 3). Last, but by no means least, it has been suggested that CLT is not appropriate for all cultures and contexts (Bax, 2003), for example where learner autonomy, pair and group-work and less obvious teacher intervention are not part of the educational tradition (see Chapter 12 for further discussion).

Despite these criticisms, however, CLT seems to offer teachers significant alternatives for their everyday teaching practices. Undoubtedly, its conception of language as communicative competence strikes a chord with many teachers and applied linguists, even if the process for achieving this is at times potentially problematic. Additionally, the broadly inclusive nature of the weak form of ELT brings us closer towards debates around Postmethod.

Tasks and Task-based Language Teaching (TBLT)

As we shall see (Chapter 6), the role of tasks in language teaching and learning is much discussed in SLA research and, of course, TBLT is currently much discussed within ELT. Although Kumaravadivelu (1993) observes that tasks can be incorporated into a variety of methods, Thornbury (2006) suggests that TBLT has emerged from the strong form of CLT.

TBLT derives in part from Prabhu's experimental Bangalore Project (1987) in which a number of primary and secondary classes focused on *what* was said in class (i.e., meaning and message) rather than *how* it was said (i.e., form and structures). In these classes, learners engaged in a series of classroom tasks rather than following a syllabus of specific language points, a task being 'an activity in which a person engages in order to attain an objective, and which necessitates the use of language' (Van den Branden, 2006: 4). Thus, the task-based syllabus outlines the types of activities and tasks that learners will encounter, but not what language items they might use. This *procedural syllabus*, which focuses on the means of learning rather than the learning outcomes themselves, uses tasks as a vehicle through which language is generated and learned (see Chapter 11 for further discussion of the procedural syllabus).

In practice, classroom tasks can take different forms. Prabhu (1987), for example, identifies three task types: information gap activities, reasoning gap activities and opinion gap activities. Meanwhile, Willis (1996) identifies six types of task: listing; ordering and sorting; comparing; problem-solving; sharing personal experiences; and creative tasks, and any one activity can fulfil more than one task role. Thus, in practical classroom terms, learners might engage in the following example activities:

- *In pairs, name your family members, then draw your partner's family tree* (i.e., a listing and ordering task).

- *In a group, read different newspaper accounts of the same incident, then share information to identify how they differ, and discuss why this might be* (i.e., a comparing task).

- *Describe your favourite place to your partner. What do you like about it?* (i.e., a sharing personal experiences task).

Tasks tend to be organized in three stages:

- Pre-task: teachers and learners prepare for the task performance, considering the topic or task goal, and activating prior knowledge.

- Task cycle: learners carry out the task, individually or in pairs or groups, and discuss and report back to the whole group on their task outcomes, strategies and any obstacles they encountered.

- Language focus: learners analyse and practise the language that was used.

(Van den Branden, 2016)

Thus, TBLT focuses on form, not forms, although there are differing accounts of how this may be achieved. While it is possible to leave all language focus until the end of the cycle (e.g., Prabhu, 1987), some accounts allow for the introduction of some vocabulary in the pre-task phase (e.g., Willis, 1996), while others still both introduce useful language to learners, examine how native or expert English speakers might perform the same task and provide an opportunity for controlled practice before reaching the task phase (Nunan, 2004). Thornbury (2006), however, questions how this final approach differs from PPP.

Although, as Johnson observes, 'the 'Age of the Task' is certainly not yet over' (2008: 189), there are a number of concerns around TBLT in addition to those already highlighted regarding CLT. First, as we have seen, it is difficult to identify what, exactly, TBLT is, as significant differences can be seen in the way its various proponents have conceptualized the approach (e.g. to pre-teach or not pre-teach task-relevant language). Second, is it possible to teach solely though tasks? Seedhouse (1999) acknowledges that tasks are clearly effective vehicles for learning, but doubts their ability to sustain an entire pedagogical approach. As an example of this, we could ask how tasks might be graded to form a full and coherent syllabus; what makes some tasks easy and others difficult? Additionally, how systematic and wide-ranging in terms of language development can TBLT actually be? V. Cook (2016: 289) observes that classroom tasks may limit learners to knowledge of the language for classroom tasks, and acknowledges Skehan's concern that relating classroom tasks to later L2 uses is 'desirable, but difficult to obtain in practice' (Skehan, 1998: 96). To summarize, then, we shall turn to Richards and Rodgers' (2014: 194) conclusions about Task-based Language Teaching:

> Few would question the pedagogical value of employing tasks as a vehicle for promoting communication and authentic language use in second language classrooms, and, depending on one's definition of a task, tasks have long been part of the mainstream repertoire of language teaching techniques for teachers of many different methodological persuasions . . . [However] it is the dependence on tasks as the primary source of pedagogical input in teaching and the absence of systematic grammatical or any other type of syllabus that characterizes current versions of TBLT . . . And despite extensive studies of various aspects of task definition and design, one prominent researcher comments: 'We are really little further forward in answering the question, "What kind of tasks are needed to promote language acquisition?"' (Ellis, 2003: 101)

Content-based instruction (CBI) and Content and Language Integrated Learning (CLIL)

Like other approaches to language teaching, the origins of using a second language to teach other academic subjects, such as geography or science, are not as recent as often portrayed (Mehisto *et al.*, 2008). Yet in recent years, the idea of integrating content and language instruction has taken hold in an increasing range of contexts and in a variety of ways. These include relatively long-standing *immersion* programmes, such as those in Canadian Quebec from the 1960s onwards, in which English-speaking children were placed in French-speaking kindergarten classes and addressed only in French (with instruction in English introduced at higher grades in the curriculum); *Content-based instruction* (CBI) programmes, typically in North America, in which language teachers work with subject teachers to co-teach subject content through the learners' second language, the learners often being immigrants or minority-language speakers learning through the majority or dominant language; and *Content and Language Integrated Learning* (CLIL), which emerged in Europe in the 1990s with a 'dual focus' (Georgiou, 2012) on the teaching of both language *and* content in contexts where the L2 is foreign, for example, English in France or Spain (from this perspective, therefore, the starting point of CBI is the *content* classroom, while CLIL originates from the *language* classroom (Richards and Rodgers, 2014)).

Despite these distinctions, however, the terminology around content-oriented approaches is hotly debated, often overlapping, and 'bedeviled by confusion' (Morton, 2016: 253). Thus we shall follow Dalton-Puffer *et al.*s' call to 'move on from the terminological puzzle' (2014: 213), and deal with CBI and CLIL as essentially the same (Cenoz, 2015), with the use of one term over another being a question of 'contextual or accidental considerations' (Morton, 2016: 254).

For many, CBI and CLIL approaches are seen as a logical development in the application of the principles of Communicative Language Teaching (e.g., Georgiou, 2012; Richards and Rodgers, 2014). As we have seen, in CLT (and TBLT), learners talk about a topic or task in order to facilitate authentic and meaningful communication; content-based approaches achieve this by organizing the syllabus around a single, academic subject (e.g., history or science). Meanwhile, increased global migration and a recognition and promotion of bi- and multi-lingualism led, in Europe, to strong European Union support for CLIL as part of its response to globalization and 'the need for knowledge-driven economies and societies' (Richards and Rodgers, 2014: 118). Again, therefore, trends in language teaching can be linked to wider academic and social trends.

Central to language learning in CBI and CLIL is the notion of 'learn as you use' rather than 'learn to use' (Mehisto *et al.*, 2008: 11; see also Chapter 4). Beyond this, however, there is 'no single CLIL pedagogy' as classes follow the 'effective practice pedagogies associated with individual subjects' (Coyle *et al.*, 2010: 86), while also, according to Coyle *et al.*, integrating a '4Cs framework' of content (i.e., subject matter), communication (i.e., language learning and using), cognition (i.e., learning and thinking processes), and culture (developing inter-cultural understanding and global citizenship). The more language-focused 'communication' element of this 4Cs framework consists of the 'language *of* learning' (i.e., the language necessary to express content-related concepts and knowledge, with a key emphasis on subject-specific vocabulary), 'language *for* learning' (i.e., the language used to participate in the classroom, such as asking questions, giving opinions, and explaining), and 'language *through* learning' (i.e., the unpredictable language that emerges during learning activities, as part of meaning-making).

In practice, therefore, interaction and the negotiation of meaning are central to CBI and CLIL classes, and typical activities involve cooperative, task-based, experiential, and project-based learning, often using authentic texts and materials (Crandall, 2012). Talk is often 'scaffolded' (see Chapter 4) in order that content is comprehensible and new knowledge created. Meanwhile, an integrated skills approach (where, for example, learners listen and take notes, or research written texts before presenting findings orally) helps bring together knowledge, language and thinking skills (Richards, and Rodgers, 2014). Yet in much content-based pedagogy (especially on those programmes labeled CLIL), there is also an explicit focus on language; subject-specific vocabulary is a key concern, with a grammar focus emerging when relevant to the communication of ideas about content. This can involve corrective feedback in order that learners notice what constitutes effective language use in a particular subject (Richards and Rodgers, 2014).

Strong claims are often made in favour of content-based approaches; Coyle *et al.* (2010) suggest that CLIL is the 'ultimate communicative methodology', while Mehisto *et al.* (2008: 11) maintain that it is 'an innovative methodology' that has emerged to cater for a globalized and technologically enabled 'new age'. Yet a number of concerns have been raised. For example, are content-based approaches effective in both supporting learners' development of language *and* content? Investigations into learners' language outcomes have found mixed results, while investigations into content learning are few and far between. Furthermore, to what extent can teachers, originally trained in either language or content pedagogy, manage to deal with and balance both elements effectively in the classroom? Meanwhile, CLIL in particular has been accused of being 'elitist' (Bruton, 2013), its programmes alleged to attract high-achieving students while excluding, either deliberately or unintentionally, lower level students. Additionally, the dominance of English as the target language in the vast majority of CBI and CLIL programmes around the world raises concerns about the extent to which they promote English at the expense of other languages, thereby reinforcing the dominant position of English in the world by *replacing*, rather than *complementing*, other languages (see Chapter 12 for further discussion of English in the world).

Overall, therefore, strong institutional support and CBI/CLIL's evident links to key concepts underpinning communicative and task-based language teaching mean that their recent expansion will be maintained. However, key debates surrounding their overall effectiveness and the implications for other languages will no doubt also continue.

Task 5.5 Thinking about communication and meaning in the classroom: CLT, TBLT and CBI/CLIL

Consider the meaning-focused language teaching methods outlined in this chapter – CLT, TBLT and CBI/CLIL:

- To what extent do you see these three approaches as similar, or related? In what ways do they differ?

- 'Strong' CLT, TBLT and CBI/CLIL emphasise 'learning the language as it used'; we have also encountered the idea of 'learning the language to use it', which is arguably the approach of 'weak CLT'. What are the implications of each perspective for the organisation of classroom tasks and activities, and, more generally, for the organisation of the ELT syllabus and materials?

- Have you ever learned a language through CLT, TBLT or CBI/CLIL? Based on your experiences, what do you consider to be their strengths and weaknesses?

- To what extent do you think meaning-focused approaches are appropriate in your own teaching context? To what extent does their focus on communication meet the learners' needs and expectations?

This brief review of the most influential methods in ELT has outlined the social context in which they emerged, their key principles, and some of the problems theorists and teachers have suggested are inherent to each. However, as we have already noted, the concept of Method and methods has been questioned in recent years, accompanied by the suggestion that ELT has moved into a Postmethod era. We shall now investigate these issues in more detail.

Challenges to 'Method': plausibility, power and 'a label without substance'

Task 5.6 'Method', and methods in practice

Consider the methods we have reviewed:

- Does the way in which methods are applied within ELT vary? If so, how and why – what factors may influence how methods are actually used in practice?

- Do you follow a method, or methods, in your own professional context?

- Do you follow one method all the time, or do you 'mix and match' various elements of them as you teach? How and why / why not?

- How does this method translate into classroom techniques (i.e., what kind of things do you do in the classroom and how does this relate to the method(s))?

- What view of language and of learning does the method, or do the methods, you teach through hold? Is this consistent with your own beliefs?

- If you 'mix and match' aspects from different methods, what theoretical beliefs do your classroom approaches hold? Are they theoretically consistent with each other?

- What happens to the concept of Method if teachers do not teach in a theoretically consistent way?

- Which do you think has more impact on what happens in the classroom – the method or the teacher who implements it?

- What is your opinion of the concept of Method? Why is it such a powerful concept?

- Is it reasonable to say 'there is no best method'? (Prabhu, 1990)

From 'best method' to 'plausibility'

When discussing methods, teachers often, and quite reasonably, suggest that there is no such thing as a 'best method'. Prabhu (1990) identifies two typical arguments that support this claim – that best method depends on context, and that every method has some value. Perhaps you reached these conclusions when discussing Task 5.6!

Prabhu (1990) notes that comparing methods to find out which is 'best' is fruitless as what takes place in the classroom, i.e., how methodological principles are implemented in practice, depends on teachers' beliefs and their subjective understandings of teaching in their own particular contexts. Prabhu calls this the teacher's *sense of plausibility* – 'a personal conceptualization of how their teaching leads to desired learning' (172). A consequence of this sense of plausibility is that methodological principles may be realized in different ways by different teachers, and elements from different methods may be mixed and blended. In effect, teachers' classroom methodologies are 'eclectic'.

Such eclecticism, while transforming how methods are seen in practical terms, also challenges the concept at a theoretical level, as to pick and choose elements from several methods is to undermine the concept, central to traditional views of Method, that there is a single best way to teach (see earlier discussions).

In whose interests? Method as control

A more critical strand of discussion has examined the relationship between method and issues of power and control within ELT. Pennycook (1989), for example, argues that all knowledge is 'interested' (i.e., knowledge reflects a political perspective of how society is, or should be, organized); the concept of Method therefore represents and maintains a specific set of interests that favour some groups at the expense of others. Pennycook suggests that Method favours 'Western' approaches to learning over non-Western practices, as methods have generally originated in the USA or UK and been 'exported' around the world. Similarly, Richards (1984) has also identified a 'secret life of methods' that depends on commercial publishers. Additionally, Method favours (largely male) academic experts and theorists over (largely female) teachers. Consequently, teachers are 'de-skilled' and become merely 'technicians' who deliver other people's ideas, the imposition of a method acting as a form of control (Pennycook, 1989; Allwright and Hanks, 2009). There are echoes of Prabhu's sense of plausibility in Pennycook's suggestion that teachers need to re-engage with classroom decision-making as 'transformative intellectuals' who are able and willing to reflect on practice (we shall return to this point, and to the issues of interested knowledge and the politics and purpose of education, in Part IV). These arguments are brought together by Canagarajah (2006) who notes that:

> We are no longer searching for yet another more effective and successful method; instead, we are now questioning the notion of *methods* itself. We are rightly concerned about their neutrality, instrumentality and their very constitution [12] . . . we have given up our march toward uniform method and materials. More important, we have become aware that assumptions about English and its teaching cannot be based on those of the dominant professional circles or communities. [29]

Methods, stereotypes and 'myths'

The apparently contrasting accounts of methods presented towards the beginning of this chapter – that the development of methods reflects 'progress' or that methods are context-dependent 'products of their time' – share a perspective, that a succession of methods *can* be identified and labelled across 'bounded periods of history' (Hunter and Smith, 2012: 430). This view has been critiqued in a number of ways.

Pennycook (1989), for example, supports Clarke's assertion that '"method" is a label without substance' (1983: 109). He argues that, despite the best attempts of many writers to define and explain Method and individual methods clearly, 'there is little agreement as to which methods existed when, and in what order; [and] there is little agreement and conceptual coherence to the terms used' (602). Indeed, the differing explanations of Method itself and the different lists of methods offered by teacher development texts (e.g. Larsen-Freeman and Anderson (2011) and Richards and Rodgers (2014) that we have explored in this chapter could serve as an example of these tendencies!

These points are developed by Hunter and Smith (2012: 430–431, and noted earlier in the chapter), who suggest that a 'mythology' has developed around methods which 'packages up', simplifies and stereotypes complex classroom practices from around the world. For example, although many accounts suggest that the Direct Method replaced Grammar-translation in the early twentieth century, a more nuanced view of ELT pedagogy finds Grammar-translation approaches still being used today in many parts of the world. Meanwhile, PPP-oriented classrooms can still be found in the current, apparently more communicative era.

For Hunter and Smith, therefore, accounts of Method and methods too often emphasise change and 'revolution', and overlook continuities in ELT practice (as noted earlier in the chapter, with regard to CLT). Hunter and Smith therefore contend that accounts of methods tend to emphasise the experiences and interests of Anglo-American methodologists, but do not reflect the experiences of teachers working in a near limitless range of contexts around the world. From this perspective, theoretical outlines of methods rarely reflect classroom reality.

The principles and practice of Postmethod

As the above arguments have taken hold and the limits of Method both in practice and as a theoretical concept have become clear, applied linguists have begun to speak of 'The Death of the Method' (Allwright, 1991), of the 'Postmethod Condition' (Kumaravadivelu, 1994) or of a move 'Beyond Methods' (ibid.; 2006; 2012). Initial forms of Postmethod practice may be identified as 'principled eclecticism' in which teachers purposefully plan and adapt their classroom procedures by absorbing practices from a variety of methods and use for specific and appropriate purposes (Rivers, 1981). However, whereas this is clearly a practical approach to classroom teaching, the 'Postmethod Discourse' (Akbari, 2008) has developed further via three principles –

particularity, *practicality* and *possibility* (Kumaravadivelu, 2012: 12–16), whereby:

- pedagogy must be sensitive to the local individual, institutional, social and cultural contexts of teaching and learning and of teachers and learners (i.e., particularity);

- the superiority of theorists over teachers is broken, with teachers encouraged to theorize from their own practices and put into practice their own theories (i.e., practicality);

- the socio-political consciousness of teachers and learners is fostered in the classroom, so that they can 'form and transform their personal and social identity' (i.e., possibility).

These three principles take into account the teachers' sense of plausibility and critical concerns within ELT. But how reasonable is this in practice?

What is evident throughout the above discussion is that Postmethod envisages teachers assuming an 'enhanced' role, with the freedom and power to make informed decisions based on local and contextual expertise. Thus, when concluding an informative overview of ELT, Waters expresses the hope that teachers will be 'better informed' and make 'sounder' decisions (2009: 115), while Brown recommends that language teachers must be 'well-versed in the pedagogical options available to meet the needs of the various ages, purposes, proficiency levels, skills and contexts of language learners around the globe' (Brown, 2001: *xi*).

However, there is a potential difficulty with this perspective. As Crookes (2009: 201) notes, 'the field of ELT is insufficiently sensitive to the constraints that the majority of English teachers are under'. Teachers are not completely free to pick and choose how they teach; they are bound in by social convention, learners' expectations and school and ministry policies about how to teach and what methodology to follow. Thus, Akbari (2008) argues strongly that Postmethod asks too much of teachers, ignoring and misrepresenting the realities of the classroom and projecting a hypothetical reality that does not acknowledge the social, political and cultural realities of teachers' and learners' everyday lives. He recognizes that not all teachers have the time, resources or the willingness to shoulder the responsibility and decision-making Postmethod asks of them, and suggests that the 'death of Method' often leads not to a Postmethod era but to the replacement of methods by textbook-defined practice. Hence, Akbari highlights the contradiction of trying to teach critically and within a Postmethod framework via generally non-critical, 'neutralized and sanitized' published textbooks (Gray, 2016; see Chapter 11 for further discussion).

Additionally, as noted in Chapter 4, there is ample evidence that many teachers still think in terms of methods, if only as resources for their subsequent 'principled eclecticism' and methodological practices. Indeed, that is the rationale behind the review of selected methods in this chapter.

So, does Postmethod offer a new methodological alternative within ELT? The more overt recognition of the socio-political nature of ELT in the world, and of the varying *local* contexts of ELT, links Postmethod thinking to ideas associated with *postmodernism* (Crookes, 2009). However, while Postmethod writers acknowledge the dangers of portraying methods' development over time as inherently progressive with each method better than what came before, there is a danger that discussions of Postmethod do fall into providing an overarching historical narrative with Postmethod as the most recent and inherently 'best' approach for teachers to follow (i.e., Postmethod becomes, in effect, another method). Equally, despite the emphasis on teacher (and learner) empowerment:

> Postmethod must become more responsible and practical to be able to win the trust of practitioners . . . adopting the language of practice, not academic discourse as its point of departure.
>
> (Akbari, 2008: 649–50)

That said, Postmethod does seem to offer a different way of conceptualizing classroom practice compared to Method, whereby the realities of teachers' classroom practices, and how these practices emerge from the interrelationship of teachers' knowledge, beliefs and contexts, are recognized as a starting point for understanding teachers' classroom methodologies. In Part IV, we will investigate further the contexts in which teachers' methodological decisions and interventions take place.

Summary: changing perspectives

This chapter has reviewed the 'array of realizations' (Canagarajah, 2006) surrounding language teaching methods. The search for the 'best method', which dominated thinking in ELT and applied linguistics for much of the twentieth century, has resulted in the range of approaches outlined in this discussion. However, we have also explored the idea that methods are 'products of their times', that is, individual methods emerge at particular moments and in particular places as a result of the social and academic philosophies that are current in those contexts.

We have also seen that, in recent years, the notion of 'Method' has been increasingly challenged. The potentially unhealthy and controlling relationship between 'experts' and teachers has been increasingly problematized, to the extent that some now suggest that the idea of Method and methods hinders rather than helps our understanding of the classroom experiences and realities of teachers and learners around the world. Meanwhile, the differing ways in which teachers may understand and implement methodological possibilities in their own professional contexts has been acknowledged. This has led to suggestions that we are now entering a Postmethod era, an idea that is itself potentially problematic as it may ignore the realities of, and constraints upon, teachers' working lives.

That said, the ways in which teachers negotiate methodological dilemmas in the ELT classroom will clearly depend upon their 'sense of plausibility' about how second languages are learned. In the next chapter, we shall explore the ways in which researchers have conceptualized L2 learning and the insights this might provide into teachers' classroom practices.

6 Theoretical insights for a Postmethod era

> The jury is still out and people, in the absence of hard evidence, can apparently believe what they will. Teachers, in other words, should remain sceptical, still play safe and not commit themselves one way or the other, and do what works. Researchers cannot do this because their job is precisely to find out why something works and something else does not.
>
> (Sharwood Smith, 2008: 189)

This chapter will:

- examine the various ways in which research conceptualizes second language learning;

- explore the links between theories of language learning, methods and potential Postmethod classroom practices;

- encourage readers to reflect upon those theoretical perspectives that contribute to an understanding of their own beliefs and everyday practices as English language teachers.

Introduction: making sense of theories

We have already noted (Chapter 1) that English language teachers' beliefs about the nature of language and language learning inform their classroom practices. We have also explored how language teaching methods, which until recently were seen by many to offer *the* mechanism for making English language teaching more effective, also reflect theories of language and L2 learning (Chapter 5). In this chapter, therefore, we shall investigate further theoretical approaches to L2 learning, and then explore the relevance of these ideas for teachers negotiating methodological dilemmas in the English language classroom.

As Gass and Selinker (2008: 3) observe, it would be counterproductive to base language-teaching methodologies 'on something other than an understanding of how language learning does and does not take place'. Similarly, Corder (1981: 7) suggests that 'efficient language teaching must work with, rather than against, natural processes, facilitate and expedite rather than impede learning', while Ellis and Shintani (2014: 27) state that 'good teaching is teaching that proceeds in accordance with how learners learn'. However, the relationship between language learning theories and pedagogic practice is not unproblematic, as acknowledged by researchers such as Larsen-Freeman and Long (1991), who suggest that teachers' expectations about what research can tell them should be modest.

This is due in part to the relatively recent emergence of Second Language Acquisition (SLA) as a field of academic study, developing in the fifty or so years since innatist and cognitivist perspectives replaced behaviourism as ways of explaining language learning. Thus although much has been discovered about *what* L2 learners know and do, there is still much to find out about *how* learners know and do these things, and theorists are even further from saying what teaching practices might follow (Larsen-Freeman and Long, 1991: 3–4). Additionally, Long observes that there are around sixty theoretical approaches and models that aim to explain L2 learning (2007), the theories complementing and contradicting each other in complex ways (Ellis, 1998). Hence, no single and unified picture of how second languages are learned has yet been found. This presents a serious challenge for teachers hoping to discover what SLA research can tell them about classroom practice.

Yet to conceive of SLA theory as a source for teachers of straightforward 'discovery' about ELT classrooms is itself too simplistic. As Ellis (1998: 12) comments:

> Teachers, in fact, do not just take a theory or research off the shelf . . . Rather they are selective consumers, buying from what is on offer in accordance with their particular needs and purposes. Teachers filter what they are told about language learning through the schemata they have developed from their own experience of classrooms as learners and as teachers. The idea that research can in some way tell teachers what to do is in fact naïve and hopelessly mistaken. All it can ever do is to offer . . . 'provisional specifications' which teachers may choose to act on or not in accordance with their own theories of learning.

Such an approach to the theory/teacher relationship parallels the relationship between teachers and methods noted in the previous chapter, with teachers filtering methods through the prism of their own experience and beliefs.

Of course, theories of L2 *learning* are not the same as theories of L2 *teaching*, and few theorists make *direct* claims about the relevance of SLA findings for specific classroom practices. Thus while SLA research may hint at universal methodological principles, it generally says little about specific classroom procedures, where, as Long (2004) acknowledges, the teacher, not the theorist, should always be the expert.

Task 6.1 Getting started: research, theory . . . and your teaching

- In what ways, if any, does 'theory' influence your own teaching and classroom decision-making? To what extent are you guided by theories of language teaching and learning, and how far are you guided by what seems 'plausible' to you as a teacher in your particular professional context? (Of course, theoretical insights and your 'sense of plausibility' may overlap).

- To what extent do you consciously think about and engage with theories of language learning and teaching in your everyday professional life, for example, by reading books or journal articles, by talking through ideas with your colleagues, etc.?

Exploring second language learning: key theoretical debates

At the heart of SLA theory is the issue of how far L2 learning is like first language acquisition (Thornbury, 2008); as we noted in Chapter 4, some theories of L2 learning draw on concepts that are similar to those put forward to explain how children learn their first language, while others see the two processes as significantly different.

From 'learning' to 'acquisition': innatism and Universal Grammar

As we have seen, in the late 1950s and 1960s, ideas about how language is acquired changed radically as the limitations of behaviourism as a comprehensive theory of language learning were exposed. Chomsky's 1959 review of Skinner's (1957) *Verbal Behaviour* argued that behaviourism cannot possibly account for the fact that children routinely produce new sentences above and beyond any language that they may have heard. This ability to generate sentences depends on a knowledge of rules; it would be impossible if children only imitated what they encountered. Consequently, Chomsky argued, the mind has an innate ability to hypothesize and discover rules based on relatively limited language samples. Given the complexity of language, and the undoubtedly 'messy' nature of the language input that children hear (including, for example, false starts and hesitations, and language slips and mistakes), what is particularly notable is that, with some trial and error along the way, the rules children ultimately discover are inevitably correct. Chomsky thus hypothesizes that children are born with an innate knowledge of the principles of a Universal Grammar (UG) that shapes all human languages, and are biologically programmed to acquire language in much the same way as people are born with, for example, the ability to learn to walk. Associated with the UG concept is the *Critical Period Hypothesis* (see Chapter 4).

Chomsky's theory focused on L1 acquisition and, in an often-cited quotation, he asserts that he is 'frankly, rather sceptical about the significance, for the teaching of languages, of such insights and understanding as have been attained in linguistics' (1966: 152). And yet, the concept of Universal Grammar has continued to resonate in approaches to L2 learning and teaching, based around evidence that, like L1 learners, L2 learners manage to acquire and produce more language than they have been exposed to. The suggestion is that UG must be available to L2 learners, whether in the same form as is available in L1 acquisition, or in a modified form (Lightbown and Spada, 2013).

In the context of L2 learning, therefore, Universal Grammar implies that learners have their own internally developing form of the target language (i.e., an interlanguage; see Chapter 1) and follow 'an in-built learning programme' (Corder, 1967 and Selinker, 1972, in Sharwood Smith, 2008: 188).

In the 1970s and early 1980s, these ideas influenced a fuller model of second language acquisition, the Monitor Model, which appeared to make very direct claims about, and have very direct consequences for, language teaching methods and classroom practices. Having touched on these claims and consequences in Chapter 4, we shall now explore them in more detail.

Theory and practice: the Monitor Model and the 'Natural Approach'

First developed in the 1970s and influenced by the ideas of Chomsky and UG, Krashen's Monitor Model of second language acquisition (1982; 1985) was based around five key hypotheses:

The *Acquisition-Learning Hypothesis* suggests that language *acquisition* and language *learning* are separate processes. Acquisition is conceptualized as a 'natural' and subconscious process that is identical to the way in which children pick up their first language through meaningful communication; learning is a conscious process that results in explicit knowledge of language and is usually developed in classrooms via a focus on language forms and rules. According to the model, items that are consciously learned cannot be converted into acquired language.

The *Monitor Hypothesis* proposes that only acquired language can initiate spontaneous language use. Learned language only 'monitors' or 'edits' spontaneous output, and checks and corrects acquired language. Monitoring cannot take place all the time as it is dependent on the learner being focused on issues of accuracy and correctness, consciously knowing the relevant rules and having enough time to apply them. Key to the Monitor Hypothesis is the idea that learned knowledge fulfils *only* this monitoring function.

Based on research into sequences of morpheme acquisition (see Chapter 9), the *Natural Order Hypothesis* posits that L2 acquisition follows a predictable sequence. This order, Krashen contends, 'does not appear to be determined solely by formal simplicity and there is evidence that it is independent of the order in which rules are taught in language classes' (1985: 1). For example, in English, 'add an –s to the third person singular verb in the present simple tense' is an easy rule to state and learn (consciously), but even advanced learners often omit this inflection in spontaneous speech.

Next, the *Input Hypothesis* suggests that acquisition occurs when L2 learners receive comprehensible input or *i+1*, where '*i*' is the language competence already acquired and '*+1*' is language input just above this level. If the input is too simple or too complex, acquisition will not take place. Thus i+1 enables acquisition to follow its natural order (see previous hypothesis).

According to Krashen, comprehensible input is necessary for language acquisition, but not sufficient; learners also need to be receptive to the input. Thus, the *Affective Filter Hypothesis* suggests that the emotions and attitudes of learners form an 'affective filter' that can block or impede input from being acquired when it is 'high'. Thus learners who are de-motivated, bored, anxious or low on self-confidence may tend to 'filter out' input while motivated, confident and relaxed learners will have a low affective filter and be ready to acquire comprehensible input.

As Richards and Rodgers (2014: 267) note, the implications of the Monitor Model for language teaching and language teaching methodology are obvious:

1. As much comprehensible input as possible must be presented.

2. Whatever helps comprehension is important. Visual aids are useful, as is exposure to a wide range of vocabulary rather than study of syntactic structure.

3. The focus in the classroom should be on listening and reading; speaking should be allowed to 'emerge'.

4. In order to lower the affective filter, student work should center on meaningful communication rather than on form; input should be interesting and so contribute to a relaxed classroom atmosphere.

Indeed, Krashen and Terrell developed the Natural Approach (1983) in an attempt to put these principles into practice. This emphasized the role of exposure to language (i.e., input) and comprehension rather than practice, and the need for learners to be affectively ready to learn.

Although elements of the Monitor Model are 'intuitively appealing' (Sharwood Smith, 2008), it has been heavily criticized. Larsen-Freeman and Long (1991) contend that, in part, this is because it was one of the first theories that focused on L2 acquisition and, as such, was *the* theory to test. Additionally, the Monitor Model is somewhat unusual for an SLA theory in that it directly resulted in clear recommendations for classroom methods and practice; it therefore needed to be tested and, if appropriate, challenged. Finally, it questions many teachers' 'common-sense' assumptions about the importance of language practice and production in language learning.

The five hypotheses have also been criticized for being untestable and therefore speculative. For example, is it really possible to distinguish between language produced as a result of learning or as a consequence of acquisition? Is it impossible to convert learned knowledge into acquired knowledge through processes of automatization and skill-development (which we shall examine shortly)? Is there sufficient evidence to sustain the Natural Order claim and is there really a 'universal' natural order for language acquisition; if so, what does this mean for individual learners and the influence of L1 transfer in L2 learning? And are comprehensible input and attention to affective factors sufficient for acquisition? (For further detailed critiques, see, for example, McLaughlin, 1987; Larsen-Freeman and Long, 1991; Mitchell, Myles and Marsden, 2013.)

Yet despite these and several other criticisms, the Monitor Model holds a central place in the development of ideas surrounding L2 acquisition. It stimulated further research, not least by critics opposing Krashen's ideas, and its emphasis on meaning and comprehensible input, while not wholly compatible with ideas behind Communicative Language Teaching that were developing at the same time, certainly chimed with moves away from learning rules and rote learning.

Further developments: the Interaction and Output Hypotheses

Brown (2007: 297) observes that the Monitor Model leaves the learners 'at the mercy of the input that others offer' while failing to explain how exposure to language actually leads to intake and language acquisition. Long's *Interaction Hypothesis*, in part, attends to these concerns.

Negotiating and constructing meaning: the Interaction Hypothesis

The Interaction Hypothesis suggests that interaction plays a key role in generating comprehensible input for language learners. Hence, in conversations between L1 speakers and L2 learners, and between more and less fluent L2 learners (i.e., class peers), speakers follow a range of conversational modification strategies in order to make themselves understood (Long, 1983c; 1985; Ortega, 2009). Strategies might include:

- *comprehension checks* by the more fluent speaker to make sure the learner understands what has been said (e.g., 'do you understand?', 'are you with me?');

- *confirmation checks* by the learner aim to establish whether they have understood correctly (e.g., 'so, what you mean is . . .');

- *clarification requests* by the learner asking the more fluent speaker to modify and further clarify a point they have already made (e.g., 'sorry, I didn't follow', 'Pardon');

- *repetition* – the more fluent speaker repeats or paraphrases their speech to assist understanding.

Interaction is thus a cooperative engagement in which speakers *negotiate meaning*. This process of interactional modification provides comprehensible input for learners, the Interaction Hypothesis thus implying that complexity and increased input are necessary for L2 acquisition, rather than just slower or simplified *caretaker talk* and reduced input (see Chapter 1). And, as it is the learners themselves who engage in interactional strategies which lead to comprehension, the focus of their learning is 'at the right point of need' (Ortega, 2009: 62).

However, a revised interpretation of the hypothesis has been suggested – rather than the sole relevant outcome of interaction being the generation of comprehensible input, it is the process of interaction itself, and the effort learners make when negotiating meaning, that results in language acquisition (Allwright and Bailey, 1991). Long's revised Interaction Hypothesis (1996) subsequently proposes that, during the negotiation of meaning, learners' 'selective attention' to language, for example during comprehension checks and clarification requests, and the engagement of their 'developing L2 cognitive processing capacity' can lead L2 input to be acquired (414). This perspective links the Interaction Hypothesis to cognitive approaches to learning (see later in this chapter).

The Interaction Hypothesis and role of interaction in L2 classrooms has been widely discussed by researchers exploring whether it is possible to design tasks that create 'optimal environments' for the negotiation of meaning and generation of comprehensible input. Such discussions are a cornerstone in the development of Task-based Language Teaching. Similarly, theorizing that input is generated by learners in a socially constructed environment suggests that input, and therefore the language that is eventually learned, is in part unpredictable, and that learning outcomes are 'co-produced' by learners and teachers. This is very different from behaviourist models of language learning and also from input-led models of L2 acquisition (where teachers direct the input). However, most research into interaction has taken place in Western cultural settings, with little being known about the negotiation strategies followed by L2 learners in other cultural contexts (Mitchell, Myles and Marsden, 2013). Thornbury also points out that learners may be reluctant to negotiate meaning when they encounter difficulties in understanding. He notes that a 'wait and see' policy may instead be adopted (2006: 108).

To summarize, the Interaction Hypothesis concurs with Krashen's perspective that input is necessary for L2 acquisition, but suggests that it is not sufficient and that modified interaction and therefore output is necessary. It is to output that we now turn.

Task 6.2 Making input comprehensible

Tsui provides the following example of interaction in an ELT classroom. The teacher is giving instructions about a homework task. What role do the learners (**S1**, **S2** and **S3**) play in making the input comprehensible? What does the teacher (**T**) do? Which of the conversational modification strategies listed on p. 123 can you identify?

T: It's twelve questions about the picture and twelve answers. So what you have to do is look at the pictures, write a question about each picture and then answer the question that you have written and underline the verb in each sentence. There are twelve pictures. Number one has already been done for you. You have to make eleven questions and eleven answers only. That is your homework.

S1:   Do we need to draw a picture?

T: Draw what pictures?

S1:   The –

T:	No, you don't have to draw the pictures, just write the sentences. All right, now, will you take out your green book four?
S2:	Mrs. Kent, do we need to write number one on the book?
T:	No, you don't have to write number one, otherwise it will be twelve pairs of sentences, wouldn't it? Eleven pairs.
S3:	Do we get the green book four?
T:	Green book four, yes.

(Tsui, 1995: 71)

From input to output: the Output Hypothesis

In contrast to Krashen's Monitor Model, the Output Hypothesis proposes that language production, especially spoken output, is necessary for L2 acquisition to take place. Swain (1995) maintains that producing output requires more mental effort and is therefore more challenging than understanding input. She observes that learners can feign understanding in a conversation by nodding or smiling, but cannot do this when it comes to L2 production in which they have to 'create linguistic form and meaning and in so doing, discover what they can and cannot do' (127).

Swain notes that producing language provides learners with practice and thus enhances their fluency. However, she also suggests that output can have a significant effect on learners' accuracy and grammatical competence (1985; 1995). As learners struggle to produce output when speaking (or writing), they are forced to pay attention to grammatical features and use language that is slightly beyond their current level. For example, in the following short extract, meanings are clear, but the learner attends to grammatical form and adjusts her output to produce more target-like language:

Learner 1: two small bottle
Learner 2: two small what?
Learner 1: bot . . . small bottles.
> (Shehadeh, 2001: 456, cited in Ortega, 2009: 68)

In the Output Hypothesis, therefore, learners move from 'semantic processing to syntactic processing' (Swain, 1985: 249), the thesis being that they are more likely to encounter language difficulties when they are 'pushed' to produce the L2. Learners may then consciously recognize the difficulty as something they do not know, which draws their attention to the 'gaps' in their linguistic knowledge. This, in turn, can trigger the cognitive processes necessary for L2 learning (Swain, 1995).

Additionally, learners test their hypotheses about how the L2 works via output, either consciously or unconsciously. They may receive feedback as they try new language forms, either in the form of being understood or through more explicit forms of correction, causing them to modify their interlanguage. De Bot (1996) suggests that output can also help learners develop their control over language items they have already partially learned.

Thus, in emphasizing the importance of conversation, the Output Hypothesis clearly resembles the Interaction Hypothesis. However, unlike Long's model, it contradicts rather than complements Krashen's ideas. In terms of ELT classroom methods and methodologies, spoken language is clearly to the fore, and more opportunities for learner output and practice may be provided. There is also a place for teacher feedback on learner output and conscious attention to language forms and structures, although how this takes place will vary. Again, it is possible to discern links with CLT and TBLT.

As we have moved beyond Krashen's ideas surrounding input and comprehension, our discussion of language learning has increasingly suggested that speaking and participation form a basis for L2 acquisition in the ELT classroom. Unlike the Monitor Model, which does not specify *how* input becomes intake, both the Interaction and Output Hypotheses indicate that the learners' cognitive processes play a central role in L2 development. Additionally, both also assume that cognitive development is a result of social interaction, language learning being seen as both a cognitive and a social activity (Swain, 2000: 97). It is to cognitive models of L2 development that we now turn, before subsequently exploring more social conceptualizations of second language learning.

Inside the learners' mind: cognitive perspectives on second language learning

Cognitive models of L2 development draw upon aspects of cognitive psychology and cognitive linguistics to examine the way the mind stores and controls linguistic knowledge. Cognitive psychology likens the human mind to a computer that can retain and process information in a way that facilitates its immediate retrieval; cognitive linguistics suggests that language and mental development are closely linked, that is, that language development is not a separate and autonomous element within people's minds, but is part of their wider mental development. Consequently, cognitive theories suggest that language learning is little different from learning other kinds of knowledge, that there is no separate system of Universal Grammar within our minds and that general theories of learning can explain language development. Consequently, there is no need to distinguish between 'learning' and 'acquisition' as distinct and separate processes. From a cognitive perspective, conscious and unconscious knowledge are in some way connected and it is the links between them, and what this means for language use and learning, which are of interest.

'Bringing consciousness back into learning': paying attention and noticing

'Attention' is central to this conception of second language acquisition, learners needing to 'pay attention' to or 'notice' language before they can understand and produce it (Lightbown and Spada, 2013; Gass and Selinker, 2008). Thus, Schmidt and Frota (1986) propose that language can only be acquired if it is available in comprehensible input *and* is consciously noticed. Here, we can see a link *to* Krashen's ideas surrounding comprehensible input and a step *away* from his approach as conscious knowledge becomes a central element within L2 acquisition.

Schmidt and Frota do not claim that noticing is the *only* condition for learning, but highlight its importance to the overall process of L2 acquisition. Schmidt (1990) goes on to suggest that noticing is: *frequency related* (i.e., the more an item occurs in input, the more likely it is to be noticed); depends on a language item's *perceptual salience*, that is, whether its 'noticeability' is reduced in some way, perhaps through reduced forms and contractions (e.g., *we would* becomes *we'd*); and is affected by *task demands*, whereby learners have to attend to (and therefore notice) certain language items to complete the activity.

There is some debate as to whether learners have to be consciously aware that they have noticed a language item. While Johnson comments that Schmidt's ideas 'put consciousness back into learning' (2008: 101), Lightbown and Spada (2013: 115) note that anything that uses up 'mental processing space', whether learners are aware of it or not, is a result of 'paying attention'.

Dealing with limited 'mental space': 'information processing' and 'automatization'

According to information-processing models of learning, then, language items have to be noticed before they can be employed automatically by learners, and noticing requires learners to utilize their cognitive resources. However, learners have a finite channel capacity (or 'room in the mind', Johnson, 2008: 102), suggesting that there is a limit to the amount of information they can attend to and engage with at any particular time (see also the discussion of Working Memory, below). For example, when beginner level learners are introduced to language for the first time, they may concentrate on understanding meaning and not be able to pay attention to producing accurate language forms. Over time, however, as they process the new information, understanding meaning becomes more automatic, and cognitive resources are freed to deal with form and accuracy.

Automatization thus involves moving from what McLaughlin (1987) characterizes as *controlled* cognitive processes, where tasks require a significant degree of control and processing capacity, to *automatic* cognitive processes where little attention is required and the mind can manage all the necessary information with little cognitive effort. When this move occurs, controlled processes are freed to deal with more complex language and skills.

However, how might automatization take place? Lightbown and Spada (2013) identify 'practice' as a key facilitating process. This is not, however, the mechanical practice associated with behaviourist approaches to language learning, and is not limited to production or output. Instead, exposure, comprehension and, indeed, anything that involves cognitive effort by learners can be termed 'practice', whether conscious or not (ibid.). Ellis, for example, while rejecting the term practice, suggests that tasks can fulfil this role (1992; 2009).

The role of 'working memory' (WM)

Working memory (WM) is the system through which we store information in the short term, while simultaneously being able to process that information; through these processes, which include hypothesis formation, reasoning and decision-making (Ortega, 2009), new information is integrated with already known information stored in long-term memory. WM is the system through which we control what we do with new information, but it has limited capacity compared to longer-term memory.

Often linked to notions of language aptitude (see also Chapter 7), WM helps learners retain information about language forms while that information is being 'assimilated into comprehension' (Collins and Marsden, 2016: 283). For example, a learner may 'hold' the *-s* verb ending while linking this form to the already known notion of 'third person singular', or link a *-ed* verb ending to the concept of 'pastness' (ibid.). Learners with a higher WM capacity are therefore thought to notice form–meaning links more effectively than those with a lower capacity (Révész, 2012).

In the classroom, therefore, the demand on learners' WM is likely to be lower if there are fewer new elements to consider at any one time, for example, by not asking learners to comprehend input *and* notice new language forms at the same time. Similarly, if lesson topics or tasks and activities are already familiar, then learners' WM capacity may be freed up to process form and meaning more effectively (Collins and Marsden, ibid.)

From gradual development to sudden progress: 'restructuring'
McLaughlin (1987; 1990) observes that there is more to the process of L2 learning than the steady development of automaticity through practice. He argues that as people learn, the way they envisage what is being learned also changes, not always gradually but often in short bursts of understanding that account for and accommodate new information. Thus:

> Restructuring is what occurs when learners are so flooded with information that goes against their initial hunch that they eventually decide to abandon the hunch altogether for a new hypothesis.
>
> (Scovel, 2001: 79)

The learner's new hypothesis (assuming it is correct) allows their inter-language system to function more efficiently. For example, in the acquisition of English as both a first and second language, a point is typically reached where learners (or children) cease learning past tense verb forms as individual items, and apply an –*ed* ending to all past verbs. This enables their interlanguage system to work more quickly and efficiently. There is, however, a well-noted difficulty with restructuring in both L1 and L2 contexts, when learners *overgeneralize* their hypothesis to include irregular verbs. This leads to incorrect verb forms such as *comed, goed* and *breaked* rather than *came, went* and *broke* (McLaughlin, 1990). Eventually, learners will restructure their linguistic knowledge again and produce irregular past forms correctly, having completed a 'correct-deviant-correct' (Lightbown, 1983), or 'U-shaped' (Ortega, 2009), pattern of development.

Language learning as skill learning
Applied linguists working from a cognitive perspective have conceived of learners' linguistic knowledge in several ways. One of the most useful frameworks, within which second language acquisition is seen as a form of 'skill learning', is that of *declarative* and *procedural* knowledge, that is, 'knowing about' language and 'knowing how' to use language (Anderson, 1983; Johnson, 1996; DeKeyser, 2007). Bialystok (1982) suggests a similar framework of *explicit* and *implicit* knowledge where knowledge is 'analysed' and 'unanalysed'. This overlaps but is not fully synonymous with the *declarative/procedural* framework, both frameworks noting the difference between being able to talk about language and being to use it, and being able to summarize a grammar point and being able to use it spontaneously. Clearly, a key issue for language learners and teachers is whether 'knowing about' language can help learners 'know how' to speak it.

From a 'skills learning' perspective, automatization converts declarative knowledge to procedural knowledge. Johnson (1996) terms this

DECPRO learning and also identifies the importance of PRODEC sequences in L2 development, suggesting that without declarative knowledge, learner language may fossilize.

Task 6.3 Learning a skill, learning a language

'Skills learning' perspectives suggest that the processes involved in learning a second language are similar to those we draw upon when we learn other skills in life.

Think of a skill you have learned, for example, learning to play a musical instrument, learning to drive a car or learning a sport (or a particular skill within a sport).

- How did you go about it? What did you do?

- Which elements of the skill did you learn first, and which came later? Why do you think you learned things in this order?

- Did you practice? If so, how did this help?

- Did someone help you? If so, what did they do?

- Was there a point when you realized you no longer had to think consciously about the skill but could do it anyway?

- Now think about learning a language. In what ways might this be similar to learning other skills? In what ways might it be different?

Other cognitive approaches

Information processing is not the only cognitive approach to SLA. *Connectionism* similarly conceives of language learning as a process of learning (generally) rather than as the result of innate language-specific knowledge. However, it differs in emphasis from the information-processing models already explored in that declarative knowledge has a less important role. Learners (subconsciously) identify patterns within the input they are exposed to, connecting elements and finding regularities as they hear items again and again. Acquisition thus depends in part on the frequency with which learners hear specific language items (Gass and Selinker, 2008).

Meanwhile, *Processibility Theory* proposes that the acquisition of some grammatical structures follows a reasonably fixed order, each structure only becoming 'learnable' when the previous stages have been processed and acquired. The order of structures depends on how complex they are for learners to process (Pienemann, 2003). There is a similarity here to Krashen's Natural Order Hypothesis (although

Pienemann (1989) emphasizes the researched nature of his claims in comparison to those of Krashen). We shall investigate sequences of acquisition and 'learnability' in more detail in Chapter 9.

Sociocultural perspectives on language learning

In spite of their differences, all the perspectives on second language acquisition reviewed in this chapter so far share one common characteristic – they present language learning as a primarily individual activity, in which language input becomes intake via cognitive processes which are either explicitly outlined or remain implicit. As seen in Chapter 4, however, sociocultural approaches draw on a very different theoretical framework to explain L2 learning, building on Vygotsky's (1978) research into the relationship between thought and language.

Central to this view is the idea that language learning is a 'transformative activity' (Negueruela-Azarola and García, 2016: 295), in which learners do not just acquire new knowledge (i.e., the L2) nor just engage in meaning-focused interactions. Rather, as they engage in strategic social interaction (DiPietro, 1987), operate within their Zone of Proximal Development, and perform at a higher level due to scaffolded support from their peers and 'more expert others' (see Chapter 4), learners co-construct new knowledge through 'shared' activity, and are 'transformed' as they appropriate and internalize these new understandings (i.e., as they make the new knowledge 'their own'). Here, transformation is defined as 'change based on conceptual development', which, from a sociocultural perspective, contrasts with understanding language through limited explanations and superficial language rules (Negueruela-Azarola and García, 2016: 298).

Sociocultural approaches thus emphasize that the learners' social world (e.g. their social *inter*-actions) is inseparable from their world of private cognition (i.e., their *intra*-action), with language being a tool to make sense of the world both socially with others, and internally, by regulating and organizing thinking (i.e., language 'mediates' thinking; see also Chapter 4).

Yet while social constructivist perspectives might superficially resemble the Interaction and Output Hypotheses, in that learning is said to take place as a consequence of interaction among learners and between learners and teachers, they differ in the importance they attach to the learners' external social world. According to the Interaction and Output Hypotheses, interlocutors and interaction are necessary to activate learners' *internal* cognitive processes. Sociocultural approaches, however, contend that knowledge is created and learning takes place during *social* activity and, ultimately, see the learners' internal and external worlds as inseparable.

SLA theories, ELT methods and classroom methodologies

Our survey of L2 learning theories has been necessarily brief, focusing on those aspects that hold most relevance to ELT methods and the associated classroom practices of English language teachers. At the start of the chapter, we acknowledged the breadth of approaches within SLA, which the subsequent discussion illustrates. Thus, what might teachers wishing to 'select and filter' theories (Ellis, 1998; see introduction to this chapter) make of the range of overlapping and contradictory theories of SLA?

'Believing and doubting'

Schumann reasons that SLA theories and theory-building are like art. Drawing upon the clearly contradictory ideas of Krashen (the *Monitor Model*) and McLaughlin (*automatization* and *restructuring*) as an example, he comments that:

> When SLA is regarded as art and not science, Krashen's and McLaughlin's views can coexist as two different paintings of the language learning experience – as reality symbolized in two different ways. Viewers can choose between the two on an aesthetic basis, favouring the painting which they find to be phenomenologically true to their experience. Neither position is correct: they are simply alternative representations of reality.
>
> (Schumann, 1983: 55–6)

Thus by playing 'both the believing and the doubting game' (Brown, 2007: 310), teachers can consider the 'usefulness' and implications of SLA theories when making sense of their own experiences and classroom reality. And, as Mitchell, Myles and Marsden (2013) note, this may or may not lead to changes in classroom practice.

Task 6.4 In practice? A return to methods and methodology

a. Your reflections

What elements of the theoretical explanations of second language acquisition that we have explored are 'intuitively appealing' to you? For example:

- To what extent do you see second language acquisition and second language learning as fundamentally different and separate processes? To what extent do you see them as closely linked and complementary?

- To what extent do you identify with the ideas proposed by the Monitor Model, the Input Hypothesis and the Output Hypothesis? What do you see as each model's strengths and weaknesses in theory and in practice?

- To what extent, and in what ways, is second language learning a process *individuals* engage in, or a fundamentally *social* experience where learners learn with and with the assistance of others?

- Have you ever experienced, or seen in your learners, a relatively rapid 'leap' in understanding or the ability to do something? Can you identify an occasion where you have experienced 'restructuring'?

- To what extent do you agree that learning a language is like learning other skills in life?

b. Theory and methods

In what ways do the language teaching methods we explored in Chapter 5 reflect the ideas about second language acquisition we have investigated in this chapter? How far can you identify the position of each method concerning concepts such as comprehensible input, affect, the acquisition/learning divide, interaction, output, automatization, declarative and procedural knowledge and the role of L1 in the classroom?

c. Theory and classroom practice

In Chapter 4, you explored everyday classroom dilemmas, which underpin ELT methods and methodology. We will now revisit these issues – how might the theoretical approaches to second language acquisition we have explored in this chapter inform your classroom practices?

- How is/might comprehensible input be provided in your classroom?

- Are there any opportunities for modified interaction in your classroom? If so, what are they and how might they affect learning?

- What is the role of output and language production in your classes?

- Is there a place for 'paying attention' and 'noticing' in your classroom? What do/might the learners do? Try to be as specific as possible.

- In what ways do you as a teacher create opportunities for learners to 'co-construct' knowledge and understandings through collaborative social activity? In what ways are learners supported and 'scaffolded' in their learning, either by you as the teacher, or by peers and classmates who may be 'more expert others'?

Method and methodology: practice, intervention and theory

A number of key themes have emerged in our discussion of second language learning theories. How might they relate to ELT methods and classroom methodology? Ellis and Shintani (2014: 22–27; see also Ellis, 2005: 210–21) summarize the key links in eleven 'Principles of instructed language learning', as follows:

1. Instruction needs to ensure that learners develop both a rich repertoire of formulaic expressions and a rule-based competence.

2. Instruction needs to ensure that learners focus predominantly on meaning.

3. Instruction needs to ensure that learners also focus on form.

4. Instruction needs to be predominantly directed at developing implicit knowledge of the L2 while not neglecting explicit knowledge.

5. Instruction needs to take into account the learner's 'built-in syllabus'.

6. Successful instructed language learning requires extensive L2 input.

7. Successful instructed language learning also requires opportunities for output.

8. The opportunity to interact in the L2 is central to developing L2 proficiency.

9. Instruction needs to take account of individual differences in learners.

10. Instruction needs to take account of the fact that there is a subjective aspect to learning a new language (i.e., learning a new language involves developing as a person, with opportunities, for example, to develop a new identity, new perceptions of the world, and even new personality; see Chapter 9 for further discussion).

11. In assessing learners' L2 proficiency it is important to examine free as well as controlled production.

These principles clearly synthesize the dilemmas and debates that have underpinned approaches to methods and methodology in ELT subsequent to the decline of behaviourism and Audiolingualism in the 1960s, albeit informed by largely cognitive rather than sociocultural concerns (principle 10 being notable for its emphasis on the subjective aspects of language learning). They provide a broad overview of current thinking but not (quite) prescriptions for classroom practice – there is still a lot of thinking to do for teachers who may wish to develop these ideas!

In this very balanced approach, Ellis and Shintani provide a broad conception of what learners' language is or needs to be (principle 1), and see a role for both input and output, for a focus on meaning and on form, for the development of implicit and explicit forms of knowledge and so on. Implicit in their position is the importance of meaning-focused production ('opportunities for output' and 'the opportunity to interact'), but not form-focused controlled practice. Ellis and Shintani posit a role for consciousness-raising activities when focusing on form.

Interestingly, Ellis and Shintani make no explicit mention of the role of learners' L1 in the L2 classroom within these eleven principles. Although the principles clearly outline the importance of L2 input, interaction and output, and it is possible to suggest that using the learners' L1 might mean they do not maximize these learning opportunities, it is equally possible to hypothesize a role for the L1 in, for example, the development of explicit knowledge or in a focus on form. In effect, Ellis and Shintani's principles seem to encourage a non-dogmatic approach to the use of L1 in the ELT classroom.

Summary: the death of Method? Continued methodological debate!

Throughout this chapter, we have noted the complex and at times contradictory nature of SLA theory, and the acknowledgement by SLA researchers that English language teachers will and should act according to their own sense of plausibility (see also Chapters 4 and 5). Indeed, the focus on acquisition and learning within SLA studies has also contributed the shift in attention away from Method and methods as the central issue within ELT, and towards learners and pedagogical contexts, as we shall see in the second half of this book.

Yet it would be wrong not to acknowledge the debates that continue among applied linguists about the implications of current theories for everyday classroom practices. The role of TBLT, seen by some as the most likely pedagogical outcome of SLA research (e.g., Ellis, 2005 and 2009; Skehan, 1998), is the subject of heated discussion, as is the associated focus on form or forms debate, Sheen (2003) going as far as to claim *focus on form* is 'a myth' while Long labels *focus on forms* 'Neanderthal' (1988: 136 cited in Sheen, 2003).

Thus while theories of L2 learning offer ELT professionals an array of insights into methodological dilemmas, they also perhaps raise more questions than they answer. Thus as ELT enters a Postmethod era, or at least an era where the grand narrative of methodological certainty has ended, 'one may say that language teaching is still what it essentially has always been: the art of the possible' (Widdowson, 2004: 553). Theory may inform teachers' decisions, but with regard to methods and classroom methodology, teachers will still be guided by their sense of what is and what is not plausible.

Part III

Learners

7 Focus on the language learner

Individual attributes and attitudes

> We can no longer assume that our students are 'simply' students, nor that they are bundles of discrete variables. They are complex human beings who bring with them to the classroom their own individual personality as it is at a given point in time, and this influences how they interact with what we do as teachers.
>
> (Tudor, 2001: 14)

This chapter will:

- develop an understanding of learners' contributions to the ELT classroom and to L2 learning;
- examine how *who* individual learners are might affect their L2 development, identifying age, aptitude, personality and gender as potential sources of variation between learners;
- investigate *how* individual learners' approaches to L2 learning may vary, focusing on motivation, beliefs and learning styles;
- explore the practical implications of learner individuality for the ELT classroom, encouraging readers to reflect upon the possible implications for their own English language teaching context.

Introduction: 'learners are interesting too!'

When exploring ELT classrooms, classroom interaction and language teaching methodologies, there is sometimes a tendency to refer to learners in a rather generic way or treat classes as homogeneous entities. As we focus on teachers' actions and classroom practices, what learners contribute, as individuals, to the language classroom and to L2 learning can be overlooked. Additionally, as Skehan (1998) observes, many second language acquisition and learning theories (such as those examined in the previous chapter) focus upon the processes *all* learners might have in common when acquiring an L2. These 'universalist' accounts naturally tend to overlook the individuality of learners, assuming that they all 'bring the same basic equipment to the language learning task' (ibid.: 185).

However, there are obvious reasons why any exploration of ELT needs to focus on language learners and their individual characteristics. As Allwright and Hanks (2009: 2) note, 'only the learners can do their own learning,' and it is learners 'that either will or will not effectively complement the efforts of teachers and other, more "background" language professionals (like textbook writers and curriculum developers) to make language classrooms productive' (ibid.). Additionally, it is self-evident that learners differ from one another in a variety of ways including, for example, age, personality, motivation and attitudes. Teachers are likely to focus upon these differing attributes and attitudes as they search for what is and is not plausible within their own professional contexts. As Harmer (2007: 85) comments:

> The moment we realise that a class is composed of individuals (rather than being some kind of unified whole), we have to start thinking about how to respond to these students individually so that while we may frequently teach the group as a whole, we will also, in different ways, pay attention to the different identities we are faced with.

Thus, in an era of methodological uncertainty (see previous chapters), attending to the contributions learners make to language learning may provide teachers and other ELT professionals with insights into L2 classrooms, teaching and learning.

Furthermore, experience tells us that some individuals are more successful language learners than others. In any L2 class sharing the same teacher, textbook and curriculum, where the learning experience is ostensibly very similar for all learners, achievement levels will vary. In common parlance, some people seem to have a 'knack' or 'flair' for languages while others do not (Spolsky, 1989; Johnson, 2008). In addition to confirming the notion of individual difference between learners, this observation has led several researchers to attempt to identify the characteristics of 'good language learners', examining the qualities and behaviours that individuals have which might promote or hold back L2 learning.

We shall examine the practical implications of 'good language learner' surveys (and, indeed, whether it is really possible to discover what a 'good' language learner is) in Chapter 8. However, this chapter will continue by exploring how 'learner characteristics' raise a series of practical questions for ELT professionals concerning *how* English might be taught and, indeed, *who* it might be taught to. Although the chapter will again address the complexity inherent in L2 classrooms, the discussion does not intend to present learners as a 'problem' to be solved, but as 'interesting, at least as interesting as teachers' (Allwright, 1980: 165).

Approaches to learner individuality: terminology and frameworks

Applied linguists have approached the idea of language learner individuality and variation in a number of ways. Stern (1983) refers to 'learner factors' as he reviews how factors such as age, aptitude and personality might both affect classroom practice and raise questions surrounding level-based learner selection and placement. Skehan (1989), meanwhile, discusses 'individual differences' between learners, those 'background learner variables that modify the general acquisitional processes', helping to explain *'why, how long, how hard, how well, how proactively,* and *in what way* the learner engages in the learning process' (Dörnyei, 2009: 182; original emphasis).

Inevitably, reviews of what language learners bring to the language learning process tend to simplify a range of complex issues, and different accounts will frame the discussion in particular ways. Brown (2007), for example, examines age and aptitude alongside a framework of cognitive, affective and linguistic 'principles' (e.g., learning style, self-confidence and the learners' L1 respectively). Larsen-Freeman and Long (1991: 172) frame the same discussion in terms of 'cognitive and non-cognitive explanations for differential success', drawing on SLA research to identify age and aptitude as 'cognitive' variables, while non-cognitive factors include motivation and attitudes, personality, learning styles and learning strategies.

In this chapter, therefore, we will follow Larsen-Freeman's (2001) example and consider what learners bring to L2 learning and class-rooms in terms of their *attributes* (i.e., *who* they are, including age, aptitude, gender and personality) and their attitudes or *conceptual-izations* (i.e., *how* they approach L2 learning, including motivation, attitudes and beliefs and learning styles). Larsen-Freeman (2001) also discusses learner *actions* (i.e., what they *do* in terms of, for example learning strategies). We will investigate these in more detail, as potential 'interventions', in Chapter 8.

Task 7.1 Language learners: some initial thoughts

- Why do you think some people seem to be more successful language learners than others?

- Do you think that age matters when it comes to language learning? If so, what do you think the relationship is between age and language learning? Consider, for example, issues such as the rate of learning, the way people of different ages might learn, success in learning pronunciation or grammar . . .

- Do you think some people have a flair or 'natural talent' for language learning?

- What might we mean when we talk of an 'aptitude' for language learning? Can aptitude be measured or tested? If so, what implications might there be for language teaching?

- Does aptitude inevitably lead to success in language learning? If not, why not?

- Do you think that a learner's gender matters when it comes to language learning? If so, how?

- What do you think the relationship might be between personality and language learning? Do you think an extrovert might be a more successful learner than an introvert? Why/why not?

- What might cause anxiety in language learning?

- What are the possible effects of anxiety on language learners and learning? Is anxiety always a problem?

- What do we mean when we say a learner is motivated?

- How important do you think motivation is for success in language learning, compared to, for example, aptitude or age?

- How important is a person's past success in language learning for their current and future motivation?

- Why might what learners believe about language learning and teaching be important in the L2 classroom?

Language learning, language classrooms and learner attributes: *who* learners are

Age: the younger, the better?

According to popular belief, or, as Cohen (2004: 22) puts it, 'anecdote and assumption', children are faster and more successful language learners than adults; most people can identify both children who have appeared to learn a second language quickly and easily and adults who have struggled with language learning. This belief partly accounts for the expansion of English language teaching to younger and younger children in many parts of the world.

However, although age clearly influences language learning in some way and is thus a key consideration within ELT, the exact nature of the relationship is rather less clear than popularly imagined, with evidence in favour of younger learners' superiority in L2 learning being contradictory (Muñoz and Singleton, 2011). Hence, a number of questions concerning age and language learning require clarification, each with implications for the ELT classroom. Is there a 'best age' at which to start learning? Do children and adults learn languages in different ways? Are all elements of second language learning (e.g., learning phonology or syntax) affected by age in the same way? And what is the relationship between age and the many other linguistic and contextual factors which affect learning (ibid.), for example, the amount and quality of input, or the learners' attitudes, beliefs and orientations towards the L2?

Pronunciation is regularly cited as one area where learners who begin to acquire an L2 before puberty tend to be more successful than adult learners (Larsen-Freeman, 2001; Ortega, 2009). In other aspects of language acquisition, however, the evidence is much less clear. Both Brown (2007) and V. Cook (2016) highlight the superior retention of vocabulary by adults, while Stern (1983) and Larsen-Freeman (2001) suggest that grammar acquisition is not necessarily affected by age. Thus, the existence of a critical period for L2 learning remains rather uncertain (Ortega, 2009) (see Chapters 4 and 6 for further discussion of the Critical Period Hypothesis).

However, the ways in which younger and older learners learn *are* likely to differ. Adults are able to draw upon cognitive capabilities, which enable them to learn about and understand language in more abstract ways than children. This may explain why, in more formal classroom settings that involve reasoning and, perhaps, the mapping of new language onto existing cognitive frameworks, adults and older children appear to learn more quickly in the early stages of learning (over time, however, this initial advantage appears to fade and children who started learning at a younger age tend to catch up (Ortega, 2009)). It may also account for the success of children compared to adults in more naturalistic language learning settings where learning is more informal and involves less abstraction and analysis (Spolsky, 1989).

Thus the ideal age to start second language learning and teaching seems unclear. V. Cook (2016) suggests that if L2 learners aim to study for many years, it may be logical to start learning as children rather than adults as young starters will eventually be better speakers; however, he also speculates that should L2 learning only last a few years, it might be better for this period to be in adulthood, as older learners might achieve a higher L2 level over a short period of time. Overall, however, there is little conclusive evidence as to when L2 learning should start.

It is likely, though, that classroom methodologies will change according to the learners' age. More informal or naturalistic learning opportunities that require fewer abstract or analytical reasoning skills will favour younger learners while, dependent on factors such as personality and learning style (which we shall examine shortly), older learners might prefer more formal classrooms (V. Cook, 2016).

Before moving on, however, one further caveat is required. Exceptions to all age-related patterns can be found across age groups. An early start to learning in an informal or naturalistic setting does not guarantee success; similarly, not all adults will retain L2 vocabulary more effectively than children. Thus, when dealing with age and with the other learner characteristics that follow in this chapter, there is a risk of stereotyping learners, paradoxically removing 'the individual' from our discussion of learner individuality. We shall return to this issue at the end of the chapter.

Aptitude: language learning as a 'natural talent'?

The notion of *language aptitude*, that is, that some people have a 'flair' for language learning, has both popular and theoretical support. Most teachers, for example, recognize that within any class, some learners learn more quickly than others and may attribute this to 'natural ability'. Meanwhile, applied linguists have suggested that language aptitude is 'consistently one of the most successful predictors of language learning success' (Skehan, 1989: 38).

Broadly speaking, language aptitude can be defined in terms of 'speed in language learning' (Ranta, 2008: 142), and is a concept that 'accepts that everyone can acquire; it is just that some people do it *faster* than others' (Johnson, 2008: 118; original emphasis). Beyond this, however, what language aptitude involves or how it functions has been widely debated.

Originating in the 1950s, the Modern Language Aptitude Test (MLAT) (Carroll, 1990) offers the most influential early characterization of aptitude, testing learners':

- 'phonemic coding ability', the ability to identify sounds and remember and link them to phonetic symbols;
- sensitivity to grammatical structures in a sentence;
- ability to learn inductively, i.e., to infer rules about language from examples;
- ability to rote learn vocabulary items.

From this perspective, aptitude was seen as a stable ability, determined early in life and not subject to training or based on prior experience (MacIntyre *et al.*, 2016).

However, as V. Cook (2016) points out, the MLAT rests upon a series of assumptions that favour audiolingual language teaching methods, for example, that rote learning and a focus on grammatical patterns are important in language learning. This is perhaps not surprising given that Audiolingualism and the MLAT emerged in the same era (for further discussion of Audiolingualism, see Chapter 5), but consequently, it might favour analytical and grammar-focused learners over those who are more 'holistic' and 'message-focused'. It also, Krashen suggests, presents a view of aptitude that is more relevant to formal, classroom-based settings and less relevant to informal real-world situations (1985; see also V. Cook, 2016). From the 1970s onwards, therefore, enthusiasm for research into and the testing of aptitude faded. With the rise of communicative language teaching, the MLAT's audiolingual orientation was seen as irrelevant; meanwhile teachers and researchers questioned the value of testing and consequently labelling learners based on an aptitude score (Wen, 2012). For some, aptitude was seen as an anti-egalitarian concept, especially if it resulted in the streaming of learners into groups, while focusing on aptitude in isolation from other learner characteristics, such as motivation and other affective factors, seemed to overlook the 'whole learner' (MacIntyre *et al.*, 2016).

In recent years, however, there has been renewed interest in aptitude, but in ways that differ significantly from past understandings. Thus, aptitude is now an 'umbrella term' (Wen *et al.*, 2017: 2) which refers to a range of cognitive abilities that interact in dynamic and complex ways, both with each other and with other factors such as motivation and language learning opportunities. Robinson (2007), for example, suggests that learners' cognitive abilities (such as 'processing speed', 'pattern recognition', or 'working memory capacity'; see Chapter 6 for further discussion of Working Memory) combine to form 'aptitude complexes' (such as 'noticing the gap' or 'consciously rehearsing rules'), which come together during specific learning tasks. Meanwhile, Skehan (2016) proposes that different aspects of aptitude operate at different stages of the learning process, for example, 'attention control' and 'working memory' during the processing of language input, or 'phonetic coding ability' and 'working memory' during noticing. These and other frameworks are summarized in, for example, Wen *et al.* (2017).

Yet, however it is understood, the concept of aptitude raises practical dilemmas for language teachers and other ELT professionals. If traditional perceptions of aptitude as a stable and 'given' attribute that cannot be improved upon linger, 'the implications for pedagogy appear to be discouraging . . . [as] teachers may feel their efforts are not worthwhile' (Byram, 2004b: 37). If, however, aptitude is realized more dynamically, through differing 'complexes' of cognitive abilities that combine to address the needs of a particular language learning task or at different stages of the learning process, then language teaching might be modified and differentiated to recognise this. Ranta (2008), for example, proposes that teachers might help less analytical learners work out language rules and patterns, or intensively focus upon phonological skill development with learners whose abilities are weaker in these areas (we shall focus further on the development of learning strategies in Chapter 8).

Furthermore, as the discussion suggests, while language aptitude is a recognizable learner attribute that in part shapes how language courses and classes are designed and managed, it does not, by itself, explain language learning success and learner behaviour. There is inevitably a complex interplay between aptitude and other learner attributes and attitudes. Thus, aptitude, while an important learner characteristic, perhaps needs to be treated with some caution when making broader decisions about who, what and how to teach. As Spolsky (1989: 100) points out:

> To say that older or younger learners are better or worse is not normally considered a breach of egalitarian principles, for most of us have our turn at being young and old. Proposing some other explanation for difference is more questionable, for labelling one learner as inherently less qualified than another runs the risk of establishing or justifying permanent divisions among people.

Task 7.2 Aptitude: implications for teaching

- To what extent do you regard aptitude as a fixed capacity that learners are 'born with'? To what extent do you see it as something which can change over time, or that is realized in different ways in different learning situations?

- V. Cook (2016: 163) suggests four possible ways in which teachers might use information about learners' aptitude:

  - select learners who are likely to succeed in the classroom . . . and bar those who seem likely to fail;

  - stream learners with differing levels of aptitude into different classes;

  - teach learners with different types of aptitude, for example, those with and without phonemic coding ability, in different ways and with different final examinations. This might lead to different activities in the same classroom, parallel classes, or self-directed learning;

- excuse learners with low aptitude from compulsory language classes.

- What are the strengths and weaknesses of each possibility? Which do you prefer and why?

- How are students grouped in your institution? Is language aptitude a consideration?

- How do you deal with differences in learner aptitude in your classroom?

Personality: 'who we are' affects 'what we do'

Learners bring a wide range of 'personality variables' to language learning and the L2 classroom. Larsen-Freeman (2001) lists *extroversion/ introversion, self-esteem, anxiety, risk-taking, sensitivity to rejection, empathy, inhibition* and *tolerance of ambiguity* as those key traits that are thought to facilitate or inhibit learning. MacIntyre *et al.* (2016), meanwhile, draw on Goldberg and Rosolack (1994) to identify 'the Big Five' personality traits: *extroversion/introversion, conscientiousness, agreeableness, emotional stability/neuroticism,* and *openness to experience/sophistication/intellect*. We shall return to some of these characteristics in more detail in Chapter 8 when examining ideas surrounding 'good language learners' (said, for example, to be tolerant of ambiguity) and learning strategies (of which risk-taking is an often-cited exemplar); but in this discussion, we shall examine those issues that seem particularly relevant to classroom interaction and the creation of L2 learning opportunities – *extroversion/introversion* and *anxiety*.

Extroversion and introversion in L2 learning: challenging stereotypes

Skehan (1989: 100–1) outlines two main characteristics of an *extrovert* – sociability (including gregariousness, people-orientation and a fear of isolation) and impulsivity (including the need for excitement, change and risk-taking). In contrast, introverts are said to be quieter and more introspective, are reserved and perhaps even rather distant, and tend to plan ahead (Eysenck, 1965, in Skehan, ibid.). It might seem, therefore, that extroverts have an advantage in language learning as they create learning opportunities through interaction and consequently expose themselves to input while generating output. However, while there may be links between extroversion and speaking skills, there does not appear to be a relationship between extroversion and overall success in language learning. Indeed, a study undertaken by Ehrman (2008) found that the logical and precise thinking that *introverted* learners may bring to the language learning process led to more successful L2 learning. As Ehrman (2008: 70) notes, however:

> It is clear from the fact that there are high-level language learners in a wide variety of personality categories that motivated individuals can become good language learners whatever their personalities.

That is not to say, however, that personality is not an important learner characteristic in the L2 classroom. It might be, for example, that introverted learners prefer teaching tasks that emphasize individual learning and knowledge while extroverts may prefer group participation tasks. Thus, in classrooms that include a range of personality types (as most do), some learners might prefer a more 'academic' style of teaching and learning, and others a more communicative type of class (V. Cook, 2016: 171), a situation with considerable implications for classroom practice. Arnold and Brown remind us, however, that 'teachers should also take into account any cultural norms, which may make an outsider confuse cultural patterns of correct behaviour with individual feelings of inhibition or introversion' (1999: 11). We shall return to the issue of cultural norms in Part IV.

Anxiety and anxieties

MacIntyre and Gardner have suggested that language anxiety, 'the feeling of tension and apprehension specifically associated with second language contexts', is experienced by many learners (1994, in Larsen-Freeman, 2001: 17). It is 'quite possibly the affective factor that most pervasively obstructs the learning process' (Arnold and Brown, 1999: 8) although as well as *causing* poor performance, it seems that anxiety may also *be caused by* poor performance (MacIntyre *et al.*, 2016).

As Arnold and Brown (1999: 9) observe:

> There are few, if any, disciplines in the curriculum which lay themselves open to anxiety production more than foreign or second language learning. There is a great deal of vulnerability involved in trying to express oneself before others in a shaky linguistic vehicle . . . [and] with the advent of methods which focus on communication . . . the chance for the development of anxiety-provoking situations can increase greatly.

Thus, language learners may experience '*Acceptance anxiety.* Will I be accepted, liked, wanted? . . . *Orientation anxiety.* Will I understand what is going on? . . . *Performance anxiety.* Will I be able to do what I have come to learn?' (Heron, 1989: 33), while Gregersen and MacIntyre (2014) suggest that further sources of anxiety in the classroom include: learner competitiveness, that is, wanting to be 'the best' (or avoid being 'the worst'); mismatches between teacher and learner beliefs; harsh error correction; and perfectionism. These considerations re-emphasize our earlier conception of the L2 classroom as a social and pedagogical environment (see Part I), anxiety being, in part, a consequence of the relationships learners have with each other as well as their more pedagogic concerns surrounding their progress and performance in the L2.

Thus, anxiety is commonly seen as 'harmful' and 'debilitating' in language learning, creating worry, lowering self-esteem and potentially reducing learner motivation and participation in class. As we have seen, Krashen (1985) argues strongly that anxiety is never helpful in L2 development (see Chapters 4 and 6 for further reference to the 'affective filter'). However, Bailey (1983) refers to 'facilitating anxiety' while Oxford (1999) also speculates as to whether 'helpful anxiety' exists; for example, most readers will have heard phrases such as 'it helps to be nervous before an exam'. That said, the existence and role of 'helpful anxiety' remains unclear.

Although, as Larsen-Freeman (2001) points out, 'anxiety' may not fit easily into a discussion of personality characteristics, it is an essential element of classroom life and is closely linked to other aspects of learners' personalities. Oxford (1999), for example, highlights the relationship between anxiety and learners' tolerance of linguistic ambiguity in the classroom, their ability to take risks with language, and the tendency of some learners to keep silent or deliberately underperform in class (see Chapter 3). Again, we can see that learner characteristics interact with each other and with the learning context in complicated ways.

Gender matters?

Gender refers to 'the socially-shaped (as opposed to biologically determined) characteristics of women and men, boys and girls' (Sunderland, 2004: 229), and is, as Nyikos (2008) points out, an often neglected aspect of variation and individuality in L2 learning. Although there is increasing research into genetic differences in the way males and females learn (i.e., sex differences), it is perhaps more interesting for language teachers to note the ways in which boys and girls and men and women might behave in class and the possible consequences of this behaviour for learning.

A popular belief is that women and girls females are 'better' L2 learners than men and boys; certainly, girls achieve higher language-related exam results in British schools and elsewhere in the world (Sunderland, 2004). However, this is likely to be a consequence of social and cultural norms, which, from an early age, lead to the development of more effective social interaction skills and strategies in girls than boys, which, as we have seen, can be helpful in language learning. These skills are subsequently encouraged and channelled by societal pressures as women may, for example, see a greater potential benefit in their future working and personal lives from learning languages (Gu, 2002 in Nyikos, 2008). Thus, in terms of the L2 class-room, it is possible that women and girls experience different forms of motivation and may utilize different learning strategies to men and boys. In terms of classroom behaviour and management, there is also some evidence that in mixed groups male learners tend to dominate verbally (Gass and Varonis, 1986, in Sunderland, 2004).

Overall, however, as Nyikos (2008) points out, evidence that females are better L2 learners than males is scarce, partly because gender interacts with so many other aspects of social identity such as race, social class, ethnicity and age in influencing language learning experiences and outcomes. Thus:

> It would seem safe to generalize that both males and females can be good language learners. The ongoing challenge . . . for teachers [is] to discover how both their male and female students may be supported to achieve maximum success as language learners.
>
> (Nyikos, 2008: 80)

Learner attributes, teachers and teaching

The above discussion has briefly illustrated some of the ways in which who learners are might affect their L2 development. It has also suggested that the relationships between age, aptitude, personality and gender and language learning are not as straightforward as popularly supposed. Behind the discussion of these learner attributes is the assumption that they are relatively stable characteristics that teachers and institutions may attend to and accommodate, but which are not subject to much change (unlike, for example, learner motivation or beliefs, which, as we shall see below, *can* change over time and which teachers often try to address).

The attributes that learners 'bring' to language learning thus add to the complexity of the L2 classroom as any group of learners will include differing personalities and aptitudes, many will be mixed-sex groups, and some may even include learners who are significantly different in age. Teachers face the challenge of attending to *individual* characteristics in a *group* setting, and managing learning opportunities in ways which seem plausible to all participants.

Yet what *learners* find plausible will depend not only on whether, for example, the teaching methodology or materials are, or seem to be, appropriate to their age or aptitude. It will also be influenced by *how* learners approach learning, that is by their conceptualizations of language learning and L2 classrooms. It is to these learner conceptual-izations, and the further dilemmas they raise for teachers, that we now turn.

Attitudes and conceptualizations: *how* learners approach learning

Motivation: 'anyone can'?

It is difficult to imagine anyone learning a language without some degree of *motivation*. Dörnyei (2005) suggests that motivation ranks alongside language aptitude as one of the two key learner characteristics that determine success in L2 development while Corder states that 'given motivation, it is inevitable that a human being will learn a second language if . . . exposed to the language' (1967: 164); teachers regularly ascribe language learners' achievements or disappointments to the presence or absence of motivation. Yet, Scheidecker and Freeman argue, motivation is also 'the most complex and challenging issue facing teachers today' (1999: 116 in Dörnyei, 2001: 1), Dörnyei adding that 'strictly speaking, there is no such thing as "motivation"'; instead it is:

> an abstract, hypothetical concept that we use to explain why people think and behave as they do. It is obvious that in this sense the term subsumes a whole range of motives – from financial incentives such as a raise in salary to idealistic beliefs such as the desire for freedom – that have very little in common except that they all influence behaviour. Thus, 'motivation' is best seen as an umbrella term that covers a variety of meanings.
>
> (Dörnyei, 2001: 1)

English language teachers thus face a series of complex questions when considering how learner motivation might affect language learn-ing and their own classroom practices. What is meant by motivation? What factors might contribute to learner motivation? Can motivation change over time? And what is the role of the teacher in generating and maintaining learners' motivation?

Task 7.3 Thinking about motivation

- What characteristics and types of behaviour do you associate with a motivated learner?

- What factors might influence or change a learner's motivation?

What is motivation? Initial thoughts

Amid a range of possible frameworks and definitions of motivation, Williams and Burden (1997: 120) suggest that motivation is 'a state of cognitive and emotional arousal' that 'leads to a conscious decision to act'. This gives rise to 'a period of sustained intellectual and/or physical effort' so that people can 'attain a previously set goal (or goals)'. Motivation is necessary to sustain both short-term and long-term goals (e.g., completing a classroom activity, or studying a language over a period of years) and operates within a broader context of social and cultural influences. In other words, although it is commonly thought of as an individual learner characteristic, it is also a social construction – individuals aspire to certain goals as a result of their socialization in a particular context; this context can also constrain their ability to achieve these goals (Lamb, 2016).

A broad distinction can also be made between the motivation that learners bring to L2 learning more generally, and the effects of teaching and learning on motivation (ibid.). For teachers, therefore, in addition to arousing interest in the classroom, motivation necessarily involves the challenge of sustaining learners' efforts over time until their goals are achieved.

Where does motivation come from? Orientations and sources

In what became known as the socio-educational model, Gardner (1985) distinguishes between *integrative* and *instrumental* orientations in motivation, an orientation being the reason for learning and motivation being the subsequent effort to sustain learning. Learners with an integrative orientation study because they identify with the target language culture while instrumentally oriented learners learn the L2 for pragmatic reasons such as passing an exam or getting a better job. Ortega (2009) points out that these orientations and their related motivational processes are not mutually exclusive, while Brown (2007) notes that learners with either orientation can be driven by high or low levels of motivation. The integrative/instrumental framework, however, is perhaps of limited value in understanding learner motivation in L2 classrooms, as it focuses on long-term and stable learner traits rather than whether or not learners are interested in and engaged with their more immediate learning environment (Crookes and Schmidt, 1991). Additionally, in the many contexts where English is used as an international Lingua Franca (see Chapters 10 and 12), the relevance of integrative motivation seems limited.

Learners are also said to draw upon *intrinsic* and *extrinsic* sources of motivation. Intrinsic motivation arises from the activity itself and might, for example, result from the pleasure or enjoyment a learner feels when learning, while an individual is extrinsically motivated when they do something in order to achieve a goal which is not related to the activity itself, for example, learning a language to gain a reward (for instance, receive praise or approval, or gain financially) or to avoid punishment. Again, however, learner actions can be prompted by a mixture of both forms of motivation, i.e., they are not 'opposites', but can be seen as a continuum ranging from 'strongly intrinsic' to 'strongly extrinsic' (Williams, Mercer and Ryan, 2015). Hence, a learner may be intrinsically motivated by the inherently enjoyable nature of a classroom task having joined a language programme to pass an exam. As Williams, Mercer and Ryan (ibid.) note, it is important not to perceive intrinsic and extrinsic motivation as, respectively, 'good' and 'bad' – the distinctions between them are not always clear, nor fixed. Interestingly, however, and importantly for teachers and other ELT professionals, intrinsic motivation seems to be more focused and sustained than extrinsic motivation. In the classroom, therefore, as not all activities are intrinsically rewarding for learners, it may be important for teachers to explain the purpose of tasks. If learners can see the links to their overall learning goals, activities may become more intrinsically valued (ibid.).

Motivation and 'the ideal self'

Perhaps the most discussed contemporary model of second language learning motivation is Dörnyei's (2005; 2009) *L2 Motivational Self System*, which suggests that motivation lies within individuals' conceptions of themselves and who they want to become. Bringing together personal, contextual and temporal relationships (Williams, Mercer and Ryan, 2015), the model has three key elements:

- the *ideal L2 self*: a 'vision' of what or who a learner would like to be as an L2 user, for example, an international traveller, or a student in a different country. The more strongly held the vision, the more the effort to learn, as individuals work to narrow the gap between their 'actual self' and their ideal self. Here, the ideal future is the learner's own vision.

- the *ought-to L2 self*: a sense of what or who others would like the learner to be, reflecting a sense of obligations and responsibilities, for example, to parents or teachers. While the ought-to self can lead to effortful learning, learners may also try to avoid negative outcomes, rather than just working for the positive, and the future may be felt to be externally imposed (e.g., passing exams to please teachers and parents).

- the *L2 learning experience*: this is the effect of the learner's past language learning experiences (e.g., their successes and failures), and their interaction with their present learning environment (e.g., teaching methods and materials, their peers, and their current successes and failures).

Research suggests that the ideal-self and L2 learning experience are the more powerful influences on individuals' efforts to learn, and that these two elements may influence each other, i.e., interesting lessons may help learners develop their ideal self, while learners with a stronger sense of their ideal self may engage more with classes that are not intrinsically enjoyable (Lamb, 2016). Clearly, therefore, learners' images of their future 'selves' can change over time, with implications for their motivation to learn.

In summary: implications for the L2 classroom

Most theoretical approaches to L2 motivation thus recognize that it results from the dynamic interaction of a variety of factors, which are summarized in Table 7.1.

However, for teachers, perhaps the most fundamental question concerning L2 learner motivation is 'whose responsibility is it to motivate learners?' (Dörnyei, 2001: 27). Dörnyei notes that, by and large, 'teachers are supposed to teach the curriculum rather than motivate learners' but suggests that, ultimately, every teacher 'who thinks of the long-term development of his/her students' will feel responsible for learner motivation (ibid.). Thus although not *wholly* responsible for learner motivation, teachers (and institutions) can clearly play an important role in motivating L2 learners. This will include, for example, the selection of inherently motivating classroom activities, but according to Dörnyei and Csizér (1998), also involves, for instance, teachers setting a personal example with their own behaviour, creating a pleasant and relaxed atmosphere in the classroom, increasing learners' linguistic self-confidence, promoting learner autonomy, and increasing learners' goal-orientedness.

Learner beliefs, preferences and preconceptions

As the previous discussion shows, *learner beliefs* and motivation are interlinked. Learners' perceptions of, for example, the target language

Internal factors	External factors
Intrinsic interest of the language learning task.	*Significant others*, including parents, teachers and peers.
Value and personal relevance of the activity.	*Interaction with significant others*, including group dynamics, feedback, rewards, praise and punishment.
Sense of control and 'ownership' over learning.	*The learning environment*, for example, comfort, resources, time of day, and class size.
Feelings of progress, competence and mastery.	*The broader context*, for example, wider family networks and societal norms.
'Self-concept', including self-esteem, a sense of personal strengths and weaknesses and successes and failures, and the expectation of success.	
Attitude to L2 learning, the L2 itself and the target language community.	
Affective factors such as confidence and anxiety.	
Age, aptitude and *gender*.	

Table 7.1 Factors affecting L2 motivation

Source: Adapted from Williams and Burden, 1997: 137–40.

community or the type of learning activity they encounter are likely to affect their motivation. Beyond this link, however, learner beliefs, those mental constructs which they hold to be true, are important because they guide learners' thinking and behaviour (see Chapter 1 for further discussion of beliefs).

Language learners hold beliefs about themselves, about language and about language learning. Additionally, of course, 'virtually all learners, particularly older learners, have strong beliefs and opinions about how their instruction should be delivered' (Lightbown and Spada, 2013: 90). Moreover, as Larsen-Freeman (2001) points out (and as we have noted elsewhere), the beliefs of 'influential others' are also relevant within language learning and L2 classrooms, particularly the attitudes held by parents of young learners. Thus, learners (and 'influential others') are likely to hold beliefs about, for example, error correction, the role of translation, the importance of drilling and repetition, and the place of grammar teaching in L2 learning and classrooms; indeed, about most of the topics explored in this book!

Learner beliefs raise a number of issues for teachers. They mediate how learners experience the L2 classroom and can lead to mismatches between learners' and teachers' perspectives of what is desirable in the L2 classroom (Lightbown and Spada, 2013). For example, if a teacher emphasizes learner-centred communicative group work with learners who believe a teacher-led focus on forms is a more effective way of learning, classroom difficulties can arise. Additionally, a language class is not a 'unified whole' (as already acknowledged). Learners are likely to hold different and possibly diverse beliefs about classroom life, adding further complexity to the L2 classroom.

Amid this complexity, it seems useful for teachers to find out what learners believe (and for learners to find out their teacher's beliefs), although the beliefs learners (and teachers) articulate may not be consistent and may change over time (Benson and Lor, 1999). Examining learner beliefs may help teachers understand why learners behave as they do, provide insights into learners' emotional and motivational systems (MacIntyre *et al.*, 2016), and lead to a clearer understanding of classroom life. Many applied linguists also suggest that eliciting learners' beliefs allows for the presentation of alternative views that can help learners revise and expand their knowledge about language learning, thereby developing a more flexible and reflective approach to their learning (Wenden, 1999; Ellis, 2005); such ideas raise the possibility of *learner training*. At this point, however, it is worth noting that the idea that some learner beliefs may be 'erroneous or counterproductive . . . [and] viewed, compared and judged according to an idea view of a good or autonomous language learner' may lead to a 'deficit' view of learners that is demeaning and unrealistic, as it compares them to an idealized view of a 'good language learner', an ideal that does not actually exist and 'real' learners do not correspond to (Barcelos, 2003: 14 in White, 2008: 123). We shall return to the ideas of learner training and the 'good language learner', and this potentially problematic 'deficit' view, in the next chapter.

Task 7.4 Learner beliefs in your context

As we have seen, language learners hold beliefs about:

- themselves and their own ability to learn languages;
- (English) language;
- the most effective ways of learning languages;
- what constitutes appropriate classroom behaviour;
- how their instruction should be delivered.

For example, *learning a language means understanding its grammar; I'm a poor language learner; only English should be used in the classroom; learner motivation is the responsibility of the teacher . . .*

- What are the typical beliefs of a group of learners you are familiar with or of different learners within that group?

- How do some of their beliefs about the above issues influence learners' approaches to learning English? Can you identify beliefs that may, in your view, particularly support or hinder their language learning?

- How might teachers acknowledge or deal with differences between their own beliefs and learner beliefs, if at all?

Learning styles: preferred ways of working and thinking

A *learning style* is 'the characteristic manner in which an individual chooses to approach a learning task' (Skehan, 1998: 237). Skehan suggests that learning styles are interesting because they may result from personal disposition or choice, perhaps based on previous learning experiences, as much as innate endowment (see also Dörnyei, 2005). Thus, they may not be 'fixed'. Additionally, learning styles are often represented as continuums between two contrasting polarities, for example, *field dependence* and *field independence* (see below), in which the learning benefits accrue not just to one style or the other, but all along the continuum, albeit in differing ways (Skehan, 1998).

One of the difficulties with learning styles is that there is a proliferation of terms and models, some of which overlap and some of which are somewhat idiosyncratic. It is thus difficult to find a clear consensus as to what learning styles actually exist (Duda and Riley, 2004; Dörnyei, 2005). That said, commonly identified learning styles include:

- *field dependent* and *field independent*, i.e., thinking which relates detail to the overall context or thinking which separates detail from the general background;

- *wholist* and *analyst*, i.e., a focus on the 'bigger picture' or a focus on detail;

- *rule forming* and *data gathering*, i.e., learning and applying rules (i.e., deductive learning) or learning via exposure to examples (i.e., inductive learning);

- *reflective* and *impulsive learning*, i.e., a deliberate or a quick response;

- *verbal* and *visual learning*, i.e., success by working with verbal information or by working with visual or spatial information;

- *levelling* and *sharpening*, i.e., assimilating new information quickly and losing some detail or emphasizing detail and changes in new information.

(from Dörnyei, 2005)

Interestingly, Thornbury (2006) adds extroversion/introversion to this list, reflecting the possible links between learning style and personality. Meanwhile, V. Cook (2016) speculates on the possible relationship between field dependence/independence and measures of aptitude, noting that field independence seems to assist learners in conventional classroom learning and abstract learning tasks. Skehan (1998) similarly considers the links between learning style and aptitude, suggesting learners might differ in the degree of analysis and the amount of memory they tend to deploy (language analysis and processing, and working memory being central to conceptions of aptitude, as we have seen). According to Skehan, more *analysis-oriented* learners develop rule-based understandings of language, and, with their general orientation towards language form, value accuracy. More *memory-oriented* learners might retain (i.e., memorize) a wide range of language examples, which they can access quickly in order to engage in real-time communication, and speed of communication is said to be valued over accuracy. Learners may be more or less analysis-oriented and more or less memory-oriented (i.e., these dimensions are not opposites).

Several researchers have also found that learning style might be influenced by nationality (or, rather, the learners' 'culture of learning' (Cortazzi and Jin, 1996), a study by Reid, for example, suggesting that Korean L2 learners tended towards visual learning styles while Arabic and Chinese learners seemed to prefer auditory learning (Reid, 1987, in Nel, 2008). Again, this suggests that learning styles are not wholly innate and, therefore, not completely fixed.

However, how might English language teachers (and other ELT professionals such as textbook writers) respond to the inevitable differences in learning styles that seem to exist within the L2 classroom? Dörnyei (2005) suggests that classroom practices should aim to accommodate a range of learning styles in order to maximize learning opportunities for all learners, recommending, in effect, a 'principled eclecticism' (see Chapter 5) that matches classroom life to learners' preferences. He also suggests that 'style stretching' might take place, in which learners are introduced to, and subsequently may incorporate, learning styles that are not part of their usual set of preferences. Finally, learners may be 'empowered' to become more effective students if they are taught learning strategies which suit their learning style (learning strategies being the activities that learners *do* (rather than the style preferences learners *have*) in order to regulate their own learning (Griffiths, 2015)).

Yet, as MacIntyre *et al.* (2016) note, a *preference* for one learning style over another does not suggest that learners will not be able to learn through less preferred approaches. Additionally, learning styles are considered to be continuums, and labelling learners as 'either this or that' is inappropriate (ibid.). Furthermore, in practical terms, it seems unrealistic, impractical and unfair to ask teachers to vary their lessons to the extent that all learners' style preferences are accommodated equally. Indeed, given the lack of clarity as to which learning styles actually exist, it may be 'neither viable nor justified' for learning styles to form the basis of lesson planning (Yates, 2000: 359, in Dörnyei, 2005).

Overall, however, 'style stretching' and, indeed, the teaching of learning strategies, again raises the possibility of 'learner training' that, as noted, we shall examine in Chapter 8 alongside the related issue of independent and *autonomous learning*. Finally, a consideration of individuals' learning styles again reminds us that language classrooms are social spaces where individual learner concerns come together in a group setting.

Task 7.5 Reflecting on learner attributes and attitudes

a. Thinking about your language learning experiences

- Think about your own experience of learning languages. In what ways might your age, aptitude for language learning, personality, gender, motivation, beliefs and learning style have affected your learning, and, if you learned in a classroom environment, your experience in that setting?

- In what ways did these attitudes and attributes interact with each other? For example, maybe your beliefs about your aptitude for language learning affected your motivation, or maybe your perceived aptitude affected your levels of anxiety in the language classroom.

b. Thinking about your professional context

- To what extent do the learner characteristics explored in this chapter affect classroom life in your professional context? For example:

  - Are learners grouped or banded by age or aptitude to minimize in-class variation? If you have taught classes where learners have been of a significantly different ability, did you adapt your teaching? If so, how?

- Have you encountered classes that have included differing personalities? If so, how did this affect classroom life and your own teaching? What were the implications for your own classroom management and for language learning?

- How do you deal with issues of learner motivation in your professional context? To what extent do you feel that motivating learners is your responsibility as a teacher? If you do feel it is your responsibility, what do you do to try to motivate learners?

- To what extent do you deal with learner beliefs and learning styles in your teaching? Do you engage in 'learner training' with your learners?

Summary: learner individuality and the English language classroom

This chapter has surveyed a range of learner contributions to language learning and L2 classrooms. We have explored those *attributes* that are stable and not subject to change, the implication being that understanding these characteristics may enable teachers to accommodate them more effectively (e.g., age). We have also examined a number of learner attitudes or *conceptualizations* of learning, which are potentially more open to change (e.g., learner motivation). Beyond this framework, there are, of course, other variables that individual learners bring to L2 learning that readers may wish to reflect on, such as the level of their first language, their social and ethnic identity and whether they have learning disabilities (see, for example, Larsen-Freeman, 2001; V. Cook, 2016).

Additionally, we should note that although the discussion has been organized systematically, addressing each learner characteristic in isolation, in 'the real world', learners' contributions to language learning are the result of the dynamic interaction of these variables which are 'mutually dependent and intertwined' (MacIntyre *et al.*, 2016: 318). Furthermore, many learner characteristics might change over time, or according to context. For example, a learner's motivation might change as their L2 aims and goals alter, or their beliefs might change as a result of their learning experiences; or they might have a different sense of 'who they are' (in terms of, for example, anxiety, self-esteem, and inhibition) with one teacher and group of classmates compared to another. Thus, the interaction between learner attitudes and the dynamic and fluid nature of many of these characteristics, makes the relationship between what learners bring to language learning and the rate and ways in which they learn complex and difficult to predict.

As we move on, therefore, it is important to recognize that learners are 'more than discrete bundles of variables' (Tudor, 2001: 14) and address the concern that by providing insights into learner characteristics and variables, it is easy to lose sight of individuals (Williams and Burden, 1997). Thus the aim of this chapter has not been to label learners or divide them into groups (our discussion has avoided the term 'individual differences', for example). Instead, the chapter has examined how individual learners are complex human beings who bring to class a unique set of dynamically interacting characteristics that add to the complexity and diversity of classroom life. As in previous chapters, it seems clear that an eclectic approach to the organization and management of learning tasks and opportunities is more appropriate than the application of a 'one-size-fits-all' approach within L2 classrooms.

As MacIntyre *et al.* (2016: 319) state:

> Language learners arrive in classrooms as integrated, whole persons; informed teachers find ways of accessing the pressure points that drive positive change among their learners. In the ecology of the classroom, diversity is a source of strength.

It is to these ways of working constructively with diversity that we now turn.

8 Learner diversity and development

Considerations for the language classroom . . . and beyond

An 'all-inclusive' package is not an option in language teaching and learning once we take personal and cultural diversity into account. There is neither one single method nor one theory that can predict students' learning success in a comprehensive way and still do justice to the miscellany of learners in our classrooms or other learning situations. Individual and cultural diversity influence language learning decisions and choices.

(Finkbeiner, 2008: 138)

This chapter will:

- examine conceptions of 'the good language learner' and the possible implications of these perspectives for language learners and teachers, noting the dangers of over-simplifying what 'good' language learners do and recognizing that there is more than one way to be a successful language learner;
- explore the role of language learning strategies within these debates;
- investigate notions of 'learner training', asking *whether* learners can be trained and, if so, *what* they might be trained to do and *how* they might be trained to do it;
- consequently, consider the concept of learner autonomy, and its links to the debates and discussions examined in earlier chapters;
- recognize the importance of social context throughout these debates, encouraging readers to reflect on whether, and how, these discussions may be relevant to their own classroom practice.

Introduction: avoiding prescriptivism

The last chapter highlighted learner individuality and learners' potential contributions to language learning and the L2 classroom. This chapter, therefore, aims to investigate how language teachers may 'work constructively with this diversity', exploring how teaching might be centred on the learner, a goal 'to which most teachers would, in general terms at least, subscribe' (Tudor, 1996: *ix*). Yet given the variety of social contexts within which ELT takes place, what this might mean in practice will necessarily differ; as we have previously observed, ELT is a 'socially constrained activity' in which local social and cultural norms and values shape what is, or is not, possible or appropriate in the classroom (Holliday, 1994). As Tudor (1996: *xi*) notes:

> Language learners are undeniably individuals who differ from one another on a number of psychological and cognitive parameters: they are also, however, members of a given sociocultural community and are therefore likely to be influenced by the social norms, role expectations and learning traditions proper to the sociocultural group to which they belong.

Hence, the discussions that follow serve not as prescriptions for classroom practice but as starting points for reflection about what might be possible and valuable in readers' own professional contexts. Centring teaching on learners is thus 'an inescapably open-ended endeavour which cannot be made synonymous with any one pre-determined set of teaching procedures' (Tudor, ibid.).

'Good language learners': key ideas and changing conceptions

Task 8.1 'Good language learners': first thoughts

- Do you think there is such a thing as a 'good' language learner (and, therefore, a 'bad' language learner)?

- If so, what do you think are the characteristics of good L2 learners? For example, *good at guessing, willing to practice, focus on grammar* . . .

- Are you a 'good' or a 'bad' language learner?

In the 1970s, the realization that some individuals were more successful language learners than others led to an increasing interest in the characteristics of 'good language learners', and the hope that these traits might be encouraged and developed among all learners. In an early investigation, Rubin (1975) identified seven characteristics, which, she claimed, 'good language learners' share. Good language learners:

- are willing and accurate guessers who are comfortable with uncertainty;

- have a strong drive to communicate, or to learn from communication, and are willing to do many things to get their message across;

- are often not inhibited and are willing to appear foolish if reasonable communication results;

- are prepared to attend to form, constantly looking for patterns in the language;

- practise, and also seek out opportunities to practise;

- monitor their own speech and the speech of others, constantly attending to how well their speech is being received and whether their performance meets the standards they have learned;

- attend to meaning, knowing that in order to understand a message, it is not sufficient to attend only to the grammar or surface form of a language.

(from Rubin, 1975: 45–8)

Meanwhile, Naiman *et al.* (1978: 30–3) argued that good language learners:

- have an active approach and positive response to language learning tasks;

- develop or exploit an awareness that language is a system which they can make inferences about;

- understand that language is a means of communicating (i.e., conveying and receiving messages) and interacting (i.e., behaving in a culturally appropriate manner);

- manage affective demands such as inhibition and anxiety well;

- monitor their own L2 performance.

Notable among both sets of ideas are the tolerance of uncertainty, a willingness to take risks and the ability to deal with associated affective stresses; self-motivation, and the active self-management and self-monitoring of learning (i.e., not always relying on the teacher); and the attendance to both the form and meaning of language. The implications for classroom practice seem to be clear. As Rubin puts it, 'teachers can begin to help their less successful students improve their performance by paying more attention to learner strategies already seen as productive' (1975: 41).

However, these conceptualizations of 'good learners' raise a number of questions. To what extent are successful L2 learners really similar, and how far do they approach learning in the same way? We noted in the previous chapter, for example, that there does not seem to be an especially clear relationship between individual characteristics such as introversion/extroversion or learning styles and language learning success. It is, thus, easy to overemphasize commonalities among good language learners (Ellis and Shintani, 2014).

Additionally, it has been claimed that those characteristics that are seen as particularly effective in promoting language learning, such as learner self-reliance and autonomy, tend to be based on Western cultural norms and Western approaches to learning and teaching. However, this contention is itself much debated. While recognizing the importance of sociocultural factors within ELT and the value of non-Western cultural norms and traditions of learning, it could also imply that learners from some non-Western contexts are not capable of, for example, autonomous behaviour within L2 learning. Thus, while recognizing difference and diversity within ELT, it may actually create and sustain stereotypes. We shall return to this argument when we examine and develop a broader understanding of learner autonomy later in the chapter.

Furthermore, published in the 1970s, both Rubin's and Naiman *et al.*'s characterizations of 'good language learners' are very much in keeping with ideas from the same era that are central to Communicative Language Teaching, such as interaction and pair or group work (see Chapter 5). Meanwhile, the importance of, for example, rote learning or learning of a more individual nature has often been overlooked within the dominant communicative and meaning-focused approaches of recent years (G. Cook, 1994), as, perhaps, has the notion that language learning may involve 'hard work' (G. Cook, 2003: 35). Thus, the characteristics of 'good language learners' are not as straightforward as they may at first appear and cannot automatically form the basis for classroom methodologies and for learner training. As Oxford and Lee (2008) note, conceptions of *the* good language learner have evolved, now acknowledging that many different kinds of successful language learners exist across a wide range of settings.

However, although 'an abstract, fictitious and perhaps even mythological character' (Johnson, 2008: 143), 'the good language learner' provides a useful starting point for discussions of how teachers might address differences between learners in the L2 classroom. It provides insights as to what kinds of learner behaviour *might* lead to effective L2 learning, but also, when subject to critical reflection, reminds us of the diversity inherent in English language teaching and among learners.

Task 8.2 Good language learners: review and reflection

Consider the characteristics of good language learners suggested by Rubin (1975) and by Naiman *et al.* (1978):

- To what extent are their ideas similar or different to the suggestions you made in the previous task?

- Which of these characteristics do you recognize:

  - from your own language learning experience?

  - as being typical of learners in your own professional context?

- Do you think it is possible to train less successful learners to be more like successful learners?

- Do you think it is possible to train learners in your context to pursue the strategies listed by Rubin and by Naiman *et al.*, if they do not already do so? If so, which? If not, why not?

- Do you think that any of the qualities listed by Rubin or by Naiman *et al.* are particularly culture-bound?

- Are any of the characteristics listed by Rubin and Naiman *et al.* typical of particular age groups, or do they apply equally to children, teenagers and adults?

- To what extent do Rubin or Naiman *et al.* manage to convey the idea that language learning involves 'hard work'?

Language learning strategies: defining, classifying . . . and teaching?

One of the consequences of 'good language learner' investigations and their interest in what effective learners might *do* has been a focus on language learning strategies more generally, individuals' strategies and *actions* in support of their learning being a further learner contribution to, and source of variety within, L2 learning and classrooms (Larsen-Freeman, 2001; see previous chapter).

What are language learning strategies?

Chamot defines language learning strategies as 'the techniques and procedures that facilitate a learning task' (2001: 25). According to Oxford, they are 'specific actions taken by the learner to make learning easier, faster, more enjoyable, more self-directed, more effective, and more transferable to new situations' (1990: 8).

However, the concept of learning strategies has also been described as 'elusive', 'fuzzy' and 'immensely ambiguous' (Wenden and Rubin, 1987: 7 and Ellis, 1994: 529, in Griffiths and Oxford, 2014: 1; Dörnyei, 2005: 162). In practice, it is sometimes difficult to distinguish between a learning strategy and an immediate 'coping technique' or communication strategy. For example, asking the meaning of a word in a conversation is a communication strategy as it compensates for an immediate gap in a learner's knowledge. However, learners may habitually ask the meaning of new words as a way of expanding their L2 vocabulary; asking is thus also a learning strategy (Johnson, 2008).

Additionally, strategies are conceptualized as *conscious* actions, yet they may be deployed *automatically*. As Griffiths points out, this is not necessarily a contradiction – most car driving behaviour is automatic but, 'hopefully, neither sub-conscious nor unconscious', lying 'somewhere on a continuum between fully deliberate and fully automatic' (2008: 86); likewise, language learning strategies. Yet, as Johnson observes, the issue of consciousness matters if learning strategies are to be 'taught' as it might 'only really [be] possible to teach things which are at least potentially conscious' (2008: 149). We shall address questions surrounding strategy teaching and training shortly.

Despite these potential ambiguities, most accounts of language learning strategies emphasize that they are both mental and physical activities, which are, to some degree, consciously chosen by learners in order to fulfil a specific purpose or achieve a specific goal, learners using strategies to regulate and control their own language learning (Griffiths, 2008; 2015). Learners' strategy choices will thus depend on contextual factors such as: the task requirements or learning situation; individual factors such as motivation, age, learning style and personality (see Chapter 7); and their learning goals (ibid.), Ehrman *et al.* noting that 'a given learning strategy is neither good nor bad: it is essentially neutral until considered in context' (2003: 315).

Examples and frameworks

In practice, learners might engage in a range of strategies that promote their own L2 learning, from the general management of learning (e.g., finding regular times for self-study or organizing their notes in a certain way) to ways of learning a specific language item or completing a particular learning task (e.g., rote learning of vocabulary lists or working with peers to complete a classroom activity). These strategies have been categorized in various ways, Oxford (1990) providing one of the most well-known taxonomies:

- *Direct strategies* for dealing with new language itself:
  - *memory strategies* to remember more effectively; e.g., using flashcards to remember new vocabulary;
  - *cognitive strategies* to use all one's mental processes; e.g., trying to identify patterns in the L2;
  - *compensation strategies* to compensate for missing knowledge; e.g., guessing the meaning when a word is unfamiliar.
- *Indirect strategies* for the general management of learning:
  - *metacognitive strategies* for organizing and evaluating learning; e.g., noticing mistakes and using that information to develop;
  - *affective strategies* for managing emotions; e.g., noticing anxiety when using English;
  - *social strategies* for learning with others; e.g., asking people to slow down or repeat themselves.

(14–16; 293–6)

Meanwhile, O'Malley and Chamot suggest three main categories of language learning strategy:

- *metacognitive strategies* which involve thinking about and planning learning, and monitoring and evaluating how well one has learned;
- *cognitive strategies* which involve interacting with or manipulating the target language, or applying a specific technique to a learning activity such as grouping, labelling or ordering material;
- *social and affective strategies* which involve interacting with people to assist learning or managing one's emotions to help learning, for example by asking clarification questions or dealing with anxiety.

(1990: 137–9)

Although there are differences between these two approaches to language learning strategies, it is interesting to note the presence of both metacognitive strategies (i.e., the ability to organize learning) and social and affective factors in both frameworks.

Task 8.3 Your language learning strategies

- When you are learning a second language, what strategies do you use? Consider, for example, how you:

- organize and develop your knowledge of L2 vocabulary and pronunciation;

- deal with grammar;

- typically complete a writing task.

Further considerations

Central to the interest in language learning strategies is the notion that more and less effective language learners might use strategies differently, and that if researchers and teachers can find out 'what works', this might form the basis for classroom practice and intervention. However, the issues are not straightforward. As Allwright and Hanks (2009) note, does successful strategy use depend on *how many* strategies are used and *how often* they are employed, or on *how well* learners use them? Although there is some evidence that more successful language learners use strategies *more frequently* than those who are less successful (Chamot, 2001; Griffiths, 2015), it also seems that effective learners deploy a *more extensive range* of strategies, selecting and adapting those strategies that are *most appropriate* to the particular learning situation; they can also monitor their own progress (Williams and Burden, 1997).

Additionally, learners' strategy use will be affected by a range of other factors, such as their learning stage (with different strategies being deployed at different points during learning), their age (adults may use more cognitive strategies than children, who may be more active), learning style preferences, motivation, personality and so forth (Griffiths, 2015; see Chapter 7 for further discussion of these learner characteristics and the complex inter-relationships between them). For example, strategy use is likely to be affected by learners' beliefs about language learning, and these may differ from one culture to another (Griffiths, 2015). Oxford (1996: *x*) summarizes Lave's (1988) perspective that learners are 'enculturated (apprenticed into a particular learning culture that in many ways reflect the general culture) through classroom activities and through the modelling and coaching of the teacher and many others', and notes that their strategy choice will be affected by this cultural background. Oxford observes, for example, the tendency of many Hispanic learners to predict, guess from context, work with others rather than alone and to base judgements upon personal relationships rather than logic, suggesting that this derives from their preferred global or field dependent learning style. Oxford contrasts this with the apparent preference of many Japanese L2 learners to work alone and draw upon logical and analytic strategies, which aim at precision and accuracy and focus on small details (see also Johnson, 2008). Of course, such descriptions are very general and should not obscure the effects of other individual characteristics (such as gender or motivation), nor the differences between learners who share the same cultural background; however, it seems clear that culture does play an important role in learners' choice and use of learning strategies and, therefore, in any consideration of strategy training.

Implications: learning strategies, learner training and learning to learn

Learner training aims to help learners make more effective use of the learning opportunities they encounter (Thornbury, 2006). Focusing on *how* to learn rather than *what* to learn, it seeks to broaden learners' knowledge and use of language learning strategies, aiming to 'extend their existing repertoire' (Griffiths, 2015: 428). However, although strategy training dominates most discussions of learner training, 'learning to learn' can also attend to learners' beliefs and learning styles, as it:

> aims to provide learners with the alternatives from which to make informed choices about what, how, why, when and where they learn. That is not to say that they *have* to make all of these decisions all of the time. They may, indeed, choose to be teacher-dependent.
> (Ellis and Sinclair, 1989: 2; original emphasis)

Learner training aims to help learners become more responsible for their own learning, and leads towards notions of learner autonomy (see below).

Learner training has become a widely accepted part of ELT in many contexts. Many textbooks embed activities that raise learning strategy awareness. Meanwhile, separate 'self-help guides' (Brown, 2001: 220) focus exclusively on 'learning to learn'. In one such approach, Ellis and Sinclair (1989) initially ask learners a series of questions (e.g., *what sort of language learner are you?* and *how do you organize your learning?*). They then ask learners what they feel and know about, and how they prefer to learn and organize their learning of vocabulary, grammar, listening, speaking, reading and writing, providing a series of activities and self-assessment charts to help learners reflect on their own strategies and practise any that are new to them.

In addition to these strategy training 'packages' (Brown, 2001), many everyday classroom activities obviously require learners to develop and practise learning strategies on a more informal basis (e.g., information gap tasks often involve cooperation with peers, note-taking and an element of guesswork). Teachers often also give informal advice about how learners might learn (ibid.). Furthermore, teachers might provide learners with strategy checklists such as Oxford's well-known Strategy Inventory for Language Learning (SILL) (1990). Learners use the SILL to assess how often they employ a wide range of strategies, for example, *reviewing lessons often*, *reading for pleasure in English* and *reading in English without looking up every new word*, their responses then being classified according to Oxford's direct/indirect taxonomy (see p. 168). This, it is argued, helps them identify their individual strategy preferences and raises awareness of possible alternatives.

Bringing this range of activities together, Griffiths (2015) therefore argues that successful strategy training should include: explicit instruction to ensure that learners understand what they are doing, why they are doing it, and, consequently, how a strategy might be transferable across tasks; practice, so that new strategies become automatic and more easily called upon by learners when needed, and so that learners can see how strategy training can be supportive of their language learning goals; and learner evaluation of their own strategy use, so that they can adjust and adapt their strategy repertoire if necessary. However, learner training rests on the assumptions that consciously attending to learning strategies is useful and that learning strategies can be taught (V. Cook, 2016). Yet while these points seem reasonable, we have already seen that effective strategy use might not be a question of *how many* but *how well*, something which is not easily taught or learned. For example, the existence of individual learning styles or preferences (see Chapter 7) might mean that not all learning strategies are equally useful to all learners, and knowing what strategies might be effective does not mean a learner will feel able to use them (Little, 2004a). Thus, V. Cook (2016) suggests that learner training might lead to feelings of 'guilt' in learners who believe they are falling short of the 'good language learner' ideal. Furthermore, as Little points out, 'metacognition is by no means an infallible guide to cognition' (2004a: 580); just because learners say and think they are engaging in certain strategies does not necessarily mean they are doing so. Additionally, learner training presents teachers with the challenge of helping learners find effective ways of learning without inhibiting their independence, group training being inevitably in conflict with the individual's right to choose what works best for them (V. Cook, 2016: 149).

As noted in Chapter 7, there are also suggestions that learner training rests on the possibly patronizing and, ironically, disempowering and *deficit* notions that learners do not actually know what strategies are available and are being compared to an idealized 'good language learner' (see also Allwright and Hanks, 2009). Thus, if learners *are* to be introduced to new behaviours:

Instruction must take into account learners' cultural expectations and beliefs; otherwise it will fail ... the teacher must first think carefully whether such a change in beliefs and strategies is necessary, worthwhile, culturally respectful, and linguistically appropriate. Only then should strategy instruction take place.

(Oxford and Lee, 2008: 313)

Language learning strategies: a final word

In addition to their attributes and attitudes, language learners' actions, that is, their learning strategies, are a further learner contribution to, and source of variation within, the language learning process. Thus, asking how teachers may make use of strategies in the L2 classroom, V. Cook suggests that 'the students often know best. It is the learners' involvement, the learners' strategies and the learners' ability to go their own way that count, regardless of what the teacher is trying to do' (2016: 146). This perspective again highlights the essentially complex and diverse nature of L2 classrooms, and once more suggests that what learners learn as they encounter the target language is unpredictable.

Learner training builds upon this interest in learning strategies. Although its effectiveness has not yet been conclusively demonstrated (Griffiths, 2015), it aims to make learners aware of, and develop a range of alternatives to, their usual ways of learning, thereby leading to more effective learning. Learner training also encourages learners to take more responsibility for their own learning, the suggestion being that this makes learning more effective as learners learn only when they are ready to do so, and that learners who are responsible for their own learning can also learn outside the classroom, choosing their own goals, selecting their own learning materials and ways of working, and monitoring their own progress (Ellis and Sinclair, 1989; V. Cook, 2016). It is to these ideas that we now turn as we explore autonomy in language learning.

Task 8.4 Reflections on learner training

- To what extent do you teach learners 'how to learn' in your professional context? How far do you engage in learner training?

- Do you think learning strategies can be taught?

- If not, why not? If so, think of some of the language learning strategies you have identified over the course of this discussion. How might you go about teaching these to your learners? Consider, for example, the value of:

- *group discussion* (in which learners might discuss their approaches to learning activities or how they solve learning problems);

- *self- and peer evaluation* (in which learners may evaluate their abilities in a particular skill area and the development of their abilities over time);

- *peer observation* (in which one learner might observe another completing a task, taking notes to inform subsequent discussion);

- *journals* (in which learners might record how they solve specific tasks and how they deal with problems that arise).

- How might factors such as the learners' age, L2 level and culture affect the teaching of language learning strategies (and, indeed, whether learner training should take place at all)?

- To what extent do your learners engage with the notion of 'learner training'? Is it an aspect of language teaching and learning that they value, or are language classes for 'learning language' rather than 'learning how to learn'?

Towards autonomy?

As seen in earlier chapters, the 1970s was a period of change for English language teaching. As the influence of Audiolingualism faded, an interest in learners as individuals developed (reflected, for example, in the development of Humanistic and Communicative approaches to language teaching, and in the investigations into learner attributes, attitudes and actions and their implications for effective language learning). It is therefore unsurprising that interest in learner autonomy and its relationship to L2 teaching and learning first emerged in this decade. Since then, 'technical' perspectives on autonomy, which are most closely related to ideas of learner training, have emphasized learners' skills, strategies and activities; 'psychological' perspectives have examined those broader attitudes and cognitive abilities that enable learners to take responsibility for their own learning; and 'political' approaches have considered how learners may be empowered as they gain control of their own learning (Benson, 2016; Palfreyman, 2003). Clearly, autonomy is a multi-faceted concept!

Autonomy: what it is . . . and what it isn't

Most discussions of autonomy explore Holec's suggestion that it is 'the ability to take charge of one's own learning' (1981: 3). However, as Little (2004b) points out, this does not make learner autonomy synonymous with self-instruction or self-access learning. Nor does it mean that learners have to work alone. Rather, in this early conceptualization, autonomous learners were said to assume responsibility for their own learning objectives, for what is to be learned and how this will be sequenced and learned, and for monitoring and evaluating their own progress. Essentially, Holec was outlining what autonomous language learners can *do*.

Subsequently, however, autonomy has come to be seen as a *capacity*, something that learners *have* and can develop, rather than just a fixed set of procedures that they do (Cotterall, 2008); autonomous behaviour and learning is a consequence of this capacity and can encompass a range of approaches to teaching and learning. Beyond this, further definitions have emphasized the *social dimensions* of autonomy, Benson (2016) noting Jiménez Raya *et al*.'s (2007: 1) description of 'self-determined, socially responsible and critically aware' learners who are autonomous only 'in relation to some social context' (Murray, 2014: 4). Social context here could range from the educational culture of a particular context to the specific classroom in which a learner learns. Therefore, as Benson (2003: 290) puts it, 'autonomy can never be an all or nothing matter. There are degrees of autonomy, and autonomy may also take many different forms'.

Thus, autonomy is not limited to learning without a teacher; learners may take responsibility for elements of their own learning within the classroom, although this might take different forms for different individuals and in different contexts (Benson, 2016). In practical terms, autonomous behaviour can range from learners devising their own curriculum through self-access materials to reflecting on ways of learning within the classroom or finding opportunities to practise newly learned language. That said, group discussion, reflective learning journals and the use of the L2 are all common features of classrooms that aim to promote learner autonomy (Little, 2004b).

Making claims for autonomy

Autonomy in language learning seems appealing. It appears to cater for the diversity and individuality that learners bring to language learning and the L2 classroom, Benson (2001: 2) claiming that:

> The concept of autonomy is grounded in a natural tendency for learners to take control of their learning. As such, autonomy is available to all, although it is displayed in different ways and to different degrees according to the unique characteristics of each learner and each learning situation.

Benson's conceptualization of autonomy therefore accommodates learners' individual needs and learning characteristics, while learners' 'natural tendency' towards autonomy implies that the capacity for autonomy is universal (Little, 1999). This is important, as we shall see below, when we return to the claim that autonomy is a culturally specific Western concept. However, it is also significant because:

> Learners who lack autonomy are capable of developing it given appropriate conditions and preparation. The conditions for the development of autonomy include the opportunity to exercise control over learning. The ways in which we organise the practice of teaching and learning therefore have an important influence on the development of autonomy among our learners.
>
> (Benson, 2001: 2)

In effect, therefore, teachers can work with learners to develop autonomy in language learning, exchanging knowledge, consulting and negotiating with learners who take more responsibility for their own learning (Tudor, 1996). This, it is suggested, makes language learning more effective. Autonomy is also seen as an inevitable and essential element of L2 learning as all learners operate independently of others at some point, that is, 'only learners can do their own learning' (see Chapter 7).

Questions, concerns and comments

Although many applied linguists and teachers regard learner autonomy as a central goal of learning, a number of concerns can be identified. Some learners are less prepared than others to assume an autonomous role; they may lack the necessary skills and knowledge, or hold different expectations about what teaching and learning should involve (Benson, 2016). Proponents of autonomy, however, argue that these difficulties can be overcome 'given appropriate conditions and preparation' (see above). Yet teachers might also find learner autonomy challenging and experience difficulty in sharing or transferring decision-making and pedagogic responsibility to learners; it may run counter to their training and established classroom practices (Tudor, 1996).

Related to these concerns lies the suggestion noted earlier, that autonomy is, in fact, a Western cultural concept that is inappropriate in non-Western settings (Little, 2004b; Benson, 2016). While autonomy apparently emphasizes individuality, Asian learners are said to tend towards 'collectivism', conformity and a 'respect for authority from which the idea of individuality is excluded almost by definition' (Benson et al., 2003: 24). Yet this view clearly stereotypes non-Western learners as being culturally bound in a way which more 'individual' learners from the West are not (ibid.).

Additionally, as already noted, autonomy is conceived as being a *universal* capacity. Thus what differs between learners, and perhaps between societies, is not the capacity for autonomy but the ways in which autonomy is realized; that is, autonomous learning behaviour can take place in any context and classroom and 'everyone can be autonomous in their own way' (Holliday, 2003: 116). Thus, learners practise autonomy in even the most commonplace actions, Holliday identifying activities such as distributing class notes, organizing informal learning groups and coping with scarce resources as autonomous practices that are typical of all learning cultures. Indeed, drawing upon Shamin's (1996) study of a large-class environment in Pakistan (see Chapter 2), Holliday (2003: 116) observes that even the ways in which learners organize their own seating in different parts of the classroom shows they have the capacity for, and are demonstrating, autonomy in their L2 learning.

Underpinning all these debates, from concerns about teacher and learner roles in the classroom to questions surrounding the cultural appropriateness of autonomy, is the extent to which autonomy is promoted in a (problematic) top-down fashion through global education policies and through ELT methodologies and resources (see Chapter 12 for further discussion of possible tensions between global trends and local contexts in ELT), or whether it emerges from the 'bottom up' (Benson, 2016). Autonomous practices will clearly be more appropriate and, in all probability, more effective, when they evolve from the interests of teachers, perhaps working together in local networks to address issues of local relevance. This was seen, for example, in our earlier discussion of teaching large classes in difficult circumstances (Chapter 2), and the ideas put forward by Shamim and Kuchah for a 'pedagogy of autonomy' (2016).

Recap: making connections

Autonomy, classrooms and methodology

It is evident that the concept of autonomy brings together a number of themes that have been examined in this and previous chapters. For example, as noted, autonomy is directly related to issues of *control* of learning and of classroom practices. The degree to which learners might act autonomously underpins many of our earlier discussions concerning the management of classroom interaction and to notions of high and low structure in the L2 classroom (see Chapter 2).

Additionally, as Little (2004b) observes, autonomous learners are 'affectively engaged' in the planning, sustaining, monitoring and evaluating of their performance in individual tasks and in their learning overall. In other words, *motivation* is essential for the development of autonomous learning. As seen, however, the promotion of autonomy is, in turn, also viewed as a key strategy for motivating language learners (Dörnyei and Csizér, 1998; see Chapter 7), learner autonomy and motivation therefore being seen as mutually interdependent.

Conceptually, autonomy also enables teachers to accommodate and work constructively with those *individual attributes, attitudes* and *actions* that learners bring to L2 learning and classrooms (Chapter 7), thereby enhancing learning. However, this, of course, is perhaps more straightforward in theory than in practice for, no matter how autonomous learners are, most are subject to the practical constraints of institutional curricula and assessment.

Links can also be made between learner autonomy and developments in *language teaching methodology* (Chapter 5). In both Communicative and Task-based Language Teaching, learners engage with learning opportunities in differing ways and with differing language learning outcomes. Meanwhile, Postmethod pedagogy encourages learners to contribute to localized decision-making about appropriate classroom practices in support of language learning goals (Kumaravadivelu, 2012; see Chapter 5). From this perspective, 'autonomy might not be seen as an overarching goal for ELT but as one of a number of elements around which postmethod pedagogies might be built' (Benson, 2016: 343).

Autonomy thus underpins a liberal or humanistic recognition of the individual in the learning process, although this is not the only philosophical or 'political' perspective on learner autonomy. From a *critical* perspective (see Chapter 5), autonomous learners are empowered, becoming 'skilled agents' who can transform their context. Both liberal and critical perspectives on autonomy, of course, are part of wider educational traditions, which we shall return to in Chapter 12.

Autonomy and new technologies

There is an increasingly close relationship between autonomy and *new technologies* (see Chapter 2), in what Reinders and White term 'a transformative fusion of ideas' (2016: 149). While those multimedia CALL resources which provide language exercises, games and quizzes can support the development of autonomy by encouraging learners to control the selection of materials and strategies of interpretation (Benson, 2001), digital technologies and online media, supported in particular by the emergence of smartphones and other mobile devices, provide opportunities for 'a closer integration of language learning and everyday life' for many (but not all!) learners (Benson, 2016: 347). Thus, language learning-focused apps, online platforms and websites, and web-based ELT courses and programmes can be accessed flexibly at the learners' own convenience, while social media provide further, less formal, opportunities for language development, leading Benson (2016: 347) to suggest that:

> Interest in autonomy in classrooms developed because teachers sought to make autonomy relevant to learners who mainly learn languages in classrooms. The imperative in the future, however, may well be for ELT practitioners to adapt classroom teaching to their learners' autonomous learning outside the classroom.

Task 8.5 Thinking through autonomy in language learning

a. Autonomy 'in theory' . . .

Which elements of the claims made in favour of learner autonomy are 'intuitively appealing' to you, if any?

- To what extent do you agree that learners have a 'natural tendency' to take control of their learning?

- In what ways might this 'natural tendency' be affected by learners' motivation? Do you agree with the view that autonomy is inherently motivating for L2 learners?

- How might a learner's age affect notions of learner autonomy? Is autonomy equally practicable, and desirable, for children, teenagers and adults?

- How far do you agree with the claim that autonomy is a universal capacity realized differently in different cultures? What are the implications of this idea for L2 teaching and learning?

- Alternatively, do you think that autonomy is a Western cultural concept that is not equally applicable in cultural contexts? What are the implications of *this* idea for L2 teaching and learning?

- As a teacher, how do you feel about learner autonomy? Is the idea of sharing control an idea you are comfortable with? Are the concepts of autonomy and taking control ideas your learners are:

  - aware of?

  - comfortable with?

b. . . . and in practice

- To what extent do you feel learners in your professional context have control over their own learning?

- Which aspects of their learning do they take responsibility for, if any? For example, selecting materials and tasks, finding opportunities for practice outside and inside the classroom, where they sit in class . . .

- To what extent do you encourage autonomy among your learners?

- What constraints are there on the development of autonomy in your professional context? For example, those which are personal, institutional, social, cultural . . .

- What is the place of new technologies in developing learner autonomy? How might they be used to facilitate autonomous learning?

Summary: learner investment and interventions

This chapter has explored the ways in which teachers might respond to, and work with, the diverse individual characteristics of learners and their contributions to language learning and the L2 classroom. At the same time, it has outlined how ideas about the character traits and actions of effective learners have changed over time. Now, instead of looking for a single set of characteristics that are shared by 'good language learners' and are transferrable to less effective learners, it is widely accepted that no definite and ideal set of qualities and actions exists. Instead, successful language learning may look quite different from learner to learner, from classroom to classroom, and from socio-political context to context. It is also worth noting, however, the contrast between notions of learner variation outlined in this chapter and the search for 'universal' trends that typifies much SLA research (see, for example, the theories and approaches outlined in Chapter 6). We shall return to this point in the next chapter.

In this chapter, then, a number of issues *have* emerged as key considerations for teachers (and learners) when reflecting upon how to work effectively with this diversity and complexity. What is the relationship between language learning strategies and language learning *per se*, and what does this mean for teachers and learners, both in the L2 classroom and beyond? Is learner training an effective and appropriate use of class time, and how might it recognize the learners' own often culturally based beliefs and expectations? And if, as much contemporary applied linguistic and ELT thinking suggests, learner autonomy leads to more effective language learning, how might this concept be understood so that sociocultural differences of form and degree might be accommodated? Furthermore, how might autonomous behaviour be encouraged and developed among learners, including both those with greater and lesser access to new and mobile technologies?

However, when considering language learning strategies, learner training and learner autonomy, it is, of course, important to recognize that learners are more than linguistic 'processing devices' (Lantolf and Pavlenko, 2001) that teachers 'manage' (we shall examine metaphorical images of L2 learners in more detail in the next chapter). Instead, learners 'need to be understood as people, which, in turn, means we need to appreciate their human agency. As agents, learners actively engage in constructing the terms and conditions of their own learning' (ibid.: 145). This process requires an 'investment' of time, energy (Brown, 2001) and motivation, 'the fire that creates action' (Oxford and Lee, 2008: 312). We shall further investigate these ideas as we explore the theoretical contexts, insights and images of learners in the next chapter.

9 Images of language learners

From individual to social, and universal to specific

We can learn a lot by listening to language learners and any kind of foray in their worlds ... is likely to provide us with valuable information about language classes ... [and] about research itself.

(Block, 1997: 358)

This chapter will:

- explore whether learners' L2 development follows a 'natural order' and, if so, consider the possible implications of this potential 'internal syllabus' for language teaching;

- contrastingly, examine learners' orientation to learning from a more 'social' perspective, investigating 'acculturation' and the social distance learners might 'travel' when learning a new language;

- similarly, investigate issues of social identity and 'investment' in L2 learning;

- consequently, explore how different metaphors for L2 learners and learning construct and convey differing images of what and how learners might contribute to language learning and the L2 class-room;

- encourage readers to reflect upon these theoretical perspectives and the contrasts between them, considering what these conceptualizations might contribute to their own understanding of L2 learners and learning in their own professional environments.

Introduction: learning with purpose

The last two chapters have examined the possible influence of individual learners' attributes and attitudes on their L2 learning. Although what effective language learners do may differ widely from person to person and from context to context, our explorations of, for example, learner motivation and beliefs, learning styles, strategies and autonomy suggest that learners are 'agents' in, that is, they exert some control over, the construction of their own learning. As Breen (2001b: 178) remarks:

> Learners [are] thinking and feeling people acting with purpose that is generated by what they see as significant and meaningful for them *as learners* in particular social and cultural contexts.
>
> (original emphasis)

Of course, the consequences of learner 'control' and 'purpose' are not always straightforward; instead of engaging purposefully with language learning, learners might 'resist', be 'defensive' to and not participate in learning for a number of reasons, as we shall see later in the chapter.

This chapter, therefore, first examines the cognitive and social 'agendas' that learners might bring to language learning and the L2 classroom. The discussion will initially return to 'universalist' and 'asocial' (Firth and Wagner, 1997) accounts of second language acquisition. Focusing upon learners' 'internal' learning mechanisms to examine whether L2 development may follow a natural order, we will explore whether some elements of language are perhaps more 'learnable', and thus more 'teachable', than others. Subsequently, however, we shall examine how learners' *social* actions and identities might affect L2 learning, investigating more socially oriented explanations of social 'distance' and learner 'investment' in language development.

We shall then examine a number of metaphors that underpin these 'internal' and 'social' perspectives on L2 acquisition. As we shall see, they reveal different assumptions about, and understandings of, the nature of language learning and learners, reminding us that 'we always bring to our experience frames of interpretation, or schemata' (Erikson, 1986: 140).

Bringing an 'internal syllabus' into the classroom: a 'natural order' in L2 development?

The possibility that learners may have an 'internal syllabus' and that L2 development may follow a 'natural order' has been touched upon on several occasions in earlier chapters. In Chapter 1, we noted that learners have a developing internal second language system, that is, an interlanguage, with learner errors resulting from the incomplete development of this system or from the influence of the learner's L1 on their L2 (i.e., interference). In Chapter 6, we saw that one of the key tenets of Krashen's Monitor Model is the Natural Order Hypothesis, which suggests that the order in which L2 items are acquired is predictable. While the notion of interlanguage is uncontroversial, ideas surrounding a natural order of acquisition have been fiercely contested. Yet the possibility that learners *may* have an 'internal syllabus' is of interest, both as a debate within applied linguistics and SLA research, and as a further element within our current focus on learners and their contribution to L2 learning and classrooms. *If* the claims of a natural order for L2 development are valid, the implications for language teaching are potentially profound.

Initial evidence: developmental sequences and morpheme acquisition order

Research into the acquisition of English as a first language suggests that children follow the same pathway of linguistic development for many language features. For example, Brown found that children acquired the present progressive *–ing* (e.g., Mummy runn*ing*) before the plural *–s* (e.g., two book*s*), which, in turn, was learned before irregular past forms (e.g., Baby *went*) and, subsequently, the possessive *'s* (e.g., Daddy*'s* hat) and so forth (1973, in Lightbown and Spada, 2013: 7). Patterns similar to this morpheme acquisition order have been found in the way children learn negation and question forms in English, and similar fixed orders have been found in the infant acquisition of other languages. This has prompted the suggestion that L1 acquisition follows an 'internal syllabus' that establishes the route (but not the rate) of L1 development.

Researchers have investigated similar developmental sequences in L2 acquisition and seem to have discovered comparable patterns. Figure 9.1, for example, illustrates Krashen's summary of L2 morpheme acquisition order, items at the top being acquired before those found in lower boxes.

Likewise, Ellis and Shintani (2014), Lightbown and Spada (2013) and Ortega (2009) review a range of SLA evidence that suggests that, as with L1 acquisition, negation, question forms, tense and aspect and possessives follow similar developmental sequences. Johnson (2008), comparing the findings of Dulay and Burt (1974) and Bailey *et al.* (1974), notes that this 'internal syllabus' appears to be similar for both children and adult second language learners, and for learners with different L1s. It is therefore seen as 'universal', second language acquisition being 'characterized by a natural sequence of development, i.e., there are certain broad stages that [learners] pass through' (Ellis, 1985: 73). Consequently, most L2 errors are said to reflect the developmental stage of the learner's interlanguage rather than be the result of L1 interference (see Chapter 1).

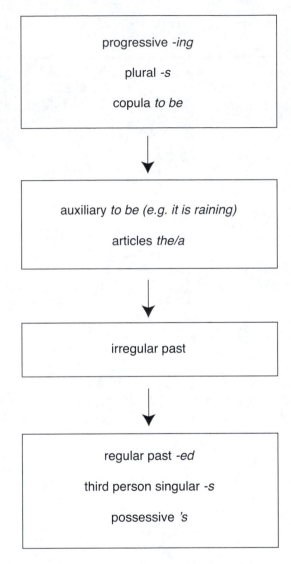

Figure 9.1 Summary of second language morpheme acquisition order
Source: Krashen, 1977.

And in practice?

The 'internal syllabus' is an appealing notion. It reflects Chomsky's ideas concerning the innate and universal nature of language acquisition (i.e., Universal Grammar), and associated perspectives around learners' 'in-built learning programmes' (see Chapter 6). It also appears to offer insights into L2 classroom practice, raising questions, for example, about the treatment of error. Acknowledging a learner's 'internal syllabus' might affect decisions about which errors should be corrected and when corrective feedback might be provided (see Chapter 1). To what extent, for example, should teachers attempt to correct the possessive *'s* before learners have acquired the auxiliary *to be* (see Figure 9.1)?

Additionally, developmental sequences and stages potentially problematize L2 syllabus design, that is, the planning of what should be learned, when and in what order (we shall refine this broad definition of a syllabus in Chapter 11). If learners have an 'internal syllabus', to what extent can an externally imposed syllabus affect learning? Maybe, as Krashen (1985) noted (see Chapter 6), the 'internal syllabus' (and Natural Order Hypothesis) makes the teaching of grammar redundant altogether; less radically, perhaps it in part accounts for why learners learn different language to that which is explicitly taught (Allwright, 1984; also see Chapter 4).

Pienemann brought such questions together through the concepts of *learner readiness*, *learnability* and the *Teachability Hypothesis* (1985). Based on the acquisition of German word order in sentences, he suggested that instruction should focus only on language that learners are developmentally ready to learn, that is, that language items should be taught in the same order as they are acquired and teachers only 'teach what is teachable' (Lightbown and Spada, 2013: 177).

Considering the claims

Developmental sequence studies and claims in support of the internal syllabus, the Natural Order Hypothesis and teachability provide teachers and applied linguists with much to think about. However, a variety of concerns and counter-arguments have been identified. Much of the research was small in scale, focusing on relatively small numbers of learners and a limited number of language items. As suggested in Chapter 6, although the evidence is interesting, is it enough to claim a 'universal' natural order for morpheme acquisition and, indeed, for second language acquisition more generally? Additionally, to what extent does one form need to be mastered before learners can acquire the next item in the sequence (i.e., how competent does a learner need to be before they are ready to move on)? Furthermore, as Ellis observes, 'it does not follow that because learners *naturally* learn one feature before another they must *necessarily* do so' (1997: 25, original emphasis), raising important questions as to the role and nature of formal instruction in L2 learning.

The relationship between instruction and developmental sequences is examined by Lightbown and Spada (2013). Drawing on a number of research studies, they suggest that the learners' L1 can affect their

L2 developmental readiness and, thus, instructional outcomes; that even if instruction is 'too advanced' in relation to the learners' current developmental stage, those samples of language provided may still be useful, with learners incorporating it into their interlanguage when the time is right; and, therefore, that instruction and interaction remain important even when the 'internal syllabus' and developmental readiness are recognized as important elements in L2 acquisition and the language classroom.

The 'internal syllabus': final comments

As the discussion above shows, the debates surrounding the 'internal syllabus' and the Teachability Hypothesis are linked to several other key questions within ELT, from aspects of classroom practice to theories of second language acquisition. Yet the 'internal syllabus' is a further important learner contribution to language learning. Drawing on 'universalist' perspectives (and thus contrasting slightly with the individual characteristics featured in Chapters 7 and 8), it adds to the complexity that teachers face in the L2 classroom.

Thus although much still remains unknown about the 'internal syllabus', and the ways in which it might interact with external factors such as instruction are still rather unclear (Littlewood, 1998), 'there is something moving in the bushes' that cannot be ignored (Larsen-Freeman and Long, 1991: 92). Consequently, Ortega (2009: 138) advises that:

> [while] language teachers should carefully consider what their students are developmentally ready to learn ... the principle of learner readiness ... should not be followed slavishly.

Task 9.1 'Teachability' in practice ... and in your practice

- Johnson suggests that the 'internal syllabus' is 'an idea that refuses to go away' (2008: 76). Why do you think this might be?

- To what extent does the idea of an 'internal syllabus' seem reasonable to you? To what extent do you think it can or might be accommodated within L2 classrooms generally ... and in your professional context?

- What might an L2 classroom based upon the learners' 'internal syllabus' rather than an external syllabus 'look' and 'feel' like?

Learners and the 'significance' of L2 learning: social and psychological considerations

As we have seen in both this chapter and earlier discussions, many theories of L2 development focus on those mental processes that are said to cause the development of learner interlanguage (Ellis and Shintani, 2014); as noted in Chapter 6, learners' minds are often metaphorically likened to computers that 'process' information. This perspective is evident in the above discussion of the 'internal syllabus'. However, SLA theorists also recognize the importance of social factors in L2 development and it is to these we now turn. Interestingly, whereas the 'internal syllabus' focuses on the *route* of interlanguage development, more social perspectives tend to focus upon issues that affect learners' eventual success (or otherwise) in language learning and, implicitly, their *rate* of acquisition. Social conceptualizations of SLA also reintroduce and further explore key concepts surrounding learner motivation and attitudes, which were first examined in Chapter 7.

Acculturation: linking 'social distance' to L2 learning

Language learning and social distance: the Acculturation Model

As Brown (2007: 193) notes, second language learning 'implies some degree of learning a second culture' and, to some extent, the acquisition of a second identity. The *Acculturation Model* (Schumann, 1978) suggests that learners need to change their social and psychological behaviour in order to adapt to, and integrate with, the target language culture, that is, they 'acculturate'; and the further learners acculturate, the more successful their language learning may be.

Developed around the metaphor of 'social distance', acculturation requires learners to move socially and psychologically from being an 'outsider' in the target-language culture to being an 'insider'. This may involve learners initially experiencing culture shock or *anomie*, that is, the feeling of social uncertainty or dissatisfaction when caught between two cultural groups (Schumann, 1978; Brown, 2007), as they recognize, and try to accept and adapt to, differences between their own culture and culture of the target language. It also involves changes in learner attitudes and motivation, both aligning more closely with the target culture (Daniels, 2004). Schumann (1978) suggests that a failure to acculturate, which may result from, for example, social isolation or the absence of motivation, means that learners will not progress beyond the early stages of interlanguage development. In effect, the L2 fossilizes, that is, it remains pidginized (see also, McLaughlin, 1987).

Difficulties with Acculturation

Larsen-Freeman and Long suggest that the Acculturation Model has 'served to turn what have otherwise been rather vague notions about the role of social and psychological factors in SLA into coherent predictions' (1991: 260). However, they also highlight a number of problems with the model. First, and like some other models we have examined, it seems untestable, that is, there is no reliable way of testing 'psychological and social distance'. Additionally, several studies have reported contradictory evidence, finding instances where learners' L2 has developed effectively in spite of apparently high social distance from the target language culture. Furthermore, the acculturation model does not explain *how* learning takes place. Ortega (2009), meanwhile, observes that attitudes, motivation and the desire to integrate are not 'fixed' but are potentially variable over time dependent on the learner's experiences, which the model does not readily acknowledge. She also suggests that explaining L2 acquisition only through acculturation is potentially 'dangerous', as it emphasizes 'individual choice' and the idea that 'everyone can learn an L2 well, if only they want it badly enough' (p. 59); this ignores the sociocultural realities of marginalization and social isolation which many learners might experience, particularly those immigrating into an English-dominant society and who do not speak the majority language Despite these concerns, however, acculturation goes some way to explaining the motivational factors that underpin L2 learning, and acknowledges learners' deeper social and psychological needs when learning the target language (Littlewood, 1998).

And in ELT contexts? The potential relevance of acculturation

As the above discussion suggests, the Acculturation Model aims to explain the relationship between 'culture learning' (Brown, 2007) and L2 development in contexts where learners might use the target language for everyday communication, that is, it seems particularly relevant to ESL learning contexts. Thus, does the model have any relevance to classroom-based and/or 'foreign' language learning contexts where learners have little contact with the L2 away from their formal learning environment, especially in a world where English is increasingly learned for international purposes without any need to integrate with, for example, predominantly English L1 cultures?

Drawing on Ehrman's (1996) notion of *language ego*, that is, the personal and egoistic side of second language learning, Brown suggests that, at some level, all meaningful L2 development involves an element of identity conflict 'as language learners take on a new identity with their newly acquired competence' (2007: 158). Applicable across the diverse range of ELT contexts, this implies that all learners might feel alienation as they learn a second language: alienation from the target language (and culture), from their home culture, from their teacher and classmates, and from themselves. Alienation, that is, psychological distance, reminds teachers of the need to be sensitive to the 'fragility' of learners (Stevick, 1976). Clearly, psychological distance also is likely to affect learner motivation in ELT contexts and classrooms, with clear implications for L2 learning. Thus, as McLaughlin comments, the concept of acculturation certainly has 'something to say to teaching practitioners' (McLaughlin, 1987, in Daniels, 2004: 3).

A more 'critical' perspective: social identity and investment in L2 learning

Learner identity and the 'right to speak'

The relationship between the social dynamics of language learning, learners' individual identities and the ways in which they consequently participate in the L2 classroom and beyond has been the focus of increasing attention since the mid-1990s. Taking a broadly 'critical' stance, Norton Pierce (1995) suggests that learners' social identities and the power relationships that exist between learners, teachers and other target language users affect, and can limit, language learning. Noting that a learner's social identity is 'multiple, a site of struggle, and subject to change' (10), she proposes that learning is most effective if learners can assume an identity that gives them the 'right to speak' and to be heard; she suggests that this is not always easy.

Norton Pierce drew upon the experiences of adult immigrants learning English in an ESL context. They were often ignored and found it difficult to assert an identity that would benefit L2 learning (for example, they found difficulty in accessing social networks that could have provided opportunities to speak, practise and develop their L2). Meanwhile, Toohey (1998) observes that in more formal classroom contexts, some learners are quickly labelled as less able, and may be subsequently excluded from practice activities and learning opportunities from which they could benefit. Investigating a specific classroom context, she noted, for example, that some learners were physically marginalized through the classroom seating arrangements while help-seeking from peers was also discouraged. In effect, the learners were engaged in a 'struggle' to be recognized and heard on their own terms.

Further perspectives on learners: from the individual to the social

Both Norton Pierce and Toohey, then, view language learning as a process in which learners have to struggle as they negotiate complex power and identity relationships within the L2 classroom and beyond. Thus, Norton Pierce (1995) suggests, several notions examined in earlier chapters need to be rethought in order to recognize fully this social complexity. Moving beyond our earlier discussion of motivation as a somewhat abstract yet personal concept, language learning is said to require learner *investment*, learners only investing in a second language if they believe that this will give them access to 'cultural capital', that is, the knowledge and ways of thinking that they need to function successfully in society (Norton Pierce, 1995; Ortega, 2009). In effect, learners will 'invest' in language learning if they think they will achieve a good social 'return'.

From this perspective, therefore, 'motivation' is seen as an individualistic and relatively fixed personality trait while the metaphor of 'investment' captures the constantly changing relationship between the L2 learner and their complex social world, and recognizes that 'an investment in the target language is also an investment in a learner's own social identity, an identity which is constantly changing across time and space' (Norton Pierce, 1995: 18). And, as Norton and McKinney (2011: 75–76) suggest, instead of asking, 'to what extent is the learner motivated to learn the target language?', we might now ask, 'what is the learner's investment in the target language practices of the classroom or community?'. A learner might be extremely motivated, but have little investment in the language practices of their classroom or community which may be, for example, sexist, racist, or in other ways exclusionary. Consequently, they could be seen as an unmotivated or 'poor' language learner, resulting in their exclusion from community or classroom language practices (ibid.).

The recognition of learner identity, struggle and investment as essential elements in language learning therefore adds to, and to some extent challenges, our earlier discussions of the 'good' or effective language learner (see Chapter 8). Clearly recognizing that what individual learners can do and that the range of behaviours available to them is limited by powerful social constraints, they again suggest that 'best practice' cannot be independent of social context (Norton and Toohey, 2001). Thus, Norton and Toohey (2001) argue that the success of effective language learners is best explained through investment and the ways in which learners assert their social identities to access 'a variety of conversations in their community' (310), rather than by listing more 'technical' characteristics of the 'good language learner' such as attending to linguistic form and meaning or exploiting learning strategies successfully. From this perspective, effective language learning depends not only on what learners do individually, but also upon their social context and relationships (ibid.).

In the classroom?

Although, like the Acculturation Model, the role of identity and investment in L2 development was first explored in ESL settings, these more social theories of second language learning again have relevance for other ELT contexts. As noted in earlier chapters, the L2 classroom is a social environment, Toohey's study (1998; see above) showing that learners face issues of identity, 'voice', inclusion and exclusion in this context as well as in society more generally. Norton (2001) additionally identifies instances of learner non-participation in class as potential acts of identity. Echoing our earlier discussion (see Chapter 7), she emphasizes that if the classroom methodologies, practices and curriculum goals do not match the learner's expectations and their beliefs about who they are, how they should act and what they can do, then learner non-participation may result, as:

> We not only produce our identities through the practices we engage in, but we also define ourselves through the practices we do not engage in. Our identities are constituted not only by what we are but also by what we are not.
>
> (Wenger, 1998: 164, in Norton, 2001: 159)

Both Greer (2000) and Tomita and Spada (2013), for example, discuss the reluctance of some motivated Japanese learners to speak English in meaning-focused communicative activities, either due to a fear of appearing superior to others or because focusing only on meaning (without attending to form or grammar) ran counter to their identities as 'language learners'. Similarly, Canagarajah (1999) documents how motivated Sri Lankan school pupils resisted participating in English language classes in which aspects of their identity were overlooked.

We can see here echoes of Allwright's ideas concerning learners' deliberate 'underperformance' in the L2 classroom (see Chapter 3), albeit approached from a different theoretical perspective. This again emphasizes that the L2 classroom is a social as well as pedagogic environment. It is worth noting, however, that, in terms of investment and social identity, non-participation is not quite the same as 'underperformance'; it is performance of a different kind and for a different purpose.

Thus, teachers and teaching cannot ignore social identity and learner investment in the L2 classroom; indeed, identity and investment are a further contribution that learners make to language learning and the complexity of L2 classrooms.

Bringing ideas together: focusing on the language classroom

Learners and 'receptivity' in language learning

The social models of second language acquisition discussed above suggest that L2 learning takes place when learners perceive it to be a 'significant and meaningful' activity (see earlier) in which they are prepared to invest. Language learning is also an activity that changes who learners are, that is, it changes their social identity and their relationship with their social (and classroom) context.

Some of these ideas are evident in Allwright and Bailey's discussion of learner 'receptivity' in the language classroom (1991: 157), receptivity being:

> a state of mind, whether permanent or temporary, that is open to the experience of becoming a speaker of another language, somebody else's language.

Allwright and Bailey propose that receptivity, and its opposite, 'defensiveness', are active states of mind, learners 'working actively to promote the learning experience . . . or taking definite steps to avoid it' (ibid.).

Although not theorizing as much personal change as Schumann's Acculturation Model, nor as 'critical' as Norton's conceptions of social identity and investment, Allwright and Bailey (ibid.) highlight a number of areas where learners' social and psychological 'openness' in the classroom might affect learning, including receptivity to: the L2 and, hence, its culture (as with the Acculturation Model); the teacher as a person; being associated with fellow learners; classroom practices and norms; class and course content; teaching materials; the idea of communicating with others; and the idea of being a successful language learner (in which learners need to feel that any investment in L2 learning brings with it rewards that outweigh the efforts made). In effect, they draw upon 'receptivity' to provide a more clearly classroom-focused account of how learners actively and critically engage with their social context when investing in language learning.

Differing perspectives, and moving on . . .

As the above discussions illustrate, social conceptions of L2 acquisition draw upon very different views of language learning to those accounts explored in earlier chapters and earlier in this chapter. While those previous accounts are primarily focused on discovering universal cognitive processes in which all individuals engage, sociocultural models of L2 learning link learners to their social context, and suggest that there cannot be a single universal language learning experience or process; learners will learn in differing ways dependent on their social identity, degree of investment and social context. Indeed, this difference is encapsulated by the various metaphors the differing approaches are built around – from learners as 'computers' to learner 'struggle', 'investment' and 'openness', as we have seen. As noted in earlier chapters, metaphors can provide useful insights into the nature of language teaching and learning and it is to these 'significant images' of learners that we now turn.

Task 9.2 Reflections on theory and practice

a. Changing identities in language learning

- Have you experienced moving from being an 'outsider' to an 'insider' in a community or culture? What did this process involve? Was it difficult or unsettling? If so, in what way or ways?

- How far do you agree that learning another language implies learning another culture?

- In what ways, if any, does the Acculturation Model add to your understanding of L2 learners, learning and teaching in your own professional context?

- How might teachers 'be sensitive to the fragility of students' who are experiencing 'social and psychological change' in the L2 classroom?

- To what extent do you think learners have to 'struggle' for the 'right to be heard', both in class and beyond (if appropriate to your professional context)?

- Thinking about a group of learners you know, what kinds of social identities do they bring to class, and how does this affect classroom life and your own practices as a teacher?

It is sometimes suggested that younger learners are often receptive to language learning at school, while teenagers are more defensive, resentful and uncooperative.

- Do you think there might be a relationship between a learner's age and issues of acculturation, investment and receptivity? If so, in what ways?

b. Differing perspectives on language learning and learners

Over the course of this chapter and in earlier discussions, a number of theories and conceptions of language learning and learners have been explored – in this chapter, for example, the 'internal syllabus', acculturation and investment; elsewhere, the input and output hypotheses, information processing, and learner attributes and attitudes. Consider some of the differences between them:

- How far does each theoretical insight or approach view L2 learning as a consequence of universal processes, which everyone shares, *or* a result of individual learner characteristics and behaviours?

- To what extent does each envisage L2 learning as a consequence of the 'internal' mental processes of learners *or* the result of learners' social behaviour in their social (and learning) context?

Further insights into language learning: images of language learners

Task 9.3 'Constructing' learners: first thoughts

- What metaphors for learners have been noted in this chapter and in earlier discussions? For example, *learners are computers, . . . are investors, . . . are strugglers . . .*

- What other metaphors for learners and learning can you think of? For example, *learners are containers (of knowledge), . . . are travellers . . .*

- Do you think that the metaphors that theorists, teachers and learners draw upon are likely to be similar or different? Why?

The value of metaphor in illuminating concepts within ELT was noted in Chapter 3, where a number of metaphors for language teaching, teachers and classrooms were explored (e.g., Breen's conception of the classroom as a 'coral garden'). As noted, although metaphors are sometimes seen as somewhat rare or particularly idiosyncratic ways of thinking, they are, in fact, commonplace and are drawn upon within many discussions of L2 learners and learning by researchers, teachers and learners alike (Lakoff and Johnson, 1980; Ellis, 2001; Kramsch, 2003). Indeed, identifying the metaphorical constructs embodied within theories of L2 learning can help clarify the differences between them. Additionally, if the metaphors that lie behind approaches to L2 learners and learning are identified, then the hidden assumptions that might direct and constrain our thinking are revealed (Ellis, 2001). Thus examining metaphors can tell us about learners and learning, but it might also tell us something about the 'world view' of those who use them. For example, Ellis (2001) highlights Firth and Wagner's (1997) critique of much SLA research, which, they argue, portrays learners as 'defective communicators' who are 'handicapped' by the 'problem' of an underdeveloped interlanguage. Firth and Wagner suggest that this metaphor has enabled SLA theory to focus on psycholinguistic aspects of L2 development (e.g., learners' internal cognitive processes) at the expense of social and contextual factors (e.g., the work of Norton Pierce, above). Indeed, the term 'second language *acquisition*' itself is a metaphor, representing language as something which, like property, can be 'obtained'. This image contrasts with, for example, L2 '*development*' or '*growth*', terms that construct L2 learning very differently.

Comparing the metaphorical constructions of learners in SLA research with images held by learners themselves, Ellis (2001) finds that the dominant metaphors drawn on by theorists are learners as *containers* (as seen) and as *machines* (resembling the *computer* metaphor discussed earlier). Both metaphors represent learners as passive, unempowered and lacking control; knowledge is 'put into' the restricted space of a container, while, according to Ellis, learners have to learn in keeping with the internal mechanism of their minds (i.e., machines) and its component parts.

As we have seen, however, other constructions of learners do exist within SLA theory, although they are less common than those above. In Chapters 2 and 6, learners were conceptualized as *negotiators* of meaning. However, although a more active image than *container* or *machine*, Ellis (2001) suggests *negotiator* in fact often supports these dominant metaphors, negotiation making 'data' available for learners' internal mechanisms to process. In contrast, Norton Pierce (1995, and above) conceptualizes negotiation very differently, suggesting that learners negotiate identities, while her image of learners as *investors* implies active, empowered individuals who have some control over their learning, the purposes for it, and its potential outcomes. Clearly, these differing images of learners underpin very different perspectives on language learning, classroom life and, indeed, the nature and purposes of ELT and education more generally (see Chapter 2; see also Chapter 12 for further discussion of the wider educational purposes of ELT).

There is thus a tension within SLA research, between those approaches that focus on psycholinguistic processes that are seen as universal to all learners, and those that take a more social perspective where individuals differ from one another. The former, which, Ellis suggests, dominate 'mainstream' SLA, tend to construct L2 learning as an automatic and unconscious process, something that mechanistically takes place 'when the right conditions prevail' (2001: 83). The latter see learners as 'agents' who exert more control over their own L2 learning. Indeed, this tension may be symptomatic of the emergence of a new paradigm within SLA research (see Chapter 5 for further discussion of paradigm change).

Of course, many ELT practitioners are likely to recognize and identify with elements of more than one approach, and one further useful metaphor from SLA theory, which identifies psycholinguistic learning processes but also acknowledges learner agency, is the image of learners as *problem-solvers* who, for example, test linguistic hypotheses when they consciously 'notice' language (see Chapter 4). This perspective portrays learners as active in shaping what they learn, and, as Ellis (ibid.) notes, the metaphor also accommodates learner difference as individuals can choose what problems to focus on and how they might address these issues.

Interestingly, learners as *problem-solvers* was also identified by learners themselves in Ellis's study, their other images including learners as *sufferers, workers, travellers* and *strugglers*. It is noticeable that all these images portray learners as active and engaged in conscious mental activity; as Ellis (2001: 83–4) summarizes:

> They saw themselves as travellers on a long journey, coping with the affective and cognitive problems that confronted them. Their journey was mapped out for them but they are the ones that must make it and in that respect they were the agents of their own learning.

There is thus an evident difference in the agency learners ascribe to themselves compared to many of the images held by SLA researchers. This difference may be unimportant; learners and researchers have different agendas and objectives. However, listening to learners' own perspectives can provide further insights into classroom life that may guide L2 teachers' classroom practices (Block, 1997; Ellis, 2001).

Summary: focus on the language learner – understandings, intuitions and instincts

This chapter has investigated contrasting theoretical perspectives on language learners and language learning. Examining ideas surrounding the 'internal syllabus' of L2 learners, the discussion initially focused on those internal mental processes that are said to be universal and also 'asocial', that is, generally unaffected by the learners' social worlds. These ideas were then contrasted with more social-cultural approaches to second language acquisition, which envisage learning as a social process in which learners' social identities and their complex social relationships change over time. SLA theorists tend to research in one tradition or another; however, ELT practitioners are not so constrained and are likely to draw upon those elements that seem intuitively appealing, plausible and recognizable in their own professional context as they search for understanding of language learners and the language classroom.

And yet, as this chapter shows, it is difficult to gain a clear picture of language learners, the ways in which second languages are learned, the activities that learners engage in and the consequences of these practices; the range of possible perspectives on classroom life is broad and, at times, appears contradictory. Thus, while Strevens observes that 'it takes better teachers to focus on the learner' (1980: 17), O'Neill offers a word of caution: 'of course, even the best teachers cannot really know what works or does not work for students. All they can do is sharpen their intuitions and instincts . . .' (1991: 302).

Of course, our understandings, intuitions and instincts, and the hidden assumptions and metaphors that we draw upon to construct our view of learners and learning, are both constrained by and serve to construct the institutional frameworks and social contexts in which we live and work. It is to these that we now turn in the final part of the book.

Part IV

Institutional frameworks and social contexts

10 From global trends to local contexts

Language dilemmas in the ELT classroom

> It is important to understand the permeability of classroom walls –
> that is to say what goes on inside the classroom is always tied to
> what goes on outside.
>
> (Pennycook, 2016: 33)

This chapter will:

- highlight those contextual factors that are likely to affect English
  language classrooms, and, indeed, the variety of English that is
  taught, in any given ELT environment;

- outline key debates surrounding the growth of English in the world,
  and examine how these debates might affect perceptions of what
  English *is*, and, hence, what variety of English might or should be
  taught and learned in specific ELT contexts;

- consider the place of 'real' or 'authentic' English in the language
  classroom;

- examine how, in English for Specific Purposes (ESP) contexts, an
  explicit focus on learners' specific language needs affects the type
  of English taught and learned, and explore the dilemmas this raises
  for ELT professionals;

- encourage readers to reflect upon whether and how these discussions
  may be relevant to their own professional context.

Introduction: the world beyond the classroom

The social, cultural and, indeed, political dimensions of English
language teaching and learning have been increasingly recognized in
recent years. Stern observes that we can investigate the 'sociology' of
ELT whereby language teaching is 'an enterprise . . . a set of activities
in society' (1983: 269), while Pennycook (2000: 89) notes that:

classrooms, both in themselves and in their relationship to the world beyond their walls, are complex social and cultural spaces.

Previous chapters have investigated in some detail the social complexity found *within* ELT classrooms. The discussions have also acknowledged, but not yet examined in detail, how all L2 teaching and learning takes place within specific institutional environments and social, economic and ideological contexts. Thus, it is to the relationship between everyday classroom practices and the wider sociocultural environment that we turn in our final three chapters, for, as Auerbach (1995: 9) maintains:

> the day-to-day decisions that practitioners make inside the classroom both shape and are shaped by the social order outside the classroom.

In this chapter, we shall ask what 'type' of English might be taught and learned in any given ELT context, linking global trends to immediate local contexts and classroom practices; the following chapter will examine how institutional and social factors might affect how this language might be organized for learners through ELT curricula and learning materials; and our final chapter will explore the wider social and educational contexts and potential purposes of English language teaching and learning.

The social context of English language teaching and learning

Given the range of environments within which English language teaching takes place, from state sector, primary level classes in low-resource contexts where most learners might share an L1 to technology-rich commercial language schools where adults who speak a variety of first languages might be taught in small groups, how can contextual factors be conceptualized? Stern (1983), adapting Mackey (1970) and Spolsky *et al.* (1974), provides the framework illustrated in Figure 10.1.

As Stern (1983) notes, at the centre of the framework is the particular language teaching and learning situation, perhaps, for example, an English class in the UK, USA or Australia for adult immigrants, or a primary or secondary school class in, for example, China, Japan or Libya. The school, institution or educational system provides the immediate environment for the language class, affecting classroom practice by providing or instituting, for instance, the language learning curriculum and broader educational policies and values. It is, in turn, located in a neighbourhood or community that provides the linguistic, cultural and socio-economic setting within which language learning takes place. For example, whether a community is multilingual

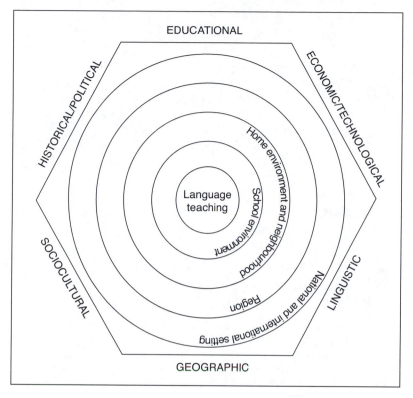

Figure 10.1 An inventory of contextual factors in language teaching
Source: Stern, 1983: 274.

or largely monolingual may affect the extent to which L2 learning is seen as a valuable activity or how 'language aware' learners might be.

Beyond this immediate environment, the model highlights the regional, national and international contexts for English language teaching and learning that may influence attitudes and policy, thereby affecting, both directly and indirectly, what happens within educational institutions and the language class itself. In multilingual Singapore, for example, the government promotes English over other official languages such as Malay, Mandarin and Tamil, in order to meet the perceived needs of the global economy. Additionally, however, the Singaporean government also strongly promotes *Standard* Singaporean English (SSE), which is grammatically and lexically similar to Standard British English (with some phonological differences), over a widely spoken *Colloquial* Singaporean English (CSE, or *Singlish*), which features a range of non-standard language features. The government promotes SSE through school curricula, class teaching and the attitudes and values that underpin the government-supported 'Speak Good English

Movement' (SGEM); fearing that CSE will harm Singapore's international competitiveness, the SGEM both promotes SSE and discourages the use of Singlish (Jenkins, 2015). Of course, as an example of the links between ELT classrooms and the wider social context, Singapore is not alone in this approach to English language and English language teaching and learning, as we shall see later in the chapter.

As Stern's model and the example of Singapore suggest, the immediate and wider social context of ELT includes a range of issues that may affect teaching, learning and the L2 classroom. According to Stern (1983), these include:

- *Linguistic factors*: for example, the extent to which English may already be used within the learners' local, regional or national community (as in Singapore), or the degree to which multilingualism is accepted as the norm.

- *Sociocultural factors*: for example, the perceived economic, political and cultural status of English or a particular variety of English and, consequently, its relationship with other languages in a community.

- *Historical/political factors*: for example, policy shifts towards, or away from, teaching English based on attitudes towards the British Empire and imperialism or towards current US influence in the world.

- *Geographical factors*: for example, Central and South American learners *may* tend towards General American English norms (i.e., the Standard English of the USA); Standard British English *may* have more importance in European countries (clearly, however, as Stern (1983) points out, 'geography' cannot be interpreted too mechanically; perceptions of the esteem and importance of a variety (i.e., sociocultural factors) will be more influential than straightforward geographical distance).

- *Economic and technological developments*: for example, English may be seen as important for economic development (as in Singapore); or, from a very different perspective, the cost of ELT materials and technological equipment (e.g., computers), and the economic resources available, will affect teaching and learning in many contexts.

- *Educational factors*: for example, the age at which children start school, whether English is a compulsory subject within the curriculum, the role of other languages within the education system and the number of hours tuition for each school subject.

As Stern (1983: 283) notes, for English language teaching (and, indeed, for all language teaching), 'society and culture are more than background and even more than context'; what happens in a language classroom is inseparable from its sociocultural context.

Task 10.1 Your classroom and the wider sociocultural context

Consider the contextual factors that affect language teaching and language classrooms in your own professional context:

- What kind of institution do you work in (e.g., primary, secondary, tertiary, state, commercial language school)?

- How does this affect teaching and learning in your classes? In what ways does your institution affect what happens in your classroom, either directly (e.g., by providing the syllabus or materials, allocating a certain number of hours for classes) or more indirectly (e.g., though its values, goals, or objectives)?

- How might the 'typical' home and neighbourhood environment of the learners affect L2 learning in your classroom or institution? For example, is language learning seen as a valuable and interesting social or educational activity; do learners come from largely monolingual or bi- or multilingual environments, and how might this affect learning (e.g., in terms of motivation and beliefs, language awareness or practice opportunities outside class)?

- In what ways do regional, national and international attitudes and policies affect what happens in your language classroom? For example, is English taught as one of several language options, or as *the* primary second or foreign language? Why? What policies are there surrounding a national curriculum or national testing system for English language?

- What historical or political trends affect ELT in your professional context, and how?

- To what extent do economic and technological resource issues affect what happens in your language classroom?

Thinking about English: 'what might teachers teach and learners learn' revisited

In Chapter 4, we recognized that 'what English language teachers teach and learners learn' is a more complex question than it might at first appear; there, we addressed the issue in terms of how *language* is conceptualized (for example, as 'innate knowledge in an individual's mind', as 'a set of sentences' or as 'a skill'). Now, however, we shall explore what is meant by *English*, and discuss the possible implications of these developing understandings for teachers and other ELT practitioners both in the classroom and beyond. As Widdowson (1992: 333) puts it: 'What, to begin with, is this English language we teach? How is the subject to be defined?' The discussion brings together global trends, national and institutional policies and values, and individual learners' needs, beliefs and reasons for learning.

Changing English, World Englishes: dilemmas for the ELT classroom

Introductory questions

The spread of English around the world is well documented, although it is difficult to calculate accurately the exact number of English speakers in the world. Crystal (2012) estimates that English is now spoken by between one and a half to two billion people globally, and in almost every country. For some, English is a first language; others use English in countries such as India or Nigeria, where it is an 'official' or institutionalized second language (used, for example, in government or law); a third group of English speakers are those who live in countries where English does not have an acknowledged official role, for example China, Germany or Mexico (Jenkins, 2015). Significantly, there are fewer English L1 speakers (somewhere between 400 and 500 million) than L2 speakers in countries where English has an official status (up to 600 million); these L2 speakers are, in turn, fewer in number than the roughly one billion people learning or using English elsewhere in the world (Crystal, 2012). Thus, between a quarter and a third of the world's population can currently speak English to some degree of proficiency (Crystal, 2012; Seargeant, 2016), although it is worth remembering that the majority of the global population does *not* speak the language, i.e., English is not 'a universal resource' (Seargeant, ibid.). Despite this, however, its global functions (e.g., as the language of business, of academic and industrial knowledge, and of online technologies) mean that it is likely to shape the environment and play a role in the lives of non-English speakers, for example, when trying to make sense of product instructions or understanding advertisements and commercial information (Seargeant, ibid.: 15).

One reason why it is difficult to establish the number of English speakers in the world is the question of who exactly to include in the figures. There are clearly differences in the *expertise* and *proficiency* of English speakers (Rampton, 1990; Seargeant, 2016), and in the *variety* of English spoken both *within* and *between* these different groups. Some speakers will be able to make themselves understood more effectively and across a wider variety of English language contexts than others (an attribute that does not necessarily depend upon being a native speaker), while varieties and dialects are a characteristic of most English language environments (e.g., in Singapore, as we have seen, but also in the UK and the USA, India, and so forth).

The global use of English raises a number of difficult questions: why has English become so important in the world – a 'happy coincidence' or a result of 'linguistic imperialism'? Are the benefits of English evenly spread or do some countries (and people) benefit more than others? What are the links between English and globalization? What are the implications of the spread of English for those who do not speak it? What is the relationship between English and other languages? How has English changed as it has spread, and should we now refer to Englishes? What are our attitudes towards this variation and the different ways in which different groups of speakers use English? Is the fact that there are fewer L1 than L2 and other speakers of English significant? What kinds of communication is English actually used for in the world? And what are the implications of these debates for English language teaching?

These key issues are reviewed in detail elsewhere (e.g., Phillipson, 1992; Pennycook, 1994, 2016; Seargeant, 2012, 2016; Jenkins, 2015) and we shall return to the political and ideological questions they raise when we discuss the wider educational purposes of ELT in Chapter 12. Yet some have direct implications for classroom practice and it is to these that we now turn.

In the classroom: which variety?

Traditionally, the question of which English to teach focused on the perceived competition between British and US English; as Jenkins (2015: 120) observes:

> The Englishes that are revered, and are the goal of teaching and testing in many parts of the world are still native speaker varieties, particularly British and North American; the methodologies and materials that are promoted are still those favoured by the ENL [English as a Native Language] centres – communicative approaches with an emphasis on 'learner autonomy' and monolingual (English-only) textbooks; the teachers who are most highly sought after are native speakers of English; and the tests which are taken most seriously measure learners' competence in relation to native-speaker norms.

However, the relevance of this perspective for many ELT contexts has been increasingly questioned. As noted above, there are fewer L1

English speakers than speakers of English as a second language or English speakers from other contexts around the world. Additionally, for many speakers, the purposes for which English is being learned and used have changed, with English increasingly used as a *Lingua Franca* (ELF) between non-native speakers who do not share an L1, rather than primarily for communication with native speakers of English (which might still be termed an *EFL*, that is, a *foreign* language, situation). Furthermore, the linguistic characteristics and associated communication strategies used in Lingua Franca contexts may differ from native speaker norms (Jenkins, 2007; Jenkins *et al.*, 2011; Kirkpatrick, 2007); Seidlhofer (2011), for example, notes that ELF communication often includes, for instance, non-use of the third person –*s* (e.g., *he play*) and use of a single question tag (e.g., *isn't it?*), features that do not hinder communication or understanding, and which appear to be accommodated by ELF speakers. Jenkins (2007; 2015) meanwhile examines the collaborative strategies that ELF speakers engage in to support successful communication, such as the avoidance of idioms, increased supportive responses (e.g., *yeah*, *right*), and adaption of pronunciation to facilitate listener understanding.

Thus, in many contexts, the assumption that British or North American English is the 'natural' variety for English language teachers and learners to focus upon is potentially problematic, or, at least, open to review. Of course, as Jenkins (2015) observes, some learners will always need or aspire to native speaker norms and varieties, perhaps for travel to, or study in, the UK, US, Australia or New Zealand, for example. Yet even here, Jenkins argues that learners should be made aware of the differences between native and Lingua Franca forms and contexts (ibid.). For learners whose main purpose is to use English in their immediate sociocultural content or as a Lingua Franca, however, it seems possible that native speaker English is less appropriate than localized non-native varieties or a focus on language features that are typical of ELF communication. At the very least, this may mean spending less time (and resources) attending to specific native speaker English features such as question tags or native speaker English idioms, and accommodating a variety of 'acceptable' ELF forms or learning about and practising supportive ELF strategies in the classroom. Alternatively, it could, in the future perhaps, mean adopting and teaching a local variety of English, such as Indian or Chinese English in South or East Asia, where English language communication may be dominated by these two powerful and influential economies or, for example, Nigerian English in Nigeria, Singaporean English in Singapore and so on (Kirkpatrick, 2007). Meanwhile, Willis identifies six possibilities for ELT in Lingua Franca contexts:

Option 1: Teach standard (British? American?) English;
Option 2: Define a form of 'international English' and teach that;
Option 3: Offer a range of Englishes in the classroom;
Option 4: Offer successful L2 speakers of English as models;
Option 5: Give learners exposure to largely native-speaker English but place a very low premium on conformity;
Option 6: Include the study of language and dialects in a language teaching programme.

(Willis, 1999, in Jenkins, 2005: 129)

The debates surrounding English and Englishes, the notion of acceptable Lingua Franca language features and the extent to which non-native varieties and variation should be recognized within the ELT classroom are fiercely contested by applied linguists and teachers alike (and, indeed, by politicians, policy-makers and other interested parties in many countries). Variation away from native speaker norms is still seen as 'worse' rather than 'different' in many contexts, while several applied linguists argue that teaching non-native speaker English fails to meet learners' needs and aspirations (e.g., Quirk, 1990). While this *may* be linked to issues of linguistic clarity and intelligibility, the apparent prestige and status of native speaker Englishes compared to other varieties clearly remains an issue for many. There are, additionally, a number of practical difficulties with the idea of teaching non-native or Lingua Franca English(es), such as resource availability, syllabus and textbook norms and standards, and international testing requirements (as Jenkins identifies, above). Of course, these could be addressed relatively easily if the prevailing discourses, which tend to promote native speaker norms within many ELT contexts, were to evolve. We shall return to this and to related issues, such as the apparently dominant status of the 'native speaker teacher' within language teaching, in Chapter 12.

Notions of English, Englishes and ELF therefore require ELT professionals to consider 'whose usage [we are] to take as the model for language learners to aspire to' (Widdowson, 2003: 30); it is to further questions surrounding which 'model' of English might be most appropriate for language learners that we now turn.

Task 10.2 In your context: which English?

• Why are learners in your professional context studying English? Who are they likely to communicate with in English, and for what purposes? Are they likely to talk to native speakers or to non-native speakers?

- What are the implications of this for the variety or varieties of English they could learn?

- What variety of English is taught in your professional context, for example, British English, North American English, another variety such as East Africa English or Hong Kong English, and why?

- Is it possible to imagine teaching a different variety of English in principle . . . and in practice? Why/why not?

- Refer back to Willis's options for the ELT classroom in Lingua Franca contexts. To what extent do you think each suggestion is a realistic possibility? Consider issues such as the needs of the learners and their learning preferences; the resources you have available; your institutional approach and other factors relevant to your social context.

- From a critical perspective, the current sociolinguistic realities of English language variation and use around the world often appear to be overlooked by materials writers and publishers, within syllabus and curriculum design, by international testing systems and, it is suggested, by ELT methodologists. How far do you agree with this perspective?

Appropriate for learning? Language description, 'real English', and corpora

As Seidlhofer (2003) notes, although the global spread of English and its implications for the ELT classroom are obviously controversial, developments in corpus linguistics and associated advances in descriptions of English at first seem less problematic for language teachers. However, notions of 'real' or 'authentic' language do, in fact, present ELT professionals with a number of dilemmas – whether to teach 'genuine' or 'artificial' language content in class, whether corpus-based language description tends to assert native speaker norms in ESL and ELF contexts, and, more philosophically, whether 'real' language can ever be 'authentic' once it is removed from its original context and studied in the language classroom (Widdowson, 1998; 2003). Although 'authenticity' and 'real' language data are issues that relate closely to debates surrounding ELT textbooks and materials, in this discussion, we shall focus specifically on questions of pedagogical effectiveness and appropriateness, addressing those issues specific to teaching and learning resources in Chapter 11.

'Real English': what and why?

Task 10.3 First thoughts: real and invented language in the classroom

Look at the two transcripts below. The first is a real conversation recorded in a hairdressing salon; the second is an invented dialogue from a popular English language textbook:

- In what ways does the language in the two extracts differ?

- How might you use each transcript in class? What would you focus upon with learners?

- What are the advantages and disadvantages of each transcript for teaching and learning? Which would you prefer to work with and why?

Example 1

[In the hair salon]

A: Do you want to come over here?
B: Right, thanks (3 secs) thank you
A: Tea or coffee?
B: Can I have a tea, please?
A: Do you want any sugar?
B: Er, no milk or sugar, just black thanks
C: Right
B: I hate it when your hair just gets so, you know a bit long [C: yeah] and it's just straggly
C: Right
B: It just gets to that in-between stage
[C: Yeah] doesn't it where you think oh I just can't stand it any more (2 secs) I think when it's shorter it tends to, you notice it growing more anyway
[C: Mm] you know it tends to grow all of a sudden
(Carter and McCarthy, 1997: 106–7)

Example 2

[At the hairdresser's]

Jane: ... Oh, yes, my husband's wonderful!
Sally: Really? Is he?
Jane: Yes, he's big, strong, and handsome!
Sally: Well, my husband isn't very big, or very strong ... but he's very intelligent

Jane:	Intelligent?
Sally:	Yes, he can speak six languages
Jane:	Can he? What languages can he speak?
Sally:	He can speak French, Italian, German, Arabic, and Japanese
Jane:	Oh! . . . My husband's very athletic
Sally:	Athletic?
Jane:	Yes, he can swim, ski, play football, cricket and rugby. . .
Sally:	Can he cook? My husband can't play sports . . . but he's an excellent cook
Jane:	Is he?
Sally:	Yes, and he can sew, and iron . . . he's a very good husband
Jane:	Really? Is he English?

(Hartley and Viney, 1978, in Carter, 1998: 46)

Extract from the Cambridge and Nottingham Corpus of English (CANCODE) "In the hair salon" in Ronald Carter, Michael McCarthy, *Exploring Spoken English*, 1997, Copyright Cambridge University Press, reprinted with permission.

The extent to which classroom texts should be 'authentic' (that is, originally written for non-teaching purposes) and tasks should replicate naturally occurring, 'authentic communication' outside the classroom has long been discussed within ELT, especially since the advent of Communicative and Task-based Language Teaching (see Chapter 5). 'Authentic' texts and tasks, it is argued, draw upon more realistic models of language use and leave learners better prepared for life outside the classroom. From the 1980s onwards, these debates have been fuelled by the emergence of new and detailed descriptions of English language use derived from the qualitative and quantitative study of corpora, a corpus being a principled (i.e., representative) collection of written or spoken texts stored on a computer (O'Keefe *et al.*, 2007; see also Cheng, 2011). And, as there are different types of texts and language varieties in the 'real world', so there are also different corpora, for example: the British National Corpus (BNC), the British Academic Written English Corpus (BAWE), the Corpus of Contemporary American English (COCA), and the Vienna-Oxford International Corpus of English (VOICE).

Corpora studies show that actual language use is often quite different to the language features recorded in standard grammars of English or invented for the purpose of language teaching, and that naturally occurring spoken language includes many features not dealt with in grammars or English language textbooks (Carter, 1998). Thus, suggesting that many teachers pay little attention to 'the facts' of English language description and, in fact, take for granted a 'mythology' about English language behaviour, Sinclair (1997: 31) argues that teachers should 'present real examples only . . . language cannot be invented; it can only be captured'. Sinclair acknowledges that teachers may think up and use quick, informal examples to exemplify a point in class, but argues that, in the presentation of language models, 'it is essential for a learner of English to learn from actual examples, examples that can be trusted because they have been used in real communication' (2005: *ix*). Sinclair (ibid.) maintains that teachers find it difficult to invent realistic examples, while learners can deal with 'real' language with less difficulty than is often supposed. Thus, according to Willis:

> Contrived simplification of language in the preparation of materials will always be faulty, since it is generated without the guide and support of a communicative context. Only by accepting the discipline of using authentic language are we likely to come anywhere near presenting the learner with a sample of language which is typical of real English.
>
> (Willis, 1990: 127, in Seidlhofer, 2003: 78)

Questions and concerns

Perhaps unsurprisingly, many teachers and applied linguists (indeed, many corpus linguists!) disagree with the suggestion that *only* 'real' language should be presented in ELT classrooms. 'Unreal', scripted or simplified language may be more accessible for learners and, thus, more appropriate, or, as Carter (1998: 47) comments, more 'real pedagogically'; 'authentic' English may be more difficult to comprehend or produce, and thus less useful or real pedagogically (ibid.). Similarly, Widdowson (1998: 714–15) suggests that:

> The whole point of language learning tasks is that they are specially contrived for learning. They do not have to replicate or even simulate what goes on in normal uses of language. Indeed, the more they seem to do so, the less effective they are likely to be.

Widdowson also argues that language in fact ceases to be 'authentic' when removed from its original context as learners cannot possibly understand it in the same ways as its original users; learners are, by their very nature, outsiders to the original discourse community and to the actual communicative purposes for which the language was used (ibid.). Additionally, as most (although not all) 'real' language descriptions within ELT are drawn from native speaker usage (e.g., the COBUILD 'Bank of English' Corpus), not only is the language potentially 'unnatural' in many English Lingua Franca ELT contexts, it is 'culturally marked', reinforcing native speaker norms (and, consequently, the status and position of native speaker teachers within ELT), leading Prodromou to ask 'whatever happened to world Englishes?' (1996: 372).

'Real English' and the role of corpora: ways ahead?

Despite these concerns, corpus-based descriptions of English and 'real' language clearly have important implications for language teachers and teaching (G. Cook, 1998). Corpora have been used to develop general language tools that learners (and teachers!) regularly draw upon in both their everyday lives and their language learning, such as document spellcheckers and autocorrect functions, and online translation apps (Frankenberg-Garcia, 2016). Additionally, most contemporary learner dictionaries are informed by corpora and provide corpus-based examples to illustrate language items in context. Meanwhile, word lists, which show word and phrase frequencies in a corpus, may be used to organize the presentation of material to learners (although frequency does not automatically equate with importance to learners). As noted above, some ELT textbook series also draw very heavily on corpora in their design and the language focused upon.

Teachers and learners may also use corpora themselves, in the classroom. Such *data-driven learning* is 'an attempt to cut out the middleman . . . and give direct access to the data so that the learner can take part in building up his or her own profiles of meanings and uses' (Johns, 1991: 3). In a 'hands-off' approach (Boulton, 2010), teachers might access corpora when preparing classes, focusing on language issues of relevance to learners which are not dealt with in their published course materials and textbooks. More 'hands-on' approaches bring the corpora 'into' the classroom, as learners explore language for themselves. Online technologies make these approaches, which enhance learner autonomy (see Chapter 8), increasingly feasible.

Yet there are clearly also several hurdles to be overcome if teachers and learners are to make more use of corpora and engage with 'real language' for themselves. As Frankenberg-Garcia notes (2016: 394), 'few teachers, and even fewer learners, are comfortable using corpora' – most existing corpora were compiled for the purpose of research rather than teaching; corpus tools are often complicated to understand; even the ability to use corpora and interpret findings effectively does not mean that classroom-based corpus work is necessarily the most effective use of classroom time (and, in the case of teachers, their preparation time); and many classrooms quite simply do not have the computer or online resources necessary for hands-on work with corpora. Thus, although there is an increasing number of corpora-informed publications within ELT, bringing 'real' language into the classroom through teachers' and learners' *direct* use of corpora seems much more problematic. It would require significant teacher and learner training, and, in many contexts, additional resources. It also depends upon a number of broader contextual factors including: the extent to which learners, teachers and other ELT professionals (e.g., textbook and materials writers) regard 'authentic' language as both the aim of learning and relevant to classroom life; the learners' social context; their reasons for learning; and the relationship between 'real' English and local Englishes.

English and learners' needs: specific English for specific purposes

The above discussion suggests that decisions about what type or variety of English should be taught and learned are not as straightforward as they may at first appear. In any classroom, the English taught reflects, either overtly or implicitly, both practical concerns and more 'ideological' perspectives about why the learners are studying English, what they need to know, the most effective ways of helping them achieve this, and the nature and role of English in the world. The ways in which ELT professionals and learners understand these issues are likely to be affected by the range of contextual factors identified by Stern (see pp. 202–205).

In some contexts, however, an additional question is the extent to which learners need to develop their *overall* linguistic competence in English, or whether they might focus in particular on learning the language and skills necessary to meet a *specific* need or to fulfil a parti-cular role, in effect, learning English for a Specific Purpose (ESP).

Like 'general English' classes, ESP teaching and learning takes place in a diverse range of settings around the world. ESP classes can thus look very different in different environments (although ESP learners are generally adults); there is no fixed language teaching methodology. However, what draws ESP approaches together is that, rather than focusing on general language structures, classes and courses are designed to help learners communicate effectively in specific work or study situations (Robinson, 2004), for example, as hotel employees, trade unionists or architects, or as students undertaking academic studies in English (a context that has its own acronym, EAP, that is, English for Academic Purposes). ESP thus provides a further perspective on the English that teachers might teach and learners might learn; the language taught is determined primarily by learner 'needs' that can be identified and specified to a much greater degree, it is claimed, than the needs of 'general English' learners (Hutchinson and Waters, 1987).

Yet in a globalized world in which ESP learners are increas-ingly mobile and multilingual, understandings of learners' needs have moved beyond an apparently objective 'language-focused' approach (Hutchinson and Waters, 1987: 54) to take account of learners' more subjective lifelong goals, motivations and investment in the language communities they are joining (Starfield, 2016; see also Chapter 9 for further discussion of investment). Needs analysis also often focuses on the skills learners need in order to learn, as well as simply what language to learn. This requires an understanding of the contexts, occupations or academic disciplines that learners are joining (ibid.).

Thus, analysing learners' current or future language needs (including functional language skills) in a particular context might typically involve shadowing or observing learners in their workplace, and the collection of authentic texts and materials that may later be used as teaching materials. Thus, the debates surrounding 'real' and 'authentic' language (see above) are particularly relevant within ESP contexts as learners work to discover and use the preferred forms of spoken or written discourse used by members of the target community, group or profession; corpus analysis can contribute to this knowledge base. Hence, the English that is taught and learned in ESP contexts is essentially genre-based.

Robinson (2004) highlights a number of dilemmas surrounding the teaching and learning of ESP such as: the extent to which ESP classes should include elements of 'general English' and aim to develop learners' broader linguistic competence; whether ESP requires a basic level of language competence (e.g., intermediate) before learners can make satisfactory progress in complex and specialized language; and how far teachers are teaching language, and how far work-related non-linguistic content, raising a more fundamental question about who might teach ESP – ESP (i.e., language) practitioners, or discipline-based content specialists. Robinson (ibid.) also questions whether some ESP programmes, particularly short introductory courses, really develop genuine linguistic competence or merely teach 'language-like behaviour'. For example, airline in-flight attendants attending a one-day ESP course may acquire a limited set of useful routine phrases, but might not be able to create their own original utterances or respond during unpredictable or unexpected interaction (ibid.).

The work-related focus of ESP teaching and learning makes clear the links between the language classroom and wider contextual factors (as documented in Stern's model, see above). Most ESP programme literature and teacher development texts refer to sponsors or stakeholders (e.g., employers, training institutes) who may organize and commission classes for learners (e.g., Hutchinson and Waters, 1987; Dudley-Evans and St John, 1998). Meanwhile, the relatively recent development of English for 'peacekeeping' or 'security' programmes in countries and contexts ranging from Angola to Azerbaijan and Latvia to Libya is impossible to imagine without the immense global geopolitical changes of the last twenty years (see, for example, Woods (2006) for further discussion). Additionally, links between ESP, international business and globalization can be seen in the emergence of 'call-centre English' programmes in India and elsewhere (Forey and Lockwood, 2010), where historical, political and economic trends link global trends to local contexts. It is worth noting how these examples bring into focus potentially difficult questions concerning the relationship between ELT and global power, politics and economics. To what extent should ESP help learners fit into rather than contest the unequal power relationships and economic outcomes that they may face at work and beyond (Starfield, 2016)? We shall return to these issues in Chapter 12; see also our earlier discussion of the role of values in ELT, Chapter 3.

Summary: English . . . and values in ELT

This chapter has investigated what is meant by *English*, problematizing an issue that is less straightforward than it might at first appear. The discussion has examined key debates surrounding the Lingua Franca function and forms of English; the extent to which 'real' English should be the goal of, and a resource for, ELT and, indeed, whether 'real' language is a coherent pedagogical concept; and the ways in which learners' specific purposes for learning can and should be prioritized through ESP. As we have seen, the issues we have examined are subject to fierce debate among applied linguists, teachers and learners, and there are clearly no simple answers to these challenging questions. A range of global and local contextual factors may affect decisions about what variety of English might or should be taught and learned in any particular ELT environment.

Implicit in much of the discussion is the notion of *values*. Classroom practice and 'ideology' or 'values' are inseparable, not only in terms of *how* teachers teach (see Chapter 3), but also, the current discussion suggests, in terms of *what* they teach. While this is extremely clear when exploring the relative prestige of varieties of English (e.g., Standard British English compared to English as a Lingua Franca), it also an important consideration when reviewing the apparent 'pragmatism' and 'neutrality' of much ESP teaching, which, from a critical perspective, accommodates a *status quo* view of the world (Pennycook, 1997). Whether one agrees fully with this perspective or not, it does invoke Davies' key question, that is, 'what are we trying to achieve in ELT?' (1995: 145).

We shall return to this question in Chapter 12. However, before we do so, we shall examine the possible ways in which ELT curricula and materials shape and organize language for teachers and learners, again linking classroom practices and interventions to broader institutional and social trends, as we move to the next chapter.

11 Planning and organizing L2 learning and teaching

Contexts and curriculum, possibilities and realities

> In deciding on [language teaching] goals, planners choose from among alternatives based on assumptions about the role of teaching and of a curriculum. Formulating goals is not, therefore, an objective scientific enterprise but a judgement call.
>
> (Richards, 2001: 112)

This chapter will:

- explore the ways in which the terms 'curriculum' and 'syllabus' have been conceptualized;

- identify the principles around which L2 syllabuses might be organized, noting the influence of course designers' beliefs, assumptions and values in this process, and recognizing that syllabus plans and principles are not necessarily realized in practice;

- examine the role and purposes of assessment and testing within ELT, and the dilemmas language testing raises for teachers and policymakers;

- explore the key debates surrounding instructional materials within ELT, encouraging readers to reflect upon how materials may support language learning, and the ways in which materials have been critiqued;

- note the links between the dilemmas, debates and interventions highlighted in this chapter and issues identified in earlier chapters concerning values in ELT, language teaching methods and theories of language and of language learning.

Introduction: the language curriculum – clarifying concepts

Previous chapters have suggested that L2 classrooms are complex social spaces in which learners engage with learning opportunities in, at times, unpredictable ways. We have also noted that, within any given teaching and learning context, teachers will be guided by their sense of what is or is not 'plausible'. However, teachers (and learners) are, of course, rarely 'free agents'; the day-to-day decisions that practitioners make inside the classroom, and the 'shape' of classroom life, are influenced by broader societal and institutional factors. One of the most obvious and wide-ranging of these is the language curriculum, which, in this chapter, we will examine as a broad set of interrelated factors and processes (Richards, 2001).

As the belief in Method as *the* central aspect of language teaching has faded (see Chapter 5), theorists and practitioners alike have paid increasing attention to L2 curriculum design (Graves, 2008), focusing, among other things, upon: learners' and teachers' expectations for a given ELT programme; the purposes of learning and programme goals; teaching and learning styles; the resources, materials and textbooks to be used; and evaluation, that is, both programme evaluation and learner assessment (Richards, 2001: *ix*). Thus, how might 'the language curriculum' be conceptualized? There are a number of competing and overlapping perspectives.

Drawing upon a British perspective (the use of terminology differs in the USA), White (1988: 4) defines the curriculum as 'the totality of content to be taught and aims to be realized within one school or educational system'. From this perspective, 'curriculum' refers 'not only to the subject matter or content, but also to the entire instructional process including materials, equipment, examinations and the training of teachers' (Stern, 1983: 434), and involves three interconnected processes – 'planning, enacting and evaluating' (Graves, 2008: 152). In some contexts, however, the curriculum may only be implicit, inferred, for example, from the textbooks or assessments used by an institution.

In the USA, 'curriculum' tends to be synonymous with British understandings of 'syllabus' and, indeed, these two terms are often used interchangeably throughout ELT (including the UK). However, in contrast to the British understanding of curriculum, a syllabus is generally understood to be the content of a particular language programme (or subject area) or the step-by-step guide that sequences and structures content, specifying what is taught (but not necessarily what is learned, as noted in earlier chapters!). Although syllabuses are public documents, their format and length can vary, ranging from 'no more than one or two pages in length' or, in some institutions, the contents pages of textbooks, to 'over one hundred pages' (Taylor, 1970: 32, in White, 1988: 3). Additionally, while syllabuses focus upon content, *what* is taught and *how* it is taught are interlinked (Richards, 2013); thus, by outlining course content, a syllabus is likely to affect classroom methodology (see Chapter 5 for further discussion of the links between language content and language teaching method-ologies).

As Graves remarks, 'while these definitions are straightforward, curriculum processes are hardly neutral' (2008: 149). White (1988) observes that any curriculum reflects the beliefs, values and theories of those who produce it, while Graves (2008: 149) suggests that a curri-culum 'is a product of someone's reasoning about what education is, whom it should serve and how', which serves 'the interests of some, but not all' (Jackson, 1992: 21, in Graves, 2008: 149). We shall return to this point later in this chapter, and again in Chapter 12. Additionally, the ways in which curriculum design is undertaken and implemented can vary widely, from potentially hierarchical, 'specialist'-designed curriculums, which aim to be 'teacher-proof' with little practitioner input and decision-making, to teacher and learner-centred curriculums whereby classroom participants determine policy according to their own perceptions of their needs (Johnson, 1989: 12). We shall examine this in more detail shortly, when we explore *process* and *negotiated* syllabuses.

To summarize, therefore, the planning and organization of L2 teaching and learning, that is, the processes of curriculum development, results from the interaction of a range of factors – from policy-based social and institutional concerns to the ways in which classroom 'cultures' might shape what is and is not possible when a curriculum is implemented or 'enacted' in practice (Graves, 2008). Thus, according to Johnson, 'a coherent language curriculum reconciles what is desirable (policy) with what is acceptable and possible (pragmatics)' (1989: 18).

This chapter does not explore every aspect of the L2 curriculum, but instead focuses on the key debates surrounding syllabus design, testing and assessment, and the role of materials in teaching and learn-ing. The discussion will develop some of the broad themes raised in this introduction, investigating how and why teachers and other ELT professionals might plan and organize L2 learning, and the implications of these potential interventions for ELT practice.

Thinking about the ELT syllabus

Syllabus design can be a complex process based around, for example, an initial analysis of learners' needs and the context for learning, and, later, an evaluation of the syllabus's effectiveness. Detailed summaries of this process can be found in, for example, Graves (2000), Richards (2001) and Nation and Macalister (2010).

In this discussion, however, we shall examine some of the possible ways in which syllabuses may be organized (i.e., syllabuses in theory), before exploring some of the broader debates surrounding the role and reality of syllabuses in practice. We shall take a 'broad' view of syllabus design (Nunan, 1988b; see also Richards, 2013), acknowledging the links between L2 content and methodology (in contrast to a 'narrow' view that focuses *only* on the selection and grading of content).

Constructing a syllabus: by content, organization and presentation

Classifying content

Perhaps the most common way of thinking about and describing syllabuses is in terms of their *content*, that is, the nature of the units into which the syllabus is divided, for example, *structures*; *functions and notions*; *situations*; *genre* and *text-type*; *processes, procedures* and *tasks*; or *language skills*.

Structural syllabuses systematically introduce learners to grammar items such as 'the present simple tense', 'modal verbs' or 'relative clauses'. Functions, situations or tasks may be introduced, but only to facilitate the central focus on L2 structures and forms. However, an evident dilemma in structural syllabus design is the extent to which it can, or should, accommodate the learners' 'internal syllabus' (see Chapter 9). Structural approaches also tend towards a 'focus on forms' approach to L2 teaching and learning, which, as seen in Chapter 4, has been criticized by applied linguists such as Long (1988). Yet despite the impact of CLT and TBLT and the widespread understanding that 'meaning matters', many ELT course books are still largely organized around structures.

In contrast, *functions*, 'the communicative purposes for which we use language' (Nunan, 1988b: 35) and *notions*, conceptual meanings such as 'logical relationships' or 'time and duration' (ibid.), offer a more meaning-focused approach to syllabus design in which the basic units of the syllabus include, for example, 'apologizing', 'requesting' or 'giving advice'. Similarly, a syllabus might be organized around *situations*, for example, 'at the bank' or 'at the railway station'. As noted in Chapter 5, *notional-functional syllabuses* first emerged in the 1970s as a reaction to structural teaching and were a central element of early, 'strong' forms of CLT. However, with the clear exception of ESP programmes in which learners' functional and situational needs remain central (and which are also often organized around *genre-* or *text-based* syllabuses – see Chapter 10; also, Johns, 2002; Bax, 2006), 'pure' notional-functional syllabuses are now rare, in part because, while it *might* in theory be possible to order and sequence grammatical structures and ultimately achieve 'total coverage' (Johnson, 2008), 'we simply cannot teach all the functions of English' (ibid.: 224); consequently, the selection and grading of functions and notions can appear arbitrary. Additionally, Thornbury (2006) suggests, functional and notional language is also less generalizable than grammatical structures and hence perceived as a less central part of the L2 syllabus. Thus, while it is 'almost inconceivable' that a contemporary syllabus will actually omit functions and notions (Johnson, 2008: 236), they are often included as a relatively minor element within a 'multidimensional syllabus' (examined shortly).

Although very different, in their own ways, structural, notional-functional and genre-based syllabuses all focus on and categorize language (Newby, 2004). In contrast, *procedural, process* and *task-based syllabuses* (seen as synonymous by some applied linguists, e.g., Richards *et al.*, 1985) attend more to principles of second language learning and acquisition, as do the language-oriented elements of *content-based* and *CLIL* syllabuses. Drawing upon similar principles, they prioritize the *route* or '*means*' of learning (Breen, 1984) rather than specifying L2 outcomes or the '*ends*' of learning. Hence, process-orientated syllabuses typically focus upon 'who does what with whom, on what subject-matter, with what resources, when, how, and for what learning purposes' (ibid.: 56), and might draw upon a bank of available activities such as planning a journey from a rail timetable, following instructions to draw a map, or continuing and completing stories (Prabhu, 1987; see also Chapter 5). Unless tasks are selected to focus upon particular language items, the actual language to be taught (and, hopefully, learned) is not specified in advance; it is likely, however, to be recorded retrospectively. Meanwhile, procedural and task-based syllabuses require learners to develop and practise their second language skills (i.e., reading, writing, listening, speaking) in order to complete activities successfully. Likewise, content-based and CLIL classrooms use academic subjects (e.g., geography or science) to create a context for meaning-making, the language emerging (and being learned) and L2 skills developing as learners focus on content-led classroom activities, tasks and projects. Thus, a distinction can be made between *product-oriented* and *process-oriented* syllabuses (Nunan, 1988b; Newby, 2004), as summarized by White (1988) and illustrated in Table 11.1.

Procedural, process, task-based, and content-based syllabuses appear to engage with many of the applied linguistic debates identified in previous chapters; for example, the learners' 'internal syllabus' appears less problematic if there is no 'external' sequence of language points to follow, they encourage a focus on form rather than forms, and they have clear implications for issues of control and decision-making within ELT. However, as noted in Chapter 5, process and task-based teaching can be problematic. In addition to the difficulties of developing a coherent syllabus, the lack of predetermined linguistic goals and outcomes raises questions concerning accountability and testing that are a concern for institutions, governments, and, indeed, many teachers and learners (Newby, 2004).

Product-orientation	Process-orientation
Focus: *What* is to be learned?	**Focus:** *How* is it to be learned?
Interventionist	
External to the learner	Internal to the learner
Other directed	Inner directed or self-fulfilling
Determined by authority	Negotiated between learners and teachers
Teacher as decision-maker	Learner and teacher as joint decision-makers
Content selected by expert	Content identified by learner
Content a 'gift' to the learner from the teacher or knower	Content what learner brings and wants
Objectives defined in advance	Objectives described afterwards
Assessment by achievement or mastery	Assessment in relationship to the learners' criteria of success
Doing things to the learner	Doing things for or with the learner

Table 11.1   Key characteristics of product and process approaches to syllabus design

Source: White, 1988: 44–5.

Thus, perhaps the most common contemporary syllabus is the *multi-dimensional* or *multi-layered* syllabus, which, drawing on the debates above, is a 'hybrid' approach to syllabus design. Typically, these syllabuses combine structures, functions and notions and elements of task-based learning and skills development, although, as Littlejohn's (1992) detailed investigation suggests, core elements of many syllabuses and textbooks tend to be structural, with other content 'grafted on' in a subsidiary role (see also Thornbury, 2006).

Organizing, sequencing and grading

There are a number of ways in which content might be sequenced in L2 syllabuses. Perhaps the most widely recognized criterion is *difficulty*, whereby language that is thought to be easier is taught before language that is thought to be more difficult. However, this apparently common-sense approach raises a number of questions. An item which has a simple linguistic form may be difficult conceptually; for example, as Johnson (2008) notes, English language articles are simple in form (i.e., *a/an/the*), but the intricacies of use are difficult to explain. We can see here links with ideas of 'teachability' (see Chapter 9). Similarly, and as noted above, the existence of the learners' 'internal syllabus' further complicates perceptions of what language items learners are ready to learn and, therefore, which language they are likely to find 'difficult'. Finally, learners who have different L1s may experience differing degrees of difficulty with some L2 items (see Chapter 1), this final point suggesting that syllabus sequencing could potentially derive from a *contrastive analysis* of the learners' L1 and the target language.

Usefulness (or *urgency*) provides another principle around which L2 syllabuses may be planned. *Usefulness* focuses upon learners' immediate needs and may be particularly relevant for learners who have recently arrived in an L2 environment and need to cope with everyday life, or for learners of ESP. *Usefulness* is also the overriding principle behind process and *negotiated* syllabuses, in which syllabuses and language content emerge through a process of negotiation between teachers and learners.

Usefulness has also been linked to *frequency*, whereby syllabuses might introduce more regularly occurring language before less frequent items. Frequency information, of course, can be increasingly obtained from language corpora (see Chapter 10). However, the relationship between usefulness and frequency is not as straightforward as it may at first appear, as, in certain contexts, relatively infrequent words such as 'ticket' and 'passport', or even 'help' and 'lost', might be more useful than more frequent words such as 'the' or 'on' (Thornbury, 2006).

Thornbury (2006) also observes that *tradition* influences syllabus design, items being included because learners and teachers expect them; for example, despite its relative infrequency, reported speech can be found in many syllabuses. Johnson (2008), meanwhile, highlights the principle of 'grouping' items that 'go' together to form simplified pedagogic rules; for example, *some* is often taught with *any*, *will* is often taught with *going to* and so forth.

Although syllabuses may be organized *linearly*, whereby language items are dealt with one after another and mastery is assumed before learners move on, content is often organized cyclically, through a *spiral* syllabus (Corder, 1973). Here, learners return to the same content area, exploring it in more depth on each occasion. Typical of this approach are syllabuses that first examine, for example, *can* as an expression of ability (e.g., *he can swim*), later, *can* as an expression of permission (e.g., *can I interrupt you for a moment?*), and, later still, as a 'general probability' (e.g., *it can get very cold here in winter*).

Links to methodology: presenting content, developing skills

Clearly, the principles around which syllabuses are organized build upon the more theoretical perspectives of language and language learning that have been explored in earlier chapters. Thus, syllabuses may present language *synthetically*, language being 'broken down' into a series of constituent parts that are taught separately; alternatively, language may be approached *analytically*, where there is much less careful linguistic control within the learning environment and language is not seen as a series of components to be progressively mastered

(Wilkins, 1976). Synthetic approaches to syllabus design are closely linked to structural syllabuses and, consequently, to Grammar-translation and audiolingual language teaching methods. More analytical approaches clearly relate to process syllabuses and underpin stronger forms of CLT and TBLT (see Chapter 5). Of course, many contemporary syllabuses draw upon both approaches, Wilkins (1976) suggesting a continuum exists between the wholly synthetic and the wholly analytical. Meanwhile, the teaching of second language skills is sometimes separated from other elements of a syllabus, with reading, writing, speaking and listening addressed discretely within an ELT programme (see Chapter 4). Alternatively, skills work may be integrated with other elements of the syllabus; this is more likely with more process-oriented approaches to syllabus design which draw on communicative or task-based approaches.

To summarize, therefore, syllabus design involves a number of decisions about language content, skills development, organization and presentation that draw upon many of the debates examined in previous chapters. Given the number of competing and conflicting perspectives, it is, as Johnson comments, 'a process full of uncertainties and compromises. Messy, and certainly an art rather than a science' (2008: 223).

We shall now further explore notions of conflict, uncertainty and 'messiness' as we examine the relationship between syllabuses and L2 teaching and learning in practice, where theory and reality may differ.

Task 11.1 Syllabuses in your context

Consider the syllabuses that are followed in your professional context:

- Are they largely product or process-oriented? What is their main 'unit of content'? e.g., largely *structural*; based around *functions and notions*; *tasks and processes* . . .

- How is the content organized and sequenced? e.g., according to *difficulty, usefulness* . . .

- What view of language and of language learning do the syllabuses draw upon?

- What is the place of language skills and skill development within the syllabuses? Is skill development integrated into other tasks or activities, or are skills focused on as separate elements of the syllabuses?

- To what extent do you think that:

  - Syllabuses should not postpone useful structures because they are difficult to teach.

  - 'Learnability' is the key difficulty within syllabus design.

  - The most effective way of teaching and learning language is to break it down into constituent parts and teach it in a specified sequence.

  - Learners should determine the pace and direction of learning.

- What are the implications of these perspectives for syllabus design?

Syllabuses in practice: realities and agendas

'Hidden' syllabuses

As Newby (2004) observes, syllabuses provide transparency, *clarifying* learning objectives for teachers, learners and other interested parties (e.g., parents and policy-makers). They also aim to *regularize* and *guide* teaching and learning, specifying what content is taught and how it is organized. Yet attempts to ensure uniformity are potentially problematic given the debates identified in earlier chapters concerning what and how learners learn and the influence of individual characteristics upon language learning outcomes; that is, what learners learn is potentially unpredictable and likely to vary from what is planned for within a given syllabus. Ylimaki (2013) therefore suggests that in addition to what is planned or *intended* (i.e., what learners are expected to learn), we might also consider what is actually taught or *enacted* through a syllabus; what is actually *learned*, either intentionally or unintentionally; the *assessed* knowledge and skills demonstrated by learners; and what is implied to learners by what or who is included or omitted from the programme of study, which constitutes a *hidden* syllabus. For example, as we saw in Chapter 10, should an ESP programme focus only on the language and skills necessary to fit in with, rather than provide learners with, the linguistic resources to challenge workplace inequalities? Are only native-speaker varieties of English focused upon, or are non-native varieties also recognized and valued (again, see Chapter 10 for further discussion)?

Nunan (1989b) suggests that learners also have a 'hidden' syllabus or agenda in the classroom, Johnson (1989: 6) noting that:

A great deal of behaviour which appears inexplicable and even bizarre in terms of the official policy can readily be understood once the 'hidden' syllabus has been identified.

This may emerge in response to, for example, the syllabus' learning aims, classroom methodologies or materials, as seen in the ways Japanese and Sri Lankan learners resisted communicative activities in which aspects of their identity were not recognized (Greer, 2000; Tomita and Spada, 2013; Canagarajah, 1999; see Chapter 9).

However, it is not only learners who may have a 'hidden syllabus'. Johnson (1989) observes that if the 'official' syllabus differs radically from teachers' beliefs about what should be taught and how this content should be organized, then L2 classroom practices are likely to conform to this 'alternative' syllabus. Indeed, all interested parties – learners, teachers, parents, school administrators and policy-makers – may have 'hidden syllabuses' and agendas that might cause mismatches between the 'official' syllabus and actual practice, for example, 'are they on course for the examination?' rather than 'are they gaining in communicative competence?' (ibid.).

In other words, what happens in the L2 classroom is not necessarily the same as outlined by the syllabus; here, there are clear parallels to the debates explored earlier concerning idealized methods and actual classroom practices (see Chapter 5). Given this potential difference between planning and practice, the 'psychological comfort' syllabuses offer teachers and learners may be as important as their clarifying and guiding role in the L2 classroom (Allwright, 1983).

Guiding or constraining?

Although syllabuses act as a guide for teaching and learning, as Newby observes, 'the dividing line between guiding and constraining can easily be overstepped' (2004: 591). Syllabuses that are too prescriptive or overly comprehensive may be viewed by teachers as controlling and 'disempowering' documents that impose both content and classroom methodologies (see Pennycook, 1989 (also, Chapter 5), and van Lier, 1996). Newby thus observes that the status syllabuses enjoy among teachers and learners depends on the extent to which they are consulted in the design process and whether a syllabus leaves scope for individual interpretation.

Syllabus design and subsequent classroom practices, therefore, take place in specific institutional and social contexts, and the form a syllabus may take results from:

the interrelationships that hold between subject-specific concerns and other broader factors embracing socio-political and philosophical matters, educational value systems, theory and practice in curriculum design, teacher experiential wisdom and learner motivation.

(Clark, 1991: *xii*, in Richards, 2001: 90)

Thus:

Rather than merely being an ordered sequence of selected and, as it were, innocuous items of content, timeless and obscure in origin, separated from the world, [the syllabus] reveals itself as a window on a particular set of social, educational, moral and subject matter values. Syllabuses seen in this perspective stand, then, for particular ideologies.

(Candlin, 1984: 30)

The wider educational and ideological nature of ELT will be further explored in Chapter 12. However, this chapter will continue by examining two further aspects of the ELT curriculum, that is, assessment and instructional materials, where debates concerning values and ideologies are never too far away.

Task 11.2 Reflections on practice

- To what extent do you think learners and teachers have a 'hidden syllabus' that might differ from the 'official' syllabus in your professional context? What kind of things might differ? e.g., *purposes for learning, language content. . . .*

- To what extent do you (and learners) find syllabuses:

  - a 'psychological comfort'?

  - a useful guide?

  - a constraint on practice?

- To what extent are you involved in the design of your own syllabus? To what extent are you able to adapt the syllabus that you work with?

Exploring language assessment and testing

Although second language assessment and testing is a 'complex and perplexing activity' (McNamara, 2000: 85), it is a key element of most L2 curricula. Tests are disliked by many teachers and learners. They are stressful for learners (and, in different ways, for teachers), divert time and resources from the perceived 'real' purpose of education, that is, learning, and are often perceived as unreliable, unfair and unduly controlling (Johnston, 2003). And yet, most learners and teachers accept that some form of testing and assessment is an essential part of education, providing learners (as well as teachers, parents, institutions, employers and other interested parties) with an indication of their progress; tests can therefore also act as a motivational tool for learners (Eklöf, 2010) Thus while Johnston characterizes testing as a 'necessary evil' (2003: 77), Johnson more positively suggests that 'teachers need testers' (2008: 302).

Terminology and test types

Although many applied linguists and teachers use the terms interchangeably (e.g., Clapham, 2004), Fulcher and Owen (2016: 109) define assessment as 'the broader term, encompassing any activity in which data is collected from learners from which we make judgements about their proficiency and progress'. This can include, for example, class quizzes and peer and self-assessment. Testing, meanwhile, is 'the more specific term that refers to formal or standardized testing for the purposes of certification or decision-making' (ibid.), and can range from the more formal and standardized tests that might be found at the end of a sequence of classes to international tests such as the TOEFL (Test of English as a Foreign Language) and IELTS (International English Language Test Score) examinations. Assessment and testing can, of course, fulfil both a *formative* and *summative* role.

Language tests can be categorized according to their method and their purpose. **Test methods** range from *discrete point testing* (e.g., multiple choice tests) to *integrative tests*, which test learners' performance more holistically (e.g., cloze tests), to more overtly *performance-focused tests*, which assess language skills in acts of communication, for example, by eliciting extended samples of speech or writing (McNamara, 2000; Johnson, 2008). Meanwhile, **test purposes** are commonly identified as being either *achievement* or *proficiency* related. *Achievement tests* relate to a course or programme of instruction and may include, for example, end-of-course tests or portfolio assessments specifically based around the programme syllabus. In contrast, *proficiency tests* do not relate to a specific programme but instead assess what learners can do in the L2, that is, their level. They may be designed with a specific end use in mind (e.g., study in an English language-medium university) or offer a more general evaluation of proficiency that may be valid for 'real' or 'general' life. Placement tests administered at the start of language programmes are also proficiency tests. As McNamara (2000) notes, language courses may prepare candidates for proficiency tests once the tests are established (e.g., IELTS or TOEFL preparation courses).

Challenges in test design

It is impossible to document the full range of considerations and innovations in language test design in this chapter (for fuller reviews, see, for example, Bachman, 1990; McNamara, 2000; Douglas, 2010; Fulcher and Owen, 2016). However, a number of key concepts are regularly cited as essential characteristics of an effective test. They are validity, reliability and practicality.

Validity

A test is *valid* 'if it measures what is it supposed to measure and nothing else', thereby providing an accurate reflection of a learner's ability to perform in the area tested (Heaton, 1988: 159, in Johnson, 2008: 310). Of course, testing 'nothing else' is extremely difficult; for example, testing writing skills through an essay question will inevitably involve learners utilizing non-linguistic topic or content knowledge as they construct an answer.

As well as including valid content (i.e., *content validity*), tests also require *face validity*, that is, they should meet the expectations of those using them (e.g., learners, teachers and policy-makers). In effect, tests need to appear convincing to test users. Clearly, although often perceived as largely 'technical' or 'asocial' phenomena (McNamara, 2000), language testing *is* a social enterprise. We shall examine this perspective in more detail shortly.

Reliability

Tests that provide consistent results are said to be *reliable*. Thus, learners at the same level should achieve similar scores, and, if learners were to take the same test twice, they should achieve similar results on each occasion. The extent to which a test is reliable depends in part on factors such as clear instructions, uniform test conditions, unambiguous test questions and consistent rating procedures (including marker training and moderation). However, as McNamara (2000) points out, rating learners' communicative ability and concepts such as 'fluency' remains 'intractably subjective' (37) with 'enormous potential for variability and hence unfairness' (45). Johnson (2008) thus notes the potential tension between reliability, which can be achieved through 'unadventurous' questions that have easily identifiable right or wrong answers, and validity, which, for the assessment of communicative effectiveness, is more likely to be established through more complex tasks and rely on marker judgement.

Practicality

Clearly, of course, language tests need to be *practical*. If a test cannot be administered effectively, the results cannot be trusted. Indeed,

Thornbury (2006) argues that test designers may in fact sacrifice validity and reliability in 'low stakes' assessment in the interests of practicability. Meanwhile, computer-based testing is increasingly seen as a practical way of administering and marking large numbers of tests (ibid.), Clapham (2004: 51) observing that:

> The competing requirements of test validity and financial practicality will maintain the distinction between tests which can be administered reliably to large numbers of students, and more holistic tests which can potentially reveal all aspects of the candidates' language proficiency.

As Johnson comments, therefore, 'testing is sometimes the art of the possible' (2008: 315).

English language testing: wider contexts

As this brief review of validity, reliability and practicality shows:

> Language testing is an uncertain and approximate business at the best of times, even if to the outsider this may be camouflaged by its impressive, even daunting, technical (and technological) trappings, not to mention the authority of the institutions whose goals tests serve. Every test is vulnerable to good questions.
>
> (McNamara, 2000: 85–6)

Thus, language testing is a social practice that, 'like language itself, cannot ultimately be separated from wider social and political implications' (ibid.: 77).

For example, tests 'sort and select' learners (Davies, 2003: 361), often with significant consequences for learners' lives ('high stakes' tests such as TOEFL and IELTS, for instance, are often used for selection and admission into North American, British and Australian universities). Tests can therefore perform a 'gate-keeping' role, including some learners and excluding others from resources and future opportunities.

Tests can also influence syllabuses and classroom learning and teaching through both positive and negative 'washback' (Taylor, 2005). For example, 'teaching for the test' is a relatively well-known phenomenon. Additionally, Jenkins (2006) suggests that international tests such as IELTS and TOEFL penalize the use of Lingua Franca forms of English (see Chapter 10), which, in turn, affects ELT syllabuses around the world.

Davies thus concludes that that tests are 'inevitably political' as they are designed to 'meet society's needs' (2003: 361). Indeed, Johnston maintains that testing, 'more than any other aspect of teaching', is value-laden (2003: 76). Shohamy (2001) refers to 'the power of tests' in shaping educational and social policy, and argues that ELT professionals should explore the rationale and motivation behind language tests; for example, why is a test being used/taken? Whose agendas underpin the test? Who gains and who loses from the test? How will the results be used? Who is interested in the results and why? What does the test mean for test-takers and their schools? And how will the test affect teaching? (ibid.: *xii-xiii*). From this perspective, the 'why' of language testing is as important as the 'how'.

Task 11.3 Your experience of language testing

For a language test you are familiar with (either as a teacher or test-taker):

- What is the test supposed to measure? Does it achieve this? If so, how? Is any other knowledge necessary for the test to be taken successfully?

- What kind of questions does the test include? To what extent do the test scores rely on marker judgement?

- How easy is the test to administer?

- What is the social context of the test? What are its 'broader purposes'?

- What do test-takers hope to achieve by taking the test? Why do they want/have to take it?

- What are the aims of the teachers, school and education system in setting and administering the test?

- Who gains and who loses from the test?

- How are the results to be used? Who is interested in them and why?

- Does the test affect classroom teaching, learning and the L2 syllabus? If so, how?

Material issues: change, controversy and the ELT curriculum

As outlined in the introduction to this chapter, teaching and learning materials are a central part of most L2 curricula, and, in one form or another, are therefore 'almost universal' elements of ELT (Hutchinson and Torres, 1994). Yet until recently, relatively little attention has been paid to their role and impact in comparison to the role of teachers, learners, methods and syllabuses (Richards, 1998). In recent years, however, discussion has been stimulated by developments in CALL (see Chapter 2) and the emergence of the 'teaching unplugged' metaphor in some contexts (see Chapter 3). Drawing on ideas surrounding the teacher's 'sense of plausibility' (see Chapter 5), this interest also reflects an understanding that teachers (and learners) do not simply 'implement' materials, but use, adapt and 'consume' (Harwood, 2014) them in different ways. Thus, in an era where textbooks are arguably more influential than methods in shaping classroom practices (Akbari, 2008; see Chapter 5), it is important to understand and reflect on the role of materials in language teaching and learning.

A 'broad' view of materials encompasses anything that assists teaching and learning, including textbooks and workbooks; blackboards and whiteboards, including interactive whiteboards (IWBs); audio and video-materials; wall-charts; Cuisenaire rods; and the hardware and software that supports the many forms of CALL (both offline and online). Clearly, the materials available to teachers and learners vary widely according to context; as noted above, teachers and learners may also use similar materials in different ways depending on, for example, their beliefs, knowledge and skills, and wider social and institutional norms and expectations (see below for further discussion).

Over time, changing conceptions of language competence and L2 learning, combined with technological development and evolving societal perspectives on education, have led to changes in ELT materials, 'older' materials being supplemented or supplanted by newer resources that may themselves, in turn, become marginalized (Sercu, 2004). Hence, like many elements of ELT, there is thus an element of 'fashion' in materials development and use that, Sercu (ibid.: 394) suggests:

> Makes it an absolute necessity that teachers are able to perceive both the strengths and weaknesses of available teaching aids, and can make well-considered judgements as to when, how and to what end they can most effectively be harnessed to particular learning or teaching tasks. Often such decisions are influenced by considerations beyond the control of the course designers and producers.

Sercu also notes the understandable tendency for many teachers to use what is familiar in the face of the hyperbole that often surrounds new L2 materials, and suggests that it is almost impossible to prove the effectiveness of one particular resource over another when the complex situational, relational, educational, cognitive and affective variables that are at play in any group of learners are considered. In effect, then, 'recommendations to use particular media remain largely based on assumptions, not on generalizable facts' (ibid.: 297).

Materials evaluation frameworks to assist ELT professionals in the process of materials evaluation and selection can be found in, for example, Breen and Candlin (1987), Tomlinson (1998) and Harwood (2010).

Task 11.4 Materials in your context

- What materials are available for teachers and learners in your professional context, both inside the L2 classroom and beyond? e.g., *textbooks, IWB, wall-charts . . .*

- Which of these materials do you use in your own teaching? Why do you use them – in what ways do they support teaching and learning? Are there any ways in which they hinder teaching and learning?

- How do you use materials in your classroom? e.g., *if you use a textbook, do you follow it precisely, adapt or add items, or omit items? In what ways do you utilize CALL resources?*

- What is your rationale for the way you use materials? Why do you use them as you do? e.g., *to save time when preparing, to motivate learners, to make the materials more relevant to your own professional context . . .*

- To what extent do the materials in your professional context affect or determine your curriculum and syllabus?

Focus on textbooks

Richards (1998) suggests that textbooks are the primary source of teaching ideas and materials for many teachers around the world, 'indeed, the extent of English language teaching activities worldwide could hardly be sustained without the help of the present generation of textbooks' (127). Yet whether they are a help or hindrance to teaching and learning has been debated by applied linguists and ELT professionals alike.

Benefits and concerns

Well-designed textbooks have a number of obvious benefits for teachers and learners. They provide language input and exposure for learners; they can provide interesting and motivating material, organized in an appealing and logical manner; and they provide a written record of what has been studied, allowing for revision and continued study beyond the classroom (contemporary textbooks often tend to be part of a wider package of resources, which include DVDs, links to websites and so forth). Textbooks also reduce the amount of time teachers require for preparation, and can provide a sense of security for teachers and learners alike. A 'difference view' of textbooks therefore suggests that professional materials writers and teachers have different and complementary areas of expertise, and that the use of well-presented, professionally published textbooks frees teachers to deal with 'practical and fundamental issues in the fostering of language learning' (Allwright, 1981: 6).

A number of counter-arguments have been put forward, however. Textbooks may create a 'dependency culture' in which they can:

> . . . seem to absolve teachers of responsibility. Instead of partici-pating in the day-to-day decisions that have to be made about what to teach and how to teach it, it is easy just to sit back and operate the system, secure in the belief that the wise and virtuous people who produced the textbook knew what was good for us. Unfortunately, this is rarely the case.
>
> (Swan, 1992: 33)

Textbooks can thus become 'reified' (Richards, 1998), attributed with qualities of excellence, authority and validity that they might not have, and, thus, seen as superior to 'deficient' teaching (Allwright, 1981). Ultimately, if teaching decisions are based largely on textbooks, teachers may become 'de-skilled', losing their ability to think critically and work independently in the L2 classroom (Richards, 1998). Textbooks are also said to fail to cater for individual and/or local needs, lead to material- rather than person-centred classes and constrain classroom creativity (e.g., Meddings and Thornbury, 2009), although these claims are strongly contested (e.g., Hutchinson and Torres, 1994).

However, criticisms of textbooks extend beyond these more peda-gogic or classroom-focused concerns. As well as being an educational resource, textbooks are commercial products, which, it is claimed, are innately conservative in order to sell as widely as possible. This caution might be methodological (Littlejohn, 1992), or it might be reflected in the cultural images that textbooks present (Gray, 2016). Most textbooks, for example, continue to focus on native speaker lives, lifestyles and language varieties, V. Cook (2016) observing that images of successful L2 learners are notably absent from ELT materials; like-wise, images of poverty, disability and many other aspects of 'real life' are difficult to find in many textbooks. Thus, like syllabuses and tests, textbooks are not 'neutral', but reflect a particular view of society. It would be unfair, however, to imply that textbook writers and publishers are not aware of or concerned about these issues; yet producing a marketable product that does not ignore global and local realities and contexts is a difficult challenge.

Textbooks in practice

Despite the reservations noted above, textbooks remain popular with teachers and learners. Yet as Edge and Garton (2009: 55) put it:

> The teacher's purpose is not to teach materials at all; the purpose is to teach the learners and the materials are there to serve that purpose.

Consequently, any discussion of textbooks needs to consider how they are actually used. Thus, McGrath (2013: 127–8) draws on Hsiao (2010) to ask 'Should a professional teacher follow the coursebook without missing a single page? Or alternatively, should a good teacher select and modify the content to be more appropriate to the target learners?'. For McGrath, this raises questions about teacher professionalism and responsibility, and the extent to which teachers should 'follow the script' or make their own judgements about what learners need.

In general, however, textbook writers, teacher trainers and educators and applied linguists suggest that teachers *should* adapt textbooks, through either omission, addition or change (McGrath, ibid.), and in practice, most do, albeit to varying degrees. Adaptions may be planned before lessons, or may be the result of in-class decision-making, and often aim to make materials more interesting, more or less challenging, more manageable (in terms of, for example, time), and more culturally appropriate. Put another way, teacher adaptions might focus on the language to be taught, the ways in which this might be taught (methodology), the topics or content, and the level of linguistic and cognitive demands placed in learners (ibid.).

Clearly, different teachers adapt textbooks to a greater or lesser extent, and different ways. The changes made depend on, for example: the textbook itself (its content); the teacher's own beliefs, training, experience, pedagogical and content knowledge, perceptions of the textbook and of the learners; the learners' level, aptitude, and learning preferences; and institutional constraints, such as time and space limitations, and cultural expectations (Harwood, 2014). Thus, the ways in which textbooks are used in the classroom vary according to context, depending on both 'the people in the room' (see also Chapter 3) and the broader institutional and social setting for teaching and learning.

Summary: from curriculum concerns to educational contexts

Stern suggests that 'language teaching can be looked upon as a deliberate intervention into ethnolinguistic relations which can be planned more or less effectively' (1983: 284). This chapter, then, has looked at the ways in which aspects of the ELT curriculum might be planned and organized. We have examined the ways in which L2 syllabuses might be organized, noting both the theoretical foundations and the practical dilemmas inherent in a variety of approaches.

We have also noted the key considerations that underpin second language testing, and the ways in which ELT materials might benefit or constrain teachers and learners. Yet even after curriculum planners navigate these debates, it is evident that ELT syllabuses and materials, like methods, are 'continually reinterpreted and recreated by the teacher and learners when it is actually used in the classroom' (Breen, 1984: 47). Thus, although curricula and textbooks aim to regularize and guide learning and teaching (indeed, Skehan (1998: 260) refers to a 'conspiracy of uniformity'), complexity and diversity remain inherent characteristics of ELT classrooms and institutions.

Furthermore, the discussions in this chapter have focused upon what might be characterized (or caricatured) as more 'technical' or 'asocial' issues such as 'structures or functions' or 'test reliability' and also wider debates surrounding the social role and purpose of English language learning and teaching. Thus, while ELT practices and interventions build upon conceptions of language and language learning, they also reflect wider, value-based conceptions concerning the purpose of, and priorities for, ELT in any given context; and it is to these possible wider purposes and priorities of ELT that we turn in the final chapter.

12 ELT in the world

Education and politics, contexts and goals

> Language education is an international business and activity. It is inevitable, therefore, that the influence of the culture of the society in which language education takes place will play a significant role in communication and miscommunication, in cooperation and conflict; in short, in politics.
>
> (Alderson, 2009: 25)

This chapter will:

- note the relevance of an educational perspective within English language teaching, exploring differing conceptions of the goals of education (and ELT) in society and for individuals;

- also acknowledge that educational and commercial discourses co-exist within ELT;

- explore the ways in which English language teaching might be understood as a political undertaking, focusing upon both the global role of English and ELT, and local contexts, agendas and goals;

- examine the notion of 'teachers as researchers', noting some of the ways in which teachers might explore their own professional environments.

Introduction: emerging debates and broadening perspectives

Until the late 1980s, theories of second language teaching and learning focused primarily on individual psychological processes or viewed the L2 classroom in isolation, a place where individual learners came together to communicate but where the broader social and political contexts of learning were largely unimportant (Johnston, 2003: 50). One of the most notable developments in ELT and applied linguistics since this time, however, is an acknowledgement of the social, cultural,

political and historical contexts of English language teaching, their
potential effects on classroom practices, and the possible implications
of the spread of English and ELT around the world for individuals
and communities. Thus:

> where before there was only really the question of what, psycho-
> linguistically speaking, was the most efficient way of acquiring a
> language, now there are matters of ideology, that is, beliefs about
> values . . . in relation to politics and power relations.
>
> (Johnston, 2003: 51)

The terms 'politics' and 'political' are, of course, potentially problematic. Many teachers do not consider themselves to be political and do
not see the L2 classroom as an environment where politics should be
discussed. However, we have touched on several issues in earlier
chapters that *are* political in nature, for example, control in the classroom, the philosophies and worldviews that inform differing language
teaching methods, decisions about what to include in the L2 curriculum
and what kind of English to teach in a changing world, and the role,
purposes and potential 'gate-keeping' function of language testing. We
have also observed on several occasions that ELT professionals are not
'free agents' as they engage with these debates in their daily working
lives, but are guided (or constrained) by institutional norms, policies
and resources and societal goals and expectations, that 'what happens
in the language classroom is intimately linked to social and political
forces' (Tollefson, 1995: *ix*).

It is clear, therefore, that ELT is much more than a 'technical' enterprise; it is also a 'profoundly and unavoidably political undertaking'
(Johnston, 2003: 50) in which *who* teaches and learns English, and
why and *how* they carry this out, can be traced back to how policy-
makers, institutions and individuals perceive the broader goals and
purposes of English language teaching and, indeed, education in any
given context (Kennedy, 2010). This chapter, therefore, brings together
these key debates, exploring the ways in which English language
teaching is talked and written about, that is, the principal discourses
that reflect and construct ELT practitioners' understandings of their
professional lives; the key debates surrounding English and ELT in the
world; and the ways in which these global trends may be understood
in diverse and complex local settings.

Towards an educational perspective

ELT in its most widespread form takes place in *educational* settings,
that is, 'mainstream' or state schools, private language schools, colleges

and universities, yet, despite this, 'it is . . . surprising to note how little thought has been given to the relationship between language teaching and the study of education' (Stern, 1983: 419). Likewise, Pennycook (1990: 304) observes that second language education is 'strangely isolated' from educational theory and suggests that, as language is both the content and the medium of the L2 classroom, language teaching theory has tended to 'look in on itself and become overly concerned with the inner workings of language and language learning at the expense of other issues'. Meanwhile, Crookes (2016) suggests that recognizing the broader philosophical foundations of applied linguistic theory will help teachers develop their own practical 'philosophies of teaching' (see Chapter 1 for the related discussion of teachers' beliefs).

The goals of education: society and the individual

Among the array of educational philosophies that have emerged since schools as we now know them first appeared from around 1000 BCE in China and 450 BCE in Greece (Crookes, 2009), a number of perspectives are regularly cited in contemporary discussions of the possible role and goals of education. Most simply and, perhaps, superficially, education is seen as the 'transmission' of information or skills, or the 'means whereby we may live and know our surroundings' (Crookes, 2003: 54). Yet, this is not a 'simple' process; as noted in Chapter 5, 'knowledge is interested' (Pennycook, 1989), that is, the knowledge identified as important within a curriculum is likely to reflect the needs of dominant interests, for example, the government, business or 'the people' (Crookes, 2003).

From this perspective, education serves the needs of society, either as currently organized, in which case it is sometimes characterized as 'traditional, conservative or custodial' (ibid.: 55), or with a view to fostering social and political change, whereby it draws upon 'progressive' principles (ibid.). Beyond this mainstream or 'liberal' approach to social change, further philosophies of 'radical' social transformation can be found in the form of 'critical' pedagogy (e.g., Freire, 1970/1993), elements of which now inform many other educational debates, albeit usually focusing upon more limited conceptions surrounding the nature of knowledge and learning rather than emphasizing radical societal change (see, for example, the discussions of 'critical' approaches in previous chapters and in the discussion of 'knowledge, learning and the curriculum' that follows shortly).

In addition to links between education and *society*, education can also be seen as a process of, or opportunity for, self-development or self-realization of the *individual*. However, although self-development and state or societal development are sometimes seen as being oppo-sitional, these philosophies of education co-exist to some degree in most societies (Crookes, 2003; 2016).

An inherent difficulty in any discussion of educational values is the degree to which philosophies become caricatured as 'Western' or 'non-Western'. For example, ideas surrounding state-building educational systems that also support personal advancement first emerged in China, yet it is notable that many texts written in English treat educational theory and philosophy as synonymous with *Western* thinking about education (Crookes, 2003; 2009). Additionally, while non-Western and localized philosophies of schooling exist (see Crookes (2016) for further discussion of what might be termed Confucian, Buddhist and Islamic educational traditions, and of more localized 'indigenous' education), the legacy of Western colonial and economic power means that some educational traditions and perspectives are shared between apparently culturally diverse countries such as China or Korea and the UK or the USA. Consequently, debates about the role and purposes of education (and ELT) need to recognize 'a complex mixture of old and new ideas, continually struggled over and rarely clearly manifested' (Crookes, 2003: 59).

Knowledge, learning and the curriculum: differing perspectives

The differing ways in which education is conceptualized, and the values, philosophies and purposes that these perspectives embody, plainly affect the curriculum and pedagogy. Writing from a critical perspective, Canagarajah (1999: 14) notes 'the "hidden curriculum" of values, ideologies and thinking that can mould alternate identities and community allegiance among the students' (see also the discussion of the 'hidden syllabus' and agendas in Chapter 11).

Hence, Canagarajah characterizes two very different orientations towards knowledge and learning – a 'traditional' or 'mainstream' view that 'separates' the classroom from its social and political context, and a 'contextualized' or 'critical' perspective that more clearly recognizes and accounts for the diverse, complex and 'situated' nature of teaching and learning, as summarized in Table 12.1.

Clearly, elements of the 'traditional' orientation offer useful insights into classroom life (e.g., 'learning is a cognitive activity'), and, as Canagarajah observes, it would be 'unwise' to argue for a 'critical' orientation 'in absolute terms, without reference to the contexts and purposes of teaching' (1999: 17). However, the latter perspective acknowledges more readily the influence and importance of social, cultural and political factors on learning and teaching.

'Traditional' orientation	'Contextualized' orientation
Learning is a cognitive activity – the mind analyzes, comprehends and interprets.	*Learning is a personal activity* – the personal background of the learner influences how something is learned, and what is learned shapes the person (e.g., their consciousness, identity, etc.).
Learning is transcendental – the learner is impartial and neutral in terms of society, culture and ideology.	*Learning is situated* – learners are deeply influenced by larger political and social contexts.
	Rules, regulations, curricula, pedagogies etc. are shaped by socio-political realities.
Learning processes as universal – teaching is value-free and efficient.	*Learning as cultural* – established methods of learning embody the preferred ways of learning/thinking of the dominant communities.
Therefore knowledge is factual and impartial, and correct for everyone.	Knowledge is socially constructed, so what is considered true and real might vary.
Curriculum is value-free.	*Curriculum is value-laden/ideological*, containing the assumptions and perspectives of the dominant group.
Curriculum is a 'bank' of established facts and is therefore transmitted.	*Curriculum is negotiated* between communities in terms of values, beliefs and prior knowledge.
	Collaboration between groups leads to the social construction of knowledge.
Learning is instrumental – teaching as an innocent and practical activity of passing on correct facts.	*Learning is political* – teachers have an ethical responsibility for negotiating the hidden values and interests behind knowledge.

Table 12.1 'Traditional' and 'contextualized' orientations to teaching and learning

Source: Adapted from Canagarajah, 1999: 15–17.

'Not only education'

Educational discourses alone offer only a partial account of English language teaching and learning. The role of commercial and quasi-commercial institutions within ELT is well-documented (Alderson, 2009: 15), and commercial concerns affect much of the 'business' or 'industry' of ELT, from private language schools to higher education programmes. The UK, for example, derives around £2.5 billion (approximately $3.1 billion USD) each year from the ELT sector alone and around £14.1 billion, or $17.7 billion USD, from education-related exports (sources: English UK (2013) and Conlon *et al.* (2011) respectively). From this perspective:

> Second language programmes can be viewed within a marketing framework. It is clear that we are suppliers of a product (or services) which consumers need and avail themselves of. Students are consumers who pay for our product directly (from their own pocket) or indirectly (through subsidies given to them or us).
>
> (Yorio, 1986: 670, in Alderson, 2009: 15)

Indeed, while not necessarily in keeping with the more pedagogic and educationally focused discussions within this book, a substantial literature addresses ELT from a more commercial and managerial perspective, often focusing on issues of leadership or innovation (e.g., Impey and Underhill, 1994; Coombe *et al.*, 2008; White *et al.*, 2008).

Clearly, in many ELT contexts, educational and commercial discourses co-exist, although one or other of the perspectives might be more influential or appear more 'natural' in any given environment. Indeed, recognizing that more than one approach exists serves to problematize the wider role and purposes of ELT as an educational or commercial undertaking. Alderson (2009) notes, for example, that many institutions (and governments!) have vested interests in promoting the teaching and use of English, and it is to these more explicitly political, and potentially problematic, aspects of the spread of English and ELT that we now turn.

Task 12.1 ELT as an educational enterprise?

- To what extent do you agree that language teaching theory is overly concerned with the inner workings of language and language learning at the expense of 'other issues'? What 'other issues' do you think ELT professionals might or should be concerned with?

- Pennycook (1990) suggests that applied linguists and ELT professionals should look beyond questions such as *what is the best age at which to start learning?', 'what is the relationship between input and acquisition?'* or *'should we teach grammar and if so, how?'* to ask *'in what ways can educational technology limit and in what ways expand the possibilities of L2 learners?', 'how can teachers (and learners) gain control over the evaluation process?'* or *'how can one work with limited language yet avoid trivializing content and learners?'.* To what extent do you share his opinion?

How appropriate are these 'critical' questions in your professional context?

- What do you understand by the notion 'all knowledge is interested'? To what extent are notions of education for change, either liberal and progressive or more radical and transformative, relevant and/or appropriate:

  - in your professional context?

  - in ELT more generally?

- To what extent are educational and/or commercial discourses recognized in your professional environment? To what extent do you attend to these debates in your role at your institution?

- To what extent do you consider ELT more generally draws upon educational and/or commercial discourses?

English and ELT: a global concern . . . and local concerns

Characterized as 'lively' by Seidlhofer, the debates surrounding the global spread of English and ELT understandably provoke 'strong feelings' (2003: 7) due in particular to their links with issues of identity and economic opportunity. Hence, the aim of this discussion is not to argue a particular case, but to draw attention to a number of key issues and contextual factors which 'people concerned with ELT cannot ignore' (Brumfit, 2001: 139).

Early debates: 'a lot of English is taught; how much is learned?'

In one of the first and most provocative critiques of English language teaching, Rogers (1982) argues that much ELT activity is unrealistic or even 'dishonest'. Arguing that Western 'experts' create rather than solve problems, Rogers suggests that English language professionals often raise false hopes among many learners who study English in order to gain well-paid jobs that utilize their language skills, but subsequently discover that few such employment opportunities exist. He also notes the high financial cost and poor results of many ELT programmes around the world, and reflects upon the 'imposition' by ELT professionals of non-local values, norms and 'solutions' in varied and diverse contexts around the world. Rogers suggests a set of causal relationships, illustrated in Figure 12.1, which sustain a situation in which 'a lot of English is taught . . . [but] how much is learned?' (11).

Thus, Rogers argues that instead of Teaching English for No Obvious Reason (i.e., TENOR), ELT could be restricted to specific and identifiable groups of tertiary level learners for whom using English is a genuinely realistic prospect. He does acknowledge, however, that this is an unlikely scenario given the widespread demand for English and for ELT around the world and the difficult issues surrounding selection that it raises (also discussed in Chapter 7, although from an SLA perspective). We should also acknowledge that this critique was first published in 1982 since when circumstances have changed (e.g., English is used by more people, in a wider range of contexts, and for a greater array of functions globally; see Chapter 10). That said, whether or not present day situations are exactly the same as in the past, Rogers' discussion facilitates the ELT community reflecting upon its responsibilities (Crookes, 2003).

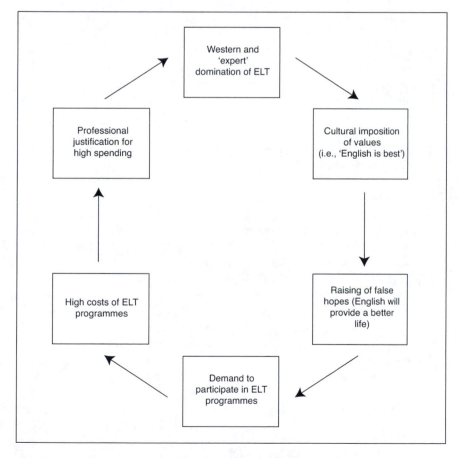

Figure 12.1 'Too much English': causal relationships within ELT
Source: Rogers, 1982.

Changing perspectives: global English, 'native speakers' and local contexts

Rogers' critique problematizes ELT in a number of ways, raising fundamental questions about the purpose of English language teaching and learning in the world, the ways in which different groups of ELT professionals are accorded unequal status and influence in the profession and, consequently, the ways in which some ELT practices may not be appropriate in particular local contexts.

English in the world: further insights

Chapter 10 identified some of the main trends associated with the spread of English, noting, for example, the emergence of non-UK or US varieties of English, and suggesting that the prestige associated with these varieties and their perceived worth to learners is, in effect, a question of values, that is, a political judgement. Beyond questions of 'which variety?', however, the spread of English itself has been critiqued.

The role of British colonialism and imperialism and the subsequent rise of US economic, political and cultural power are regularly identified as the two key processes that have sustained the spread of English (e.g., Jenkins, 2015; Seargeant, 2012; 2016), while the contemporary relationship between globalization and English is regularly commented upon (e.g., Block and Cameron, 2002; Pennycook, 2016).

All accounts acknowledge the threat posed to local languages and cultures. Johnston (2003: 54) refers to the 'predatory action' of English, while Crystal (2000) suggests that at least 50 per cent of the world's six thousand or so languages are predicted to die out in within the next century, partly as a result of the global status of English. However, accounts differ in the extent to which the growth of English is attributed to being 'in the right place at the right time' (ibid.). An alternative thesis posits that the global position of English is a consequence of 'linguistic imperialism' (Phillipson, 1992), whereby the spread and teaching of English is said to perpetuate colonial (or neo-colonial) attitudes and practices, thereby promoting the political and economic interests of English L1-speaking countries. Yet the thesis of linguistic imperialism itself has been criticized for projecting an unrealistic view of English language learners and non-native speakers as 'passive victims' of powerful global processes, thereby failing to acknowledge how English may be used, and changed, by learners for their own purposes (Bisong, 1995; Pennycook, 2016). As Canagarajah (1999: 76) notes, communities might appropriate English:

> to dynamically negotiate meaning, identity and status in contextually suitable and socially strategic ways and, in the process [modify]

the communicative and linguistic rules of English according to local cultural and ideological imperatives.

We may connect these perspectives to the debates identified above and in Chapter 10 surrounding varieties of English and English as a Lingua Franca (ELF).

Language norms, prestige and 'native speakers'

Among the many issues associated with the spread of English, perhaps the most problematic, and, indeed, paradoxical, is that of the 'native speaker'. As English has spread, more traditional descriptions such as Kachru's (1985) three-circle categorization of English have ascribed a high-status, 'norm-providing' role to 'Inner Circle' countries such as the UK and US and, therefore, to native speakers. In Kachru's model, while English is said to be 'norm-developing' in 'Outer Circle' countries where it has an official status (e.g., India and Nigeria), in the 'Expanding Circle', where it has no official capacity, English is said to depend on native speaker models of English (e.g., in China or Indonesia). In other words, according to Kachru (as summarized in Jenkins, 2015: 15), while Outer Circle varieties of English 'have become institutionalized and are developing their own standards', Expanding Circle Englishes are seen only as 'performance' varieties lacking in official status; they are therefore dependent on the norms and standards of Inner Circle native speakers.

Yet the growth of English in the world is more complex than this perspective can accommodate. The emergence and potential acceptance of Outer and Expanding Circle varieties of English challenges the assumption that native speaker norms are necessarily the most appropriate for any given context. Furthermore, and perhaps more perplexingly, it undermines traditional conceptions of who or what a native speaker is. To what extent can someone characterized as a norm-provider from Kachru's Inner Circle be thought of as a native speaker of Indian or Chinese varieties of English? Similarly, if ELF is spoken only as an L2 (see Chapter 10), do ELF forms of English have any native speakers at all? In this context, 'the native speaker of English' is an increasingly ambiguous concept that is both 'myth and reality' (Davies, 2004: 431). Despite these debates, however, the terms 'native' and 'non-native speaker' remain widely used and largely unquestioned within the 'popular discourse' of ELT (Holliday, 2006b: 385); hence, they are used in this book, albeit with some reservation.

Despite the increasingly thorough documentation of non-native varieties and ELF forms, it is evident that native speaker norms continue to be seen by many as the most appropriate model for English language teaching, as they appear to meet learners' aspirations (Timmis, 2002). Yet the notion of linguistic imperialism suggests that this is not, in fact, a free choice but is restricted by discourses of native speaker superiority, that is, by 'native speakerism' (Holliday, 2006b) – the belief that native speakers and 'Western culture' represent an ideal in terms of English language norms, English language teachers and teaching, and ELT methodology (ibid.); from this perspective, native speakers are seen to be inherently and always 'better' or more expert English users than non-native speakers, which, as Jenkins (2015: 18) notes, is 'patently untrue'. Native speakerism is thus an implicit element of Rogers' critique of ELT (see above), dividing the world into superior native speaker cultures ('Us') and problematic non-native speaker cultures ('Them'), the latter labelled, for example, as 'dependent', 'passive' and 'traditional' (Holliday, 2005; 2006b). Native speakerist attitudes were also identified in our earlier review of learner autonomy (Chapter 8).

Having problematized native speakerist discourses around language norms, we shall now move on to examine the common (but inaccurate) assumption that native speakers automatically make better language teachers, before exploring further the relationship between ELT methodologies and local contexts.

Good teachers: native and non-native, qualified and experienced

As V. Cook (2016: 197) observes, the debates surrounding Native English Speaker Teachers (NESTS) are 'divisive'. In many contexts, the recruitment of NESTs (Medgyes, 1994) rather than non-NESTS is prioritized, and native speakers are often paid more than their non-native colleagues. Thinking through the issues surrounding NESTs and non-NESTs is more than just a theoretical exercise, therefore; the debates affect the working lives of many ELT professionals.

Many discussions speculate about the apparently differing strengths and weaknesses of NESTs and non-NESTs. The most commonly cited advantage of NESTs is the model of English they are said to provide for learners (see Timmis (2002), also noted above). Yet, as we have seen, native speaker English may be only one of several L2 models that are available to learners. They may instead wish to model themselves upon the English of successful L2 users rather than that of often monolingual native speakers (V. Cook, 2016: 199). Additionally, some of the numerous regional and social accents of, for example, the UK, USA and Australia are likely to prove more or less desirable, or even accessible, models of English than others (ibid.). Thus, the apparent superiority of NEST models of English is less straightforward than it may at first appear.

Furthermore, being a good teacher is likely to be influenced by training, qualifications and experience, including knowledge of the learners' language, culture and their educational system. Thus, Medgyes (1992) suggests that, in comparison to NESTs, non-NESTs:

- can provide models of successful L2 use;

- teach learning strategies more effectively;

- provide learners with more information about and insights into how English works;

- anticipate language difficulties more effectively;

- are more empathetic to learners' needs and problems;

- can benefit from sharing the learners' mother tongue.

Clearly, of course, any discussion of NESTs and non-NESTs tends towards stereotyping. Yet, as the strengths of non-NEST teachers are increasingly recognized and as consideration is given to the knowledge and skills that *all* teachers need, it seems possible that native speaker-ist discourses surrounding teachers and teaching may gradually be challenged and, eventually perhaps, more attention will be given to what teachers can do rather than where they are from.

Task 12.2 Thinking about NESTs and non-NESTs   (TC)

- To what extent do you agree or disagree with the apparent advant-ages of NESTs and non-NESTs outlined in this discussion?

- If you work in an environment where there are both native speakers and non-native speakers, do they have the same kind of roles and responsibilities? For example, do NESTs and non-NESTs teach the same kind of classes? Who manages and plans the curriculum?

- How far do you agree with the view that 'native-speakerism' is widespread in ELT?

- To what extent does the idea of 'native' and 'non-native' English teachers *really* help us understand or identify effective or successful English language teaching? Consider the importance of native/non-native speaker status when compared to, for example, teachers': training and education, teaching experience, linguistic knowledge (both knowing *about* language and being *able to use* language), pedagogic knowledge, knowledge about learners and learning, and so forth.

Methods revisited: context, culture and appropriate methodology

A central claim of the linguistic imperialism and native speakerism hypotheses is the notion of a 'methods trade', first noted in Chapter 5. In many accounts, this is characterized as the unquestioning 'export' of teaching methodologies and practices from Western to non-Western contexts, that is, from the 'centre' to the 'periphery' (Phillipson, 1992), where they may be inappropriate.

Holliday (1994; 2005), however, refines the debate somewhat, suggesting that the transfer of language teaching methodologies takes place between two very different *cultures* within ELT, 'BANA' and 'TESEP', whereby:

> BANA comprises an innovative, often predatory culture of integrated skills which is located in the private sector or in commercially-run language centres in universities and colleges in Britain, Australia and North America. TESEP comprises a more traditional culture of academic subjects, which is located in tertiary, secondary or primary schools throughout the world... TESEP people are *mainstream* in the sense that they do very similar work, with similar initial qualifications to teachers and lecturers of other subjects ... BANA people come *from* the English-speaking West and are characterized by having an overactive professional zeal connected with the notion that English and English teaching is originally theirs. They are *not mainstream* in educational terms in that they often stand outside established academic departments in schools, colleges and universities...
>
> (Holliday, 2005: 3; original emphasis)

TESEP environments can thus be found in 'the West', while many BANA-oriented ELT professionals work in non-Western countries. (Holliday, in fact, recognizes the limitations of all terminology that divides ELT professionals into *Us/Them* categories and works against a 'common identity'; like the term 'native speaker', however, the terms 'BANA' and 'TESEP' serve a useful purpose in our discussions.)

Much of the thinking surrounding classroom practice and methodologies discussed in earlier chapters has, of course, originated in BANA contexts. Yet many ELT contexts involve the bringing together of people and ideas from both BANA and TESEP cultures and, as Johnson notes, the result 'may be a happy union. Unfortunately, there is often also an element of clash' (2008: 208). In a study of Alaskan classrooms, for example, Collier noticed differences in the way 'Anglo' teachers paced lessons compared to local Inuit teachers, suggesting that the BANA-oriented teachers followed a more rationalized and technical teaching approach which learners did not fully respond to (1979, in Holliday,

1994: 35). Drawing upon his study of an Egyptian ELT project, Holliday, meanwhile, identifies the very different ways in which group work is perceived in different contexts (ibid.). As we have seen, much SLA research argues that interaction is crucial for L2 learning (Chapter 6); groupwork may also reduce learner anxiety and motivate learners (Chapter 7); and it might help to individualize instruction (Long and Porter, 1985). In effect, Holliday argues, the 'learning group ideal' allows for process-oriented, task-based, collaborative and communicative language teaching (54). Yet both Holliday and Shamin (1996; see also Chapter 3), for example, suggest that this group ideal does not account for local contexts where large, teacher-fronted classes are the norm and 'transmission' models of teaching (see above) are embedded in local educational cultures. Similarly, Cortazzi and Jin (1996; see also Chapter 7) identify the 'cultures of learning' that account for the ways in which many Chinese learners' classroom participation might differ from BANA-oriented norms. In summary, then, although ideas with an ideological origin in BANA cultures are not necessarily and by their very nature inappropriate, 'if teachers (native or non-native speakers) grounded in English-speaking Western TESOL assume a method-ological superiority (and as a result perceive other kinds of learning as inherently inferior), they will be doing their students and themselves a potential disservice' (Harmer, 2007: 76).

Holliday (1994) suggests, therefore, that, rather than transferring methodologies unquestioningly and attempting to 'remove the differ-ences' between teachers, learners and learning environments, ELT professionals should recognize there is no single best way to teach and learn. Instead, methodology should be 'appropriate' (ibid.) while teaching should be 'context-sensitive' (Bax, 2003). Thus, Holliday (2005) refers to 'emergent practices' in the L2 classroom, whereby a focus on linguistic meaning is not necessarily equated with, for example, group-work or learner-centred, rather than teacher-led, activity. Bax, meanwhile, suggests that rather than subscribing to a predominantly CLT or TBLT methodology, ELT professionals should recognize that a variety of methods and approaches may be valid in a given context, that methodology is just one factor in learning a language, and that other factors (such as affect) may be more important than methods.

As Bax observes, however, 'good teachers naturally take account of the context in which they teach – the culture, the students, and so on' (2003: 284); notions of appropriate methodology and context-sensitive teaching are not necessarily new. Indeed, these debates are clearly related to the notions of Postmethod and principled eclectic-ism explored in Chapters 5 and 6, in which teachers are guided by their sense of what is and what is not plausible in the L2 classroom. A context-sensitive or a Postmethod approach to classroom life thus envisages an 'enhanced' role for teachers in which practitioners might develop their own understandings of classroom life and the wider professional context through teacher-led investigations.

While acknowledging concerns (already noted) surrounding the institutional constraints teachers face and the risk of teacher burnout, the final section of this chapter will examine the possible ways in which teachers may explore and research 'personally relevant' questions and issues in their own professional contexts (Maley, 2003). Before that, however, we shall briefly take note of a concern raised by some applied linguists and ELT professionals, that several of the debates explored in this chapter reflect ideologically based BANA thinking rather than the real concerns of ELT teachers around the world.

'There's more to life than politics' . . .?

This chapter has explored a number of issues that, in one way or another, can be broadly labelled as 'political', from the goals of education and ELT to notions of linguistic imperialism and native speakerism. As Sowden puts it, these discourses seek to 'empower the marginalized and give a voice to those who are often excluded by the dominant social and political discourses' (2008: 284). Yet Sowden also argues that 'there is more to life than politics', suggesting that some of these critical debates politicize ELT in ways that are 'unnecessary and potentially harmful' (ibid.). He points out, for example, that many learners and teachers regard language teaching as skills training, and suggests that, in these contexts, ideological concerns are 'largely irrelevant'. Additionally, he questions whether many ELT professionals are in fact qualified to pronounce on political and social matters.

Waters (2007) also queries what he sees as the dangers of 'political correctness' and critical theory in ELT, suggesting that, although the ideas discussed in this chapter have been influential in ELT and applied linguistic theory, many of them have had 'sparse grassroots take-up' (354), achieving little widespread popularity. While acknowledging that these debates have helped draw attention to potential abuses of power within ELT, such as the NEST/non-NEST debate or the relationship between 'global' and 'local' methodologies, Waters highlights the dangers of creating new dominant ways of thinking in ELT, which, ironically perhaps, continue to promote a 'prevailing intellectual ideology of the professionally predominant Anglophone West' (353).

Yet, as noted in earlier chapters, teachers and learners do not adopt and implement new ideas and approaches in straightforward ways. Instead they 'appropriate, delete, and add to new trends in ELT according to their own principles and the values they see as important in education' (Lima, 2009: 273, citing Brumfit, 1981). Thus while these educational and critical perspectives may 'embody the state of knowledge and understanding of language and politics we have at this particular moment in the history of English language teaching' (Lima, 2009), they will, like all other approaches within ELT, naturally be subject to debate and criticism as teachers and learners search for ways of understanding English language teaching and learning in their own specific contexts.

Task 12.3 In theory and in practice: reviewing the debates

- To what extent do you recognize some of the concerns and debates highlighted in this chapter in your own professional context? For example:

  - what elements of Rogers' critique of ELT are valid, if any?

  - to what extent are different groups of ELT professionals accorded unequal status, if at all?

  - how convincing is the idea of a 'methods trade' from BANA to TESEP cultures? Is it always necessarily a negative phenomenon?

  - how plausible are the concepts of 'appropriate methodology' and 'context-sensitive teaching'? Are they new ideas? If not, why do you think Holliday and Bax felt the need to draw attention to these concepts? In what ways do you recognize contextual factors in your own teaching?

  - to what extent do you see ELT as a 'political enterprise' that is 'infused with values'? How far are the debates raised in this chapter 'unnecessary and potentially harmful'?

Developing understanding: teacher research and inquiry

Although the debates examined throughout this book have been diverse and wide-ranging, a number of key themes have recurred, for example, that classrooms are complex social environments; that English language teaching takes place in a diverse range of social and cultural contexts that affect classroom life; that values permeate language classrooms and educational institutions; and that a teacher's (and learner's) sense of plausibility mediates ways in which, for example, methodologies, syllabuses, materials are realized in practice. Consequently, the relationships between practice and theory and between (supposedly) universal principles and local understandings have been emphasized. How might teachers and other ELT professionals develop understandings of their own professional contexts and practices?

A number of texts focus upon the ways in which teachers might systematically reflect upon and explore practice (e.g., Edge, 2002; Richards and Farrell, 2005; Mann and Walsh, 2017). Beyond immediate planning and post-class reflection, teachers may engage in, for example, peer observation, journal writing, or audio or video self-recording and monitoring. They may also engage with and reflect upon ELT and applied linguistic literature and research findings, or wish to undertake research themselves.

However, many teachers perceive an 'insurmountable gap' (Nunan, 1990) between theory and practice. Reasons for this include the different priorities of teaching and 'academic' research, which can be broadly caricatured as the difference between 'immediate, practical developments' and 'objective truths', and the ways in which the tacit knowledge of teachers is sometimes devalued at the expense of research findings (ibid.). Proposing that teachers 'can and should be involved in researching their own professional practices in their own classrooms' (ibid.: 16), Nunan suggests that teacher-research can provide new insights into classroom life, bridge the gap between theory and practice and place additional value on teachers' knowledge (see also, for example, Allwright and Hanks, 2009; Hanks, 2017).

Dikilitaş *et al.* (2016: *vii*) therefore characterize teacher research as research conducted 'by and for teachers'. This can help teachers understand and 'personally theorize' their own practice, following a research process that they design themselves, in their capacity as teachers. Although there is some debate about the differences between teacher investigations and more formal or 'academic' conceptions of research (S. Borg, 2013), and teacher research is notably under-represented within applied linguistic publications, teacher research has intrinsic worth as it supports professional development and understanding at a local level (ibid.). Additionally, an increasing range of teacher research *is* now being published (e.g., Bullock and Smith, 2015; Dikilitaş *et al.* 2016; Edwards and Burns, 2016), which not only shares teachers' insights into their own classroom practices and their understandings of how teacher research might be undertaken, but also provides a mediating link between academic researchers and teacher researchers (Dikilitaş *et al.*: ibid.).

Action research is regularly cited as a model for teacher-led inquiry, following a cycle of problem identification, the collection of relevant information about the issue, devising a strategy to address the concern, trying out the strategy, and observing its effects, i.e., observing, analysing, acting and reviewing (Richards and Farrell, 2005; Burns, 2010). Data can be collected in a number of ways including observation, teacher and learner diaries, questionnaires and interviews. Thus, central to action research are the notions of addressing and solving immediate problems, and researchers (i.e., teachers) who investigate *their own* context; the aim is not to turn teachers into 'researchers' *per se*, but to assist with understanding and professional development (Wallace, 1998). A typical action research investigation might focus on, for example, the effectiveness of feedback and repair in class, or the ways in which changes to typical classroom routines and practices might affect learner anxiety. Action research is thus different in intentions and outcomes to the research undertaken by applied linguists examining *other people's* institutions or classrooms, or investigations into second language acquisition. Wallace (1998), Edge (2001) and Burns and Burton (2008) provide numerous accounts of action research in practice.

Action research thus provides a route towards understanding classroom life either within a particular methodological approach such as CLT or TBLT, or within a Postmethod or context-sensitive framework. Yet although generally seen as 'empowering' for teachers, there is the possibility that it may add unreasonably to teachers' workloads, especially if imposed as a top-down requirement (Wallace, 1998). Allwright (2003) also suggests that the conceptualization of 'problems' that need to be 'solved' is not always helpful, suggesting instead that teachers and learners should work together to explore the 'quality of life' in the classroom without necessarily seeking to improve it. Thus while change might result from this '*Exploratory practice*', understanding is more important. Allwright (ibid.) also argues that exploratory practice should be integrated fully into the curriculum; for example, rather than developing language skills and knowledge through in-class discussion of topics such as 'holidays' or 'the environment', learners might discuss the issues surrounding language learning and teaching, and their own classroom practices in more detail (Allwright and Hanks, 2009; Hanks, 2017).

Summary: exploring ELT

Recognizing that a number of competing discourses surround English and ELT in the world, this chapter has explored English language teaching as a 'worldly' enterprise (Pennycook, 1994), in which decisions surrounding second language learning and teaching reflect broader social, cultural and political concerns. Although noting the commercial or quasi-commercial discourses inherent in much ELT activity, the chapter has placed ELT within a broadly educational framework, examining a number of ways in which English language teaching as a 'profession', 'enterprise' or 'industry' has been critiqued and problematized. Although not all aspects of this chapter's discussion are accepted by all ELT professionals and applied linguists, the challenges raised undoubtedly provide a starting point for reflection about the goals of English language teaching, that is, what we hope to achieve and how we hope to achieve it.

Although these debates might appear more overtly 'difficult' or controversial than those explored in earlier chapters, the nature of the disagreements highlighted here are perhaps not out of keeping with applied linguistic and ELT thinking more generally. As we have seen in all our discussions, there are very few clear straightforward solutions when trying, for example, to locate the 'best' or most effective ways of teaching, identify how learners learn and what conditions might promote learning, or understand the broader socio-political contexts of learning.

It is hoped, therefore, that the debates highlighted throughout this book will act as a stimulus for reflection whatever our professional environment, as we link ELT practice to theory, and classroom concerns to wider social and institutional contexts. By drawing upon our own 'sense of plausibility', we may, as Brumfit (2001: 187), suggests, edge our way towards 'tentative understandings' of English language teaching in the world and our own professional practices as we explore ELT.

Commentary on selected tasks

The tasks in this book are intended as starting points for discussion and reflection as readers consider their professional practices and contexts in light of the many debates explored, and establish their own perspectives on the links between practice and theory within ELT. Many of the tasks ask readers to reflect upon their own experiences or identify their beliefs and opinions; obviously, there is no single answer to these kinds of tasks. For other exercises, key points and interpretations are 'built in' to the main text for readers to consider within the relevant chapter.

Consequently, this commentary does not consider all the tasks in the book, but provides additional comment only where relevant. Additionally, these notes are intended as further prompts for reflection, *not* as answers to the tasks.

You may also be able to see connections between different tasks as you move from chapter to chapter; for example, the discussion of the Interaction Hypothesis and Output Hypotheses in Chapter 6 may remind readers of issues surrounding classroom interaction explored in Chapter 1. Thus, the tasks in this book aim to provide a starting point for the critical synthesis of practice and theory as we explore English language teaching.

Task 1.1 Thinking through 'beliefs'

It seems likely that most teachers' beliefs change over time, as a result of both practical experiences in the classroom and by sharing ideas with colleagues, participating in teacher training or teacher education programmes, and engaging in, or with, research. The ways in which beliefs change will, of course, vary from individual to individual.

Many teachers will be able to identify occasions where their classroom practices seem to run counter to their apparent beliefs, for example, teaching 'from the front' and engaging in more teacher talk than they consider appropriate or correcting learners' errors more (or less) frequently than they believe is necessary. Clearly, such occasions are influenced by the immediate circumstances of the class, that is, by 'what works', but also by the expectations and beliefs of, for example, learners, parents and institutional managers as to what constitutes 'proper' classroom behaviour and activity. Additionally, such occasions raise interesting questions about how the beliefs (and values) individuals hold may be contradictory, a point explored in more detail in Chapter 3.

Task 1.3 Teacher talk in the L2 classroom

Listening to teachers talking in the target language can be a source of comprehensible input for learners (see Part II). While the benefits of making teacher talk comprehensible are clear (i.e., it is a source of comprehensible input for learners), the extent to which teacher talk is modified touches on the debates that surround the place of 'real' or 'authentic' language in the classroom (see Chapter 10). How 'real' is modified or simplified teacher talk and what are the implications of this for L2 learning?

Task 1.5 Interaction, control and class size

This task reminds us of the wide range of contexts in which English language teaching takes place, a theme to which we shall return throughout the book. By considering the effects of class size, it also leads us towards discussions, in Chapter 2, of teaching English to large classes in 'difficult circumstances'.

Task 2.3 The L2 classroom in practice: thinking about your context

Routine in the L2 classroom can provide learners (and teachers) with a sense of security; they have a general understanding of what is likely to happen in class, for example, how a class might start, the kind of activities to be undertaken, behavioural norms and so on. This can make learners less anxious and increase their readiness to learn (see discussions concerning the role of affect in L2 learning in later chapters). However, there is clearly a point at which routinization may lead to boredom and, consequently, classrooms based around unvarying routines might potentially demotivate learners.

Additionally, as Chapter 2 outlines, 'convivial' and unexpected discourse in the L2 classroom is seen as important in the creation of meaning-focused learning opportunities. From this perspective, a degree of uncertainty and unpredictability in classroom interaction is central to L2 learning.

Task 2.4 New technologies and ELT

Although teachers might 'blend' technology into their classes, and might ask learners to engage in out-of-class technology use, the extent to which this happens obviously depends a great deal on context. Furthermore, in those contexts where learners do have access to new technologies beyond the classroom, they may find (or create) learning opportunities without teacher guidance (see also Chapter 8). In such situations, the distinction between language *learning* and language *use* might be blurred (i.e., learners may use English when online, primarily motivated by the wish to communicate and participate; language learning may result, but, equally, may not be the primary aim of the activity).

One obvious difference between computer-mediated interaction (CMC) and face-to-face interaction is that CMC has, until recently, usually been written (although technological developments mean that this situation is changing, and oral interaction is increasingly common online). Written CMC may be lexically and syntactically more complex than speech, but takes place without intonation or other non-verbal cues (such as gestures). Written transcripts of CMC can often be obtained, which may be used for L2 teaching and learning purposes. Some research also suggests that written CMC discussions tend to have more balanced patterns of participation than face-to-face communication – it is more difficult for one or two participants to dominate, and all participants can 'speak' at once without having to take a formal turn in a conversation.

Task 3.1 Metaphorically thinking

Other metaphors you may think of include, for language teaching, *building bridges*; *scaffolding* or *supporting*; a *balancing act*; *conducting a band or orchestra*. . . . Language teachers might *grow*, *tend*, *plant seeds* (or be *gardeners*); *drive*, *navigate*, or *steer* . . .

Task 3.2 Your context: laboratories, culture and communities

This task emphasizes the idea that different classes have their own particular 'cultures', making each a unique social and pedagogic environment.

Task 4.2 First language acquisition and second language learning

First language acquisition and second language acquisition or learning differ in terms of both the learners' personal characteristics and the environment in which language development takes place. Innatist accounts suggest that all children successfully acquire a first language during their 'critical period' (pre-puberty), drawing upon an innate knowledge of language that everyone is born with. From this perspective, first language acquisition is an unconscious and 'natural' process.

Meanwhile, no matter what their age, all second language learners have already acquired at least one language, and whether this knowledge is an advantage for L2 learners is a key debate within SLA research. L2 learners may be able to draw upon their prior linguistic knowledge to assist their second language development. Older second language learners, for example, might approach language learning with a degree of metalinguistic awareness and a range of analytical skills that children acquiring a first language (and young children learning a second language) lack. Not all SLA researchers share this perspective, however; those from a more 'innatist' tradition suggest that conscious knowledge and analysis of language is inevitably less effective than the processes involved in first language development noted above.

Further possible differences between first and second language development include: whether learning takes place formally, for example in a classroom with a teacher, or informally, for example through immersion in a target language-rich environment; consequently, the amount and type of correction that is available and is given to L1 and L2 learners; the time that learners have for learning; the language available in the learning environment; reasons for learning; and whether learners are anxious about using the language (it is often hypothesised that L2 learners, particularly older learners, might be more anxious about speaking the second language than young children speaking either their first or a second language).

The implications for second language teaching include, for example, the extent to which language rules, patterns and forms are given explicit attention in the classroom, the ways in which learners' knowledge about language and/or their own first language might be drawn on in second language learning, the extent to which corrective feedback should be provided for errors, and so forth.

Task 5.1 Language teaching methods over time

Several of the methods and approaches you might have listed are explored further in later sections of the chapter. Both Larsen-Freeman and Anderson (2011) and Richards and Rodgers (2014) provide book-length reviews of a range of individual methods.

Task 5.2 Thinking about Grammar-translation

As noted in the chapter, a widely perceived goal of Grammar-translation is for learners 'to learn a language in order to read its literature or in order to benefit from the mental discipline and intellectual development that result from foreign language study' (Richards and Rodgers, 2014: 6). Language is conceptualized as a system of grammatical rules that are taught deductively through a focus on forms, while language learning is the memorization of these rules and other language 'facts', usually at the level of the sentence. Both teachers and learners are therefore aware of grammatical rules and structures that are analysed and discussed in the learners' L1. Several weaknesses of this approach are cited in Chapter 5 (for example, its description of language, and, perhaps stereotypically, the supposedly tedious nature of classes taught in this tradition). However, more positive conceptions of Grammar-translation suggest that it may be appropriate for learners (and societies) that 'treat academic knowledge of the second language as a desirable objective and hold a traditional view of the classroom and of the teacher's role' (V. Cook, 2016: 264). Meanwhile, G. Cook (2010) suggests that bilingual explanation and translation might be combined with periods of monolingual practice in the L2 classroom.

Task 5.3 How 'Direct' are you?

As the chapter notes, although few teachers follow the Direct Method in contemporary language teaching (the exception being in Berlitz Schools), its focus on L2-only teaching, spoken rather than written language, and little or no grammatical analysis have been influential in many classrooms.

Task 5.4 Humanistic approaches: exploring your context

The various terms used to label 'humanistic' methods and approaches reveal a number of differing perspectives. As V. Cook notes (2016), the term 'alternative methods' suggests that there is a common conventional method to which they are an alternative, and that approaches such as TPR, the Silent Way and Suggestopedia have a great deal in common. Both these assertions are debateable. Meanwhile, labelling these approaches as 'humanistic' and 'ways' suggests an almost philosophical or mystical take on classroom language learning. The term 'designer methods' may emphasize that TPR, Suggestopedia and the Silent Way all have an identifiable 'founding figure' (also, perhaps, suggesting a degree of idiosyncrasy), while the term 'fringe methods' seems to marginalize these approaches from 'mainstream' ELT.

Task 5.5 Thinking about communication and meaning in the classroom: CLT, TBLT and CBI/CLIL

There are clear theoretical similarities between CLT, TBLT and CLIL in terms of the way they conceptualise language learning taking place (i.e., through a focus on meaning). Differences *between* the approaches, but also *within* the approaches, are apparent when we consider the amount of attention given to meaning and to form (i.e., to the language itself). Thus, 'strong' and 'weak' CLT focus approach language learning in different ways ('learning by using' or 'learning to use'); within TBLT, there are differing perspectives on when learners should focus on language; and different CBI/CLIL programmes might attend to language through parallel language classes, or by focusing on language before or after content-oriented tasks in the CBI/CLIL classes themselves. Such variations, throughout each of the three approaches, will affect how classroom activities and the broader syllabus are organised.

Task 6.2 Making input comprehensible

In this extract, the learners engage in a number of confirmation checks and clarification requests as they attempt to understand the teacher's instructions. As this transcript reveals, it is often difficult to classify with certainty what a particular speaker and utterance is 'doing' in classroom interaction (Walsh, 2011), but one possible interpretation of this extract sees the learners as engaging in a series of clarification requests about their homework (i.e., *'do we need to draw a picture?'* and *'do we need to write number one on the book?'*). S3's final question about current classroom activity (i.e., *'do we get the green book four?'*) could be regarded as a confirmation check. Whatever our classification of the differing elements within the transcript, it is clear that the learners and teacher have to engage cooperatively and negotiate meaning to ensure the teacher's initial instructions are understood.

Task 6.3 Learning a skill, learning a language

In this task, note the differences between approaches that equate L2 learning to the learning of other skills, and those perspectives that see language learning as different to learning other kinds of knowledge (for example, those approaches that draw on ideas of innatism and Universal Grammar).

Task 7.1 Language learners: some initial thoughts

This task asks you to think through what learners bring to the language classroom in terms of their key attributes and attitudes. You can compare your answers to the points made in the discussions that follow this task in the chapter.

Task 7.2 Aptitude: implications for teaching

The literature focusing on aptitude suggests that many teachers are 'suspicious' of the concept as it seems to raise issues of fairness and equality of treatment for all learners. However, these doubts are in part based around more traditional notions of aptitude as a fixed ability. If, however, aptitude is seen as a dynamic set of abilities that combine during specific learning tasks, which learners may be introduced to and practise, perhaps these views might change over time.

In practical terms, however, the 'fixed ability' perspective continues to resonate within many educational systems, raising a series of questions and possibilities. *Selecting learners who are likely to succeed and barring those who are likely to fail* is 'unthinkable in most settings with open access to education' (V. Cook, 2016: 163), while *streaming learners according to aptitude* is a common practice in many educational settings. *Teaching learners with different aptitude in different ways with varied exercises in the same class and varied assessments* may seem desirable but, in practical terms, would seem costly in terms of staffing and resources. *Excusing low aptitude learners from L2 learning* occurs in many contexts. Thus in addition to debates focusing on classroom pedagogy, the question of how to deal with differences in learner aptitude raises wider concerns of 'access', 'fairness', and, indeed, the role of and importance attached to L2 learning in society at large (there are links here to the discussion in Chapter 3 of values in ELT).

Task 8.1 'Good language learners': first thoughts

As the chapter goes on to note, the many published reviews of 'good L2 learner' characteristics quite reasonably highlight factors such as a focus on meaning and the ability to take risks. Less often emphasized is the notion that successful language learning involves hard work as well as, for example, the ability to engage in social interaction. During this task, readers might also consider whether the characteristics of a 'good language learner' might be different for children, teenagers and adults (a point returned to in Task 8.2).

Task 9.1 'Teachability' in practice . . . and in your practice

An L2 classroom based solely around the learners' 'internal syllabus' would see little need to follow an external syllabus. Learners would encounter language in the classroom, but would learn according to their own 'natural' learning order. By not specifying the language items to be taught in advance, classes would develop a *process* or *procedural* syllabus (see Chapter 10 for further discussion). A focus on form, rather than forms, would be likely.

Pienemann's 'Teachability Hypothesis' offers a slightly different perspective to the process syllabus, suggesting that an external syllabus *can* be followed, but that it should focus only on language that learners are developmentally ready to learn, i.e., syllabuses should be organized according to what we know about learners' 'internal syllabuses' through the study of morpheme acquisition order.

An alternative viewpoint is that acquisition order studies focus on a limited number of morphemes and draw on naturalistic rather than classroom-based learning. Thus, while learners may have an internal syllabus, it is too difficult to predict and follow; classes should therefore continue to follow a pre-planned external syllabus.

Task 9.3 'Constructing' learners: first thoughts

Possible metaphors for learning include the *banking of information*; *movement* or *being on a journey* or *quest*; *growth*; *switching on a light bulb*; *travelling through fog*, etc. From earlier chapters, we can also identify ideas such as *scaffolding*, *constructing* (knowledge) and the *affective filter* as metaphorical perspectives on learning.

Task 10.3 First thoughts: real and invented language in the classroom

The real conversation recorded in Example 1 includes a range of features that are typical of spoken language, including: discourse markers (e.g., *'right'*), ellipsis (e.g., *'tea or coffee?'* rather than *'would you like tea or coffee?'*); vague language (e.g., *'you know'*); hesitations (e.g., *'er'*); back-channelling, where listeners signal that they are actually listening (e.g., *'yeah'* and *'Mm'*); the use of *'tend to'* to describe regular actions, events or habits; incomplete utterances; and speakers interrupting each other and speaking at the same time. In contrast, most of these features are absent from the invented dialogue in Example 2. There is very little vague language; speaker 2 (Sally) shows interest by using 'content' words (e.g., *'intelligent'*, *'athletic'*) rather than *'Mm'* or *'Right'*; there are few hesitations and no interruptions. Example 2 also focuses on specific language items – the modal verb *'can'* is notable as is the amount of vocabulary that is introduced.

Thus, while the scripted text of Example 2 provides an unrealistic model of real discourse, it is easier for learners to understand and, therefore, potentially more 'real' pedagogically. Meanwhile, Example 1 is likely to be more difficult for learners to understand and produce and could be considered less 'real' pedagogically. Nevertheless, learners often want to know what 'real English' is and, as the discussion in Chapter 10 makes clear, there is certainly a case for drawing upon 'real' language in the ELT classroom.

Task 12.2 Thinking about NESTs and non-NESTs

As the discussion in Chapter 12 suggests, the division of English language users into 'native' and 'non-native' speakers is increasingly problematic – far more important than where people were born or what language they first learned is how effectively people use the language in specific contexts, in effect, how 'expert' they are at using English. As Chapter 12 notes, this does not depend on 'native speaker status', and hopefully, in years to come, the attention given to whether someone is a 'native' or 'non-native' speaker will fade.

That said, in many contexts around the world, the status of a teacher as either a NEST or non-NEST does, unfortunately, result in differences in status, pay and working conditions. It is hoped, however, that by focusing on what teachers can do regardless of where they are from, 'native-speakerism' in ELT might be overcome.

Glossary

Glossary entries are cross-referenced in **bold**.

acculturation
the process of adapting socially and psychologically to a new culture, implying the creation of a second identity.

achievement test
an assessment measuring how well learners have done on a particular programme of study.

action research
research often undertaken by teachers that aims to solve immediate problems and improve practice in their own professional environment, typically following a cycle of *plan-act-observe-reflect*.

adjacency pair
in conversation, the occurrence of two consecutive utterances by two speakers in which the first turn provokes the response, e.g., a question and answer or an offer and an acceptance.

affect
feelings and emotion, including factors such as **anxiety** and **motivation**.

affective filter
a hypothetical mechanism that reflects learners' emotional readiness to learn. A 'raised' affective filter is said to block or slow down learning.

agency
portraying an active and positive image of learners, agency suggests learners approach learning with their own agendas and purposes.

anomie
a feeling of social uncertainty and lack of cultural attachment.

anxiety
feelings of nervousness, stress or tension, often associated with second language contexts.

apprenticeship of observation
the informal and largely unreflective observation and evaluation of teachers undertaken by schoolchildren who later become teachers themselves.

approach
sometimes distinguished from **method**, approach refers to the coherent set of assumptions about language and language learning that underpin L2 teaching methods and methodology. However, the term is often used interchangeably with 'method'.

aptitude
once seen as a fixed ability to learn languages, aptitude is now more often regarded as an 'umbrella term' for a range of cognitive abilities that come together in complex ways to facilitate (and usually increase the rate of) language learning.

assessment
a broad term encompassing the activities through which learners' proficiency and progress is monitored. See also **testing**.

audiolingualism/audiolingual method
a language teaching method based on **behaviourist** theories of learning and structural approaches to language, and emphasizing habit formation through repetition and controlled practice.

authenticity
a notion emphasizing 'real-world' language, language use and texts in language learning.

automatization
the process of internalizing knowledge so that a task can be performed automatically, thereby freeing up the learner's cognitive resources.

autonomy
the capacity of individuals to take charge of, and responsibility for, their own learning. Autonomy can be realized in a number of ways.

behaviourism
psychological theory that suggests learning, including language learning, is the result of habit formation via a process of 'stimulus-response-reinforcement'.

blended learning
learning through a combination of online technologies and more traditional face-to-face instruction.

bottom-up processes
focusing on the linguistic elements of a text (e.g., words, sounds, clause and sentence structure) to gain understanding of it.

caretaker talk
the modified or simplified language sometimes used by L1 speakers to address language learners. Some teacher talk can be conceptualized as a form of caretaker talk.

classroom interaction
the general term for social encounters within the L2 classroom, particularly those related to language.

cognitive learning theories
perspectives that examine the ways in which the mind receives, stores, processes and makes connections with information. Learners' internal mental processes are emphasized, language learning being seen as similar to learning other types of knowledge.

communicative competence
the ability to use language effectively and appropriately across a variety of contexts and social settings.

communicative language teaching (CLT)
an approach to language teaching that emphasizes the importance of meaning in interaction and the ability to communicate successfully.

community language learning
a 'humanistic' language teaching method in which teachers act as 'consultants', learners take responsibility for lesson content, and interpersonal relationships are emphasized.

community of practice
a group of people engaged in the same task (e.g., language learning) with a shared set of understandings and behaviours.

competence
see **linguistic competence**.

complexity perspective
a perspective that looks to understand phenomena such as classrooms holistically, making sense of them as a dynamic system of multiple, interacting and interrelated parts which cannot be separated. From a complexity perspective, the classroom system is also 'nested' in wider institutional, educational and societal systems.

comprehensible input
language that learners can understand.

computer assisted language learning (CALL)
language learning that utilizes computers, including online and offline technologies.

connectionism
a cognitive approach to L2 learning in which learners are said to subconsciously identify patterns within input, connecting elements and finding regularities.

content-based instruction
an arguably North American term for approaches which use a language other than the learners' L1 as a medium of instruction for other subjects, such as maths or geography. Overlaps significantly with **content and language intergrated learning (CLIL)**.

content and language integrated learning (CLIL)
initially developed in Europe, an approach which uses a language other than the learners' L1 as a medium of instruction for other subjects, such as maths or geography. Overlaps significantly with **content-based instruction (CBI)**.

corrective feedback
responses by teachers or peers to learner utterances that contain **errors**, and which indicates that an error has been made.

critical period hypothesis (CPH)
the suggestion that the biological mechanisms that enable children to acquire language operate most successfully before puberty.

critical pedagogy
an approach that assumes that power and politics are central elements of education and society, and that existing power structures should be critiqued and challenged.

curriculum
in British usage, the planning, implementation and evaluation of an educational programme, including, for example, its overall aims, content, instructional process, materials and assessment.

data-driven learning (DDL)
an approach that brings linguistic data (in the form of corpora) into the classroom in order that learners can research language for themselves.

declarative knowledge
knowledge that learners have and can talk about, i.e., 'knowing about'.

deductive learning
the presentation of rules, which are then applied.

developmental error
an error that is the consequence of the learner's developing internal language system.

developmental sequence/stage
the order in which certain features of a language are acquired.

direct method
teaching based on the beliefs that only the target language should be used in class, that grammar should be taught inductively, and that there should be no translation.

English as a lingua franca (ELF)
use of English between non-native speakers who do not share a first language.

English for specific purposes (ESP)
the English language and skills necessary to meet a specific need or role, for example, an occupation or academic study.

error
incorrect or idiosyncratic language resulting from the learner's developing internal second language system.

exploratory practice
a form of practitioner research in which teachers and learners work together to explore and understand classroom life.

expressive morality
the subtle acts and gestures through which teachers (and learners) send messages about their values.

extrinsic motivation
motivation to do something arising from factors 'external' to the activity itself, e.g., to receive praise or a reward from another person.

focus on form
attending to language forms and structures at any stage of instruction, often as they arise within the context of meaningful interaction. This may be achieved by simply highlighting the form, by correction, or by explicit explanation.

focus on forms
instruction that is organized around the systematic presentation of language forms.

foreigner talk
see caretaker talk.

formative assessment
assessment that aims to support learning and improve learners' performance, usually as a course is progressing.

fossilization
a lack of change in a learner's **interlanguage**, with errors becoming permanent.

global error
an error that hinders understanding and communication.

grammar-translation method
an approach to language teaching in which learners focus on grammar rules and vocabulary memorization. Teaching is **deductive** and focuses on written language, requiring learners to translate example sentences.

genre
a type of discourse, spoken or written, which has a particular form or set of conventions, e.g., a sports commentary, a lecture, an email, an academic essay.

ideal L2 self
who or what the learner would like to be as an L2 user, based on their hopes and aspirations.

inductive learning
inferring rules about language from examples.

information processing
an approach to learning that suggests that there is a limit to the amount of information learners can consciously focus on at any one time. Through repeated practice, such information is processed and **automatized**, freeing learners to attend to other things.

innatism
theoretical approaches suggesting that humans are born with an innate knowledge of, and the mental ability to acquire, language.

input
the language, either spoken or written, that learners are exposed to.

input hypothesis
the theory, associated with Krashen, which suggests that L2 acquisition occurs when learners are exposed to **comprehensible input** and have a low **affective filter**, i.e., they are receptive to the input.

instrumental orientation
learning a second language for practical reasons, such as passing an exam or getting a better job.

intake
the language that a learner retains from L2 instruction and/or **input** (also referred to as uptake).

integrative orientation
learning an L2 based on the learner's identification with the target culture and even their desire to integrate with members of that community.

interaction hypothesis
the suggestion, by Long, that language learning results from the learners' ability to

process input and, furthermore, on their ability to generate input and negotiate meanings through interaction and conversation.

interference error
an error resulting from the influence of the learner's L1 on their L2.

interlanguage
a learner's developing internal second language system that lies somewhere between the learner's first language and their second language. Interlanguages are systematic, but also develop as learners revise their internalized hypotheses about the L2.

internal syllabus
drawing on evidence of **developmental sequences** in language acquisition and ideas surrounding the **natural order** of L2 development, learners are said to have an 'internal syllabus' that establishes the route of L2 acquisition.

intrinsic motivation
motivation arising from the wish to engage in an activity itself, rather than in anticipation of an external reward.

investment
learners are said to invest in L2 learning if they believe it will provide them with the knowledge and ways of thinking they need to function successfully in society. Proponents of 'investment' suggest that this social perspective contrasts with the more individual viewpoint implicit in the concept of **motivation**.

language acquisition
often used interchangeably with **language learning**. However, some theorists (e.g., Krashen) note a contrast between acquisition and learning, suggesting that acquisition is unconscious and 'natural' and takes place when the focus is on meaning rather than form.

language ego
the identity a person develops or assumes through language. Learning a second language, with the possibility of making errors and not being understood, may threaten a learner's ego.

language learning
in this book, a general term for learners' L2 development. However, learning has been contrasted with **language acquisition** by some researchers (e.g., Krashen) and involves conscious study of language.

language learning strategies
mental and physical activities that are chosen by learners in order to fulfil a specific purpose or achieve a specific goal, learners using strategies to regulate and control their own language learning.

learnability
see **teachability hypothesis**.

learner training
focusing on *how* to learn rather than *what* to learn, learner training aims to help learners make more effective use of the **learning opportunities** they encounter and encourage **learner autonomy**.

learning opportunity
learners may learn from any encounter with the target language, although what they might learn can be unpredictable.

learning styles
preferred ways of learning that are relatively stable, e.g., group-oriented or individualistic, verbal or visual.

linguistic competence
underlying knowledge of a language system and its grammar, rather than the actual use of language.

linguistic imperialism
the suggestion that the spread and teaching of English perpetuates colonial (or neo-colonial) attitudes and practices, thereby promoting the political and economic interests of English L1 speaking countries.

local error
an error that relates to only part of a message and does not prevent it from being understood.

metalanguage
the language that teachers use to explain or describe the target language; broader definitions of metalanguage include the language of classroom management such as instructions.

method
an increasingly problematic concept, but traditionally seen as a theoretically consistent set of teaching principles that would lead to the most effective learning outcomes if followed correctly.

methodology
what practising teachers actually do in the classroom to achieve their stated or unstated teaching objectives.

mistake
a performance error, or slip, in language that learners know and might usually get right.

motivation
an abstract term used to explain why people think and behave as they do, and which subsumes a whole range of motives that influence behaviour.

native speaker
a problematic term that is increasingly questioned, but, traditionally, a person who has acquired a particular language from an early age and is fully proficient in that language.

native-speakerism
the belief that **native speakers** and 'Western culture' represent an ideal in terms of language norms, English language teachers and associated ELT methodology.

natural order hypothesis
the suggestion that the order in which L2 items are acquired is predictable; see also **developmental sequences** and **internal syllabus**.

negotiation of meaning
interaction between speakers who adjust their speech to make themselves understood and to **repair** misunderstandings.

noticing
the suggestion that learners need to 'pay attention' to or 'notice' language consciously before they can understand and produce it.

notional-functional syllabus
central to the emergence of **CLT**, a syllabus primarily organized around functions (e.g., 'apologizing' or 'requesting') and notions (e.g., 'logical relationships' or 'time and duration').

ought-to self
a sense of what or who others would like the language learner to be, reflecting the learner's perceived sense of obligations and responsibilities.

output
the language that learners produce, both spoken and written.

output hypothesis
the suggestion, associated with Swain, that language production, especially spoken output, is necessary for L2 acquisition to take place.

paradigm
according to Kuhn, a widely accepted or common-sense way of thinking and behaving within 'normal science', legitimizing what counts as 'proper' theory and practice.

Postmethod
the notion that teaching and learning needs to move 'beyond methods', enabling teachers to develop a 'principled eclecticism' that is appropriate to local contexts.

presentation-practice-production (PPP)
a three-stage approach to teaching in which language is first presented to learners

who subsequently engage in controlled practice, focusing on accuracy. Finally, learners 'produce' the language creatively in 'free practice'.

procedural knowledge
knowledge of how to do something, and which underpins fluent or automatic language use.

process/procedural syllabus
a syllabus that prioritizes the route or 'means' of learning rather than specifying L2 outcomes or the 'ends' of learning.

proficiency test
a test measuring the level learners have reached in the L2, unrelated to a specific language course or programme.

recast
repeating a learner's incorrect utterance, but reformulating it into a correct form, phrase or sentence.

receptivity
with links to ideas surrounding **acculturation** and **investment**, receptivity is a readiness, either temporary or permanent, to become a speaker of another language.

reliability
the extent to which a test provides consistent results.

repair
a general term for the correction or modification of speech, either self-initiated or in response to teacher or peer feedback.

restructuring
within **cognitive learning theories**, some theorists argue that learning does not occur at a steady pace. Instead, restructuring is the process through which learners accommodate new knowledge through short bursts of understanding.

scaffolding
the interactional support given to learners that enables them to communicate successfully at a level beyond their current **competence**. See also **sociocultural learning theory** and the **zone of proximal development**.

silent way
a 'humanistic' language teaching method that draws upon the belief that language learning is a personal enterprise. In practice, the teacher keeps silent for much of the class, thereby requiring learners to create language rather than repeat it.

sociocultural learning theory
a view of learning that emphasizes the importance of social interaction, so that knowledge is 'jointly constructed' before being internalized by individuals; language

plays a central 'mediating' role in this process. See also **zone of proximal development**.

standard variety

the variety of a language that is usually used in writing, taught in schools and can be found in grammar books. English has a number of standard varieties, e.g., American English, British English and also Indian English, Singaporean English etc.

structural syllabus

a programme of study that is organized primarily around forms, most typically sequences of discrete grammatical items. See also **focus on forms**.

suggestopedia

a 'humanistic' language teaching method that proposes that learning can be accelerated via the processes of suggestion, relaxation and concentration, all of which can be enhanced by the physical environment in which learning takes place.

summative assessment

end of course tests; see also **achievement test**.

syllabus

in British usage, the content of a particular language programme or the step-by-step guide that sequences and organizes content, specifying what is to be taught.

task

a classroom activity in which attention is focused primarily on meaning as learners aim to replicate real-world communication.

task-based language teaching (TBLT)

also called task-based learning (TBL) and task-based teaching (TBT), an approach to language teaching in which **tasks** are the central organizing principle of the **syllabus** and of lessons.

teachability hypothesis

the suggestion that instruction should focus only on language that learners are developmentally ready to learn, i.e., that language items should be taught in the same order as they are acquired (see also **developmental sequences**, the **internal syllabus** and the **natural order hypothesis**).

teacher research

research carried out by teachers, usually focusing on their own professional practices in their own classrooms. Approaches to teacher research include **action research** and **exploratory practice**.

testing

a specific part of **assessment**, the formal or standardized tests for the purposes of certification or decision-making.

top-down processes
focusing on the whole text to understand it, drawing on what is known from outside of the text (e.g., context, prior knowledge of the topic and experience) for comprehension.

total physical response (TPR)
a 'humanistic' language teaching method that links physical action to learning; for example, learners follow commands.

universal grammar (UG)
the theory that all languages consist of a common set of linguistic principles, i.e., a universal grammar, of which humans have an innate knowledge (see also **innatism**).

validity
the extent to which a test measures what it is supposed to measure.

washback
the influence of a test, either positive or negative, on teaching and learning, e.g., 'teaching for the test'.

working memory (WM)
the cognitive 'space' or system where learners store new information in the short term, while also actively processing the information through processes such as hypothesis formation, reasoning and decision-making.

world Englishes
a term that recognizes (and values) the varieties of English spoken and written around the world, challenging the notion of a single **native speaker** norm.

zone of proximal development (ZPD)
associated with Vygotsky, the ZPD is the 'place' where, working with peers and 'better others', learners can work at a level that would otherwise be beyond their reach.

Further reading

Readers wishing to reflect further upon ELT can, of course, refer to specific sources cited in the preceding chapters. Beyond this, however, you may want to consider the following suggestions for further reading. Some of these titles extend topics already covered in this book, others focus on topics touched on here but not covered extensively for reasons of space.

Books

Allwright, D. and Hanks, J. (2009) *The Developing Language Learner: An Introduction to Exploratory Practice*. Basingstoke: Palgrave Macmillan.
An overview of Exploratory Practice, including a thoroughly argued rationale, case-studies and resources.

Benson, P. (2011) *Teaching and researching autonomy*. 2nd Edition. London: Pearson.
A thorough review of autonomy in language learning, taking in research and practice.

Biber, D., Johansson, S., Leech, G., Conrad, S. and Finegan, E. (1999) *Longman Grammar of Spoken and Written English*. London: Longman.
One of several corpus-based grammars that increasingly inform applied linguists' and teachers' understandings of the language component of ELT.

Braine, G. (2010) *Nonnative Speaker English Teachers: Research, Pedagogy, and Professional Growth*. London: Routledge.
A thorough consideration of the native/non-native speaker teacher issue.

Burns, A. (2010) *Doing Action Research in English Language Teaching: A Guide for Practitioners*. London: Routledge.
A guide to Action Research written for teachers and teacher educators.

Burns, A. and Richards, J. (2012) *The Cambridge Guide to Pedagogy and Practice in Second Language Teaching*. Cambridge: CUP.
Thirty chapters covering a range of topics relevant to this book.

Hall, G. (ed.) (2016) *The Routledge Handbook of English Language Teaching*. London: Routledge.
A collection of thirty-nine chapters, examining further the key issues and areas of debate outlined in this book.

Hewings, A. and Hewings, M. (2005) *Grammar and Context: An Advanced Resource Book*. London: Routledge.
A textbook that again illustrates the ways in which corpus data can add to our understandings of the English language.

Howatt, A. with Widdowson, H. (2004) *A History of English Language Teaching*. 2nd edition. Oxford, OUP.
An illuminating history of English language teaching from 1400 CE onwards.

Johnston, B. (2003) *Values in English Language Teaching*. London: Routledge.
A wide-ranging discussion of values and morality within ELT.

Liddicoat, A. and Scarino, A. (2013) *Intercultural Language Teaching and Learning*. Chichester, UK: Wiley-Blackwell.
A survey of issues in intercultural language teaching and learning, ranging from key concepts to classroom practices.

Lightbown, P. (2014) *Focus on Content-Based Language Teaching*. Oxford: OUP.
An overview of content-based teaching, its challenges and possible classroom practices.

McGrath, I. (2013) *Teaching Materials and the Roles of EFL/ESL Teachers: Practice and Theory*. London: Bloomsbury.
A discussion of language teaching materials in terms of their production and also how teachers and learners use materials in practice.

Mitchell, R., Myles, F., and Marsden, E. (2013) *Second Language Learning Theories*. 3rd edition. London: Hodder Education.
One of a number of texts reviewing SLA research in some detail.

Ortega, L. (2009) *Understanding Second Language Acquisition*. London: Hodder Education.
A further review of theories of L2 learning.

Pennycook, A. (2001) *Critical Applied Linguistics: A Critical Introduction*. Mahwah, NJ: Routledge.
A challenging introduction to critical approaches within applied linguistics and ELT.

Richards, J. and Rodgers, T. (2014) *Approaches and Methods in Language Teaching*. 3rd edition. Oxford: OUP.
A title that systematically summarizes the major language teaching approaches and methods.

Seargeant, P. (2012) *World Englishes: Language in Action*. London: Routledge.
An overview of the spread and current role of English and Englishes in the world.

Seidlhofer, B. (ed.) (2003) *Controversies in Applied Linguistics*. Oxford: OUP.
A collection of reprinted articles in which prominent applied linguists argue different positions on a series of issues.

Thomas, M., Reinders, H., and Warschauer, M. (eds) (2012) *Contemporary computer-assisted language learning*. London: Bloomsbury.
One of several texts examining developments in the rapidly changing field of CALL and new technologies.

Walsh, S. (2011) *Classroom Discourse: Language in Action*. London: Routledge.
A text that examines the relationship between classroom interaction and language learning in detail.

Williams, M., Mercer, S., and Ryan, S. (2015) *Exploring Psychology in Language Learning and Teaching*. Oxford: OUP.
An accessible book that explores key aspects of educational and social psychology, and outlines their relevance to language teaching and learning.

Wright, T. (2005) *Classroom Management in Language Education*. Basingstoke: Palgrave Macmillan.
A thorough discussion of classroom management, covering research and practice.

Journals

A wide range of relevant papers can also be found in the following journals:

Applied Linguistics
www.applij.oxfordjournals.org/
This journal publishes research into a variety of applied linguistics topics.

ELT Journal (ELTJ)
www.eltj.oxfordjournals.org/
Articles in *ELTJ* are often written by ELT practitioners and aim to link everyday practices to theoretical concepts and discussions.

System
www.sciencedirect.com/science/journal/0346251X
System publishes applied linguistic research into language teaching and learning.

TESL-EJ
www.tesl-ej.org/wordpress/
TESL-EJ is an online (and free) electronic and peer-reviewed journal publishing a range of articles and reviews concerned with ELT.

TESOL Quarterly
www.ingentaconnect.com/content/tesol/tq
   TESOL Quarterly (*TQ*) publishes research into, and explores ideas surrounding, English language teaching and learning.

References

Adamson, B. (2004) 'Fashions in Language Teaching Methodology', in A. Davies and C. Elder (eds) *The Handbook of Applied Linguistics*. London: Blackwell, 604–22.

Akbari, R. (2008) 'Postmethod Discourse and Practice'. *TESOL Quarterly*, 42/4: 641–52.

Alderson, C. (2009) 'Setting the Scene', in C. Alderson (ed.) *The Politics of Language Education: Individuals and Institutions*. Bristol: Multilingual Matters, 8–44.

Allwright, D. (1979) 'Language Learning Through Communication Practice', in C. Brumfit and K. Johnson (eds) *The Communicative Approach to Language Teaching*. Oxford: OUP.

Allwright, D. (1980) 'Turns, Topics and Tasks: Patterns of Participation in Language Learning and Teaching', in D. Larsen-Freeman (ed.) *Discourse Analysis in Second Language Research*. Rowley, MA: Newbury House, 165–87.

Allwright, D. (1981) 'What Do We Want Teaching Materials For?' *ELT Journal*, 36/1: 5–19.

Allwright, D. (1983) *The Nature and Function of the Syllabus in Language Teaching and Learning*. Unpublished paper, Lancaster University.

Allwright, D. (1984) 'Why Don't Learners Learn What Teachers Teach? The Interaction Hypothesis', in D. Singleton and D. Little (eds) *Language Learning in Formal and Informal Contexts*. Dublin: IRAAL, 3–18.

Allwright, D. (1991) 'The Death of the Method', *CRILE Working Paper*, No. 10. Lancaster: Lancaster University.

Allwright, D. (1992) *Making Sense of Classroom Language Learning*. Unpublished Ph.D. thesis, Department of Linguistics, Lancaster University.

Allwright, D. (1996) 'Social and Pedagogic Pressure in the Language Classroom: The Role of Socialisation', in H. Coleman (ed.) *Society and the Language Classroom*. Cambridge: CUP, 209–28.

Allwright, D. (2003) 'Exploratory Practice: Rethinking Practitioner Research in Language Teaching'. *Language Teaching Research*, 7/2: 113–41.

Allwright, D. (2005) 'From Teaching Points to Learning Opportunities and Beyond'. *TESOL Quarterly*, 39/1: 9–32.

Allwright, D. and Bailey, K. (1991) *Focus on the Language Classroom*. Cambridge: CUP.

Allwright, D. and Hanks, J. (2009) *The Developing Language Learner: An Introduction to Exploratory Practice*. Basingstoke: Palgrave Macmillan.

Amnpalagan with Smith, R., Ajjan, M. and Kuchah, H. (2012) 'Large class teaching and responses'. Retrieved from www.warwick.ac.uk/telc/strategies/

Anderson, J. (2015) 'Affordance, learning opportunities and the lesson plan pro forma'. *ELT Journal*, 69/3: 228–38.

Anderson, J. (1983) *The Architecture of Cognition*. Cambridge, MA: Harvard University Press.

Anthony, E. (1963) 'Approach, Method and Technique'. *English Language Teaching*, 17: 63–7.

Appel, J. (1995) *Diary of a Language Teacher*. Oxford: Heinemann.

Arnold, J. and Brown, H. (1999) 'A Map of the Terrain', in J. Arnold (ed.) *Affect in Language Learning*. Cambridge: CUP, 1–24.

Asher, J. (1977) *Learning Another Language Through Actions: The Complete Teacher's Guidebook*. California: Sky Oaks Productions.

Auerbach, E. (1995) 'The Politics of the ESL Classroom: Issues of Power in Pedagogical Choices', in J. Tollefson (ed.) *Power and Inequality in Language Education*. Cambridge: CUP, 9–33.

Bachman, L. (1990) *Fundamental Considerations in Language Testing*. Oxford: OUP.

Bailey, K. (1983) 'Competitiveness and Anxiety in Adult Second Language Acquisition: Looking *At* and *Through* the Diary Studies', in H. Seliger and M. Long (eds) *Classroom Oriented Research in Second Language Acquisition*. Rowley, MA: Newbury House, 67–103.

Bailey, N., Madden, C. and Krashen, S. (1974) 'Is There a "Natural Sequence" in Adult Second Language Learning?' *Language Learning*, 24/2: 235–43.

Bancroft, W. J. (1972) 'The Psychology of Suggestopedia or Learning Without Stress'. *The Educational Courier* (February), 16–19.

Barcelos, A. (2003) 'Researching Beliefs about SLA: A Critical Review', in P. Kalaja and A. Barcelos (eds) *Beliefs about SLA: New Research Approaches*. Netherlands: Kluwer, 7–33.

Bartel, R. (1983) *Metaphors and Symbols: Forays into Language*. Urbana, IL: National Council of Teachers of English.

Bartram, M. and Walton, R. (1991) *Correction: A Positive Approach to Language Mistakes*. Boston, USA: Thompson Heinle.

Bax, S. (2003) 'The End of CLT: A Context Approach to Language Teaching'. *ELT Journal*, 57/3: 278–87.

Bax, S. (2006) 'The Role of Genre in Language Syllabus Design: The Case of Bahrain'. *International Journal of Educational Development*, 26/3: 315–28.

Bell, D. (2003) 'Method and Postmethod: Are They Really so Incompatible?' *TESOL Quarterly*, 37/2: 325–36.

Bell, D. (2007) 'Do Teachers Think that Methods are Dead?' *ELT Journal*, 61/2: 135–43.

Benson, P. (2001) *Autonomy in Language Learning*. Harlow: Longman.

Benson, P. (2003) 'Learner Autonomy in the Classroom', in D. Nunan (ed.) *Practical English Language Teaching*. New York: McGraw-Hill, 289–308.

Benson, P. (2016) 'Learner autonomy', in G. Hall (ed.) *The Routledge Handbook of English Language Teaching*. London: Routledge, 339–52.

Benson, P. and Lor, W. (1999) 'Conceptions of Language and Language Learning'. *System*, 27/4: 459–72.

Benson, P., Chik, A., and Lim, H-Y. (2003) 'Becoming Autonomous in an Asian Context: Autonomy as a Sociocultural Process', in D. Palfreyman and R. Smith (eds) *Learner Autonomy Across Cultures: Language Education Perspectives*. Basingstoke: Palgrave Macmillan, 23–40.

Bialystok, E. (1982) 'On the Relationship Between Knowing and Using Linguistic Forms'. *Applied Linguistics*, 3/3: 181–206.

Bisong, J. (1995) 'Language Choice and Cultural Imperialism: A Nigerian Perspective'. *ELT Journal*, 49/2: 122–32.

Blake, R. (2000) 'Computer mediated communication: a window on Spanish L2 interlanguage'. *Language Learning and Technology*, 4/1: 120–36.

Block, D. (1997) 'Listening to Language Learners'. *System*, 25/3: 347–60.

Block, D. and Cameron, D. (eds) (2002) *Globalization and Language Teaching*. London: Routledge.

Bolitho, R., Gower, R., Johnson, K., Murison-Bowie, S. and White, R. (1983) 'Talking Shop: The Communicative Teaching of English in Non-English-speaking Countries'. *ELT Journal*, 37/3: 235–42.

Borg, E. (2003) 'Discourse Community'. *ELT Journal*, 57/4: 398–400.

Borg, M. (2001) 'Teachers' Beliefs'. *ELT Journal*, 55/2: 186–8.

Borg, M. (2004) 'The Apprenticeship of Observation'. *ELT Journal*, 58/3: 274–5.

Borg, S. (2006) *Teacher Cognition and Language Education: Research and Practice*. London: Continuum.

Borg, S. (2013) *Teacher research in language teaching: A critical analysis*. Cambridge: CUP.

Boulton, A. (2010) 'Data-driven learning: Taking the computer out of the equation'. *Language Learning*, 60/3: 534–72.

Breen, M. (1984) 'Process Syllabuses for the Language Classroom', in C. Brumfit (ed.) *General English Syllabus Design (ELT Documents 118)*. Oxford: Pergamon Press, 47–60.

Breen, M. (1998) 'Navigating the Discourse: On What is Learned in the Language Classroom', in W. Renandya and G. Jacobs (eds) *Learners and Language Learning Anthology Series 39*. Singapore: SEAMO Regional Language Centre, 115–43.

Breen, M. (2001a) 'The Social Context for Language Learning: A Neglected Situation?', in C. Candlin and N. Mercer (eds) *English Language Teaching in its Social Context*. London: Routledge, 122–44.

Breen, M. (2001b) 'Postscript: New Directions for Research on Learner Contributions', in M. Breen (ed.) *Learner Contributions to Language Learning*. Harlow: Longman, 172–82.

Breen, M. and Candlin, C. (1987) 'Which Materials? A Consumer's and Designer's Guide', in L. Sheldon (ed.) *ELT Textbooks and Materials: Problems in Evaluation and Development*. Oxford: Modern English Publications and the British Council, 13–28.

Briggs, J. and Moore, P. (1993) *The Process of Learning*. 3rd edition. Sydney: Prentice Hall.

Brown, H. (2001) *Teaching by Principles: An Interactive Approach to Language Pedagogy*. 2nd edition. New York: Longman.

Brown, H. (2007) *Principles of Language Learning and Teaching*. 5th edition. New York: Longman.

Brown, R. (1973) *A First Language: The Early Stages*. Cambridge, MA: Harvard University Press.

Brumfit, C. (1981). 'Talking Shop'. *ELT Journal*, 36/1: 29–36.

Brumfit, C. J. (1982) 'Some Humanistic Doubts About Humanistic Language Teaching', in P. Early (ed.) *Humanistic Approaches: An Empirical View (ELT Documents 113)*. London: The British Council.

Brumfit, C. (1984) *Communicative Methodology in Language Teaching: The Roles of Fluency and Accuracy*. Cambridge: CUP.

Brumfit, C. (2001) *Individual Freedom in Language Teaching*. Oxford: OUP.

Bruton, A. (2013) 'CLIL: Some of the reasons why…and why not'. *System*, 41/3: 587–97.

Bullock, D. and Smith, R. (eds) (2015) *Teachers Research!* Faversham: IATEFL Research Special Interest Group.

Burns, A. (2010) *Doing Action Research in English Language Teaching: A Guide for Practitioners*. London: Routledge.

Burns, A. and Burton, J. (eds) (2008) *Language Teacher Research in Australia and New Zealand*. Alexandria, VA: TESOL, Inc.

Burns, A. and Richards, J. (eds) (2012) *The Cambridge Guide to Pedagogy and Practice in Second Language Teaching*. Cambridge: CUP.

Butzkamm, W. (1989/2002) *Psycholinguistik des Fremdsprachenunterrichts. Natürliche Künstlichkeit: Von der Muttersprache zur Fremdsprache*. Tübingen: Francke. (Nature and artifice. From mother tongue to foreign language: a psycholinguistic approach.) English summary in H. Weinstock (ed.), (1991) *English and American Studies in German*. A supplement to Anglia: Tübingen: Neimeyer. 171–5.

Byram, M. (2004a) 'Audiolingual Method', in M. Byram (ed.) *Routledge Encyclopedia of Language Teaching and Learning*. London: Routledge, 58–60.

Byram, M. (2004b) 'Aptitude for Language Learning', in M. Byram (ed.) *Routledge Encyclopedia of Language Teaching and Learning*. London: Routledge, 37–8.

Cain, R. (2004) 'Total Physical Response', in M. Byram (ed.) *Routledge Encyclopedia of Language Teaching and Learning*. London: Routledge, 631–3.

Canagarajah, A. S. (1999) *Resisting Linguistic Imperialism*. Oxford: OUP.

Canagarajah, A. S. (2006) 'TESOL at Forty: What are the Issues?' *TESOL Quarterly*, 40/1: 9–34.

Candlin, C. (1984) 'Syllabus Design as a Critical Process', in C. Brumfit (ed.) *General English Syllabus Design (ELT Documents 118)*. Oxford: Pergamon Press, 29–46.

Carroll, J. (1990) 'Cognitive Abilities in Foreign Language Aptitude: Then and Now', in T. Parry and C. Stansfield (eds) *Language Aptitude Reconsidered*. New Jersey: Center for Applied Linguistics and Prentice Hall, 11–29.

Carter, R. (1998) 'Orders of Reality: CANCODE, Communication, and Culture'. *ELT Journal*, 52/1: 43–56.

Carter, R. and McCarthy, M. (1997) *Exploring Spoken English*. Cambridge: CUP.

Cenoz, J. (2015) 'Content-based instruction and content and integrated language learning: the same or different?' *Language, Culture and Curriculum*, 28/1: 8–24.

Chamot, A. (2001) 'The Role of Learning Strategies in Second Language Acquisition', in M. Breen (ed.) *Learner Contributions to Language Learning*. Harlow: Longman, 25–43.

Chapelle, C. (1997) 'CALL in the Year 2000: Still in Search of Research Paradigms?' *Language Learning & Technology*, 1/1: 19–43.

Chapelle, C. (2001) 'Opening Plenary ELT, Technology and Change', in A. Pulverness (ed.) *IATEFL 2001 Brighton Conference Selections*. Whitstable: IATEFL, 9–18.

Chapelle, C. (2010) 'The Spread of Computer-assisted Language Learning'. *Language Teaching*, 43/1: 66–74.

Chaudron, C. (1988) *Second Language Classrooms: Research on Teaching and Learning*. Cambridge: CUP.

Cheng, W. (2011) *Corpus Linguistics: Language in Action*. London: Routledge.

Chomsky, N. (1959) 'Review of "Verbal Behaviour" by B. F. Skinner'. *Language*, 35/1: 26–58.

Chomsky, N. (1966) 'Linguistic Theory'. Reprinted in J. Allen and P. Van Buren (eds) *Chomsky: Selected Readings*. Oxford: OUP, 152–9.

Clapham, C. (2004) 'Assessment and Testing', in M. Byram (ed.) *Routledge Encyclopedia of Language Teaching and Learning*. London: Routledge, 48–53.

Clark, J. (1991). *Curriculum Renewal in School Foreign Language Learning*. Oxford: OUP.

Clarke, M. (1983) 'The Scope of Approach, the Importance of Method, and the Nature of Techniques', in J. Alatis, H. Stern and P. Strevens (eds) *Georgetown University Roundtable on Language and Linguistics*. Washington, DC: Georgetown University Press, 106–15.

Cohen, A. (2004) 'Age Factors', in M. Byram (ed.) *Routledge Encyclopedia of Language Teaching and Learning*. London: Routledge, 21–4.

Coleman, H. (2006) 'Darwin and the Large Class', in S. Gieve and I. Miller (eds) *Understanding the Language Classroom*. Basingstoke: Palgrave Macmillan, 115–35.

Collier, M. (1979) *A Film Study in Classrooms in Western Alaska*. Fairbanks Center for Cross-Cultural Studies: University of Alaska.

Collins, L. and Marsden, E. (2016) 'Cognitive perspectives on classroom language learning', in G. Hall (ed.) *The Routledge Handbook of English Language Teaching*. London: Routledge, 281–294.

Conlon, G., Litchfield, A. and Sadlier, G. (2011) 'Estimating the value to the UK of Education Exports'. *Department for Business, Innovation and Skills (BIS) Research Paper 43*. London: BIS, UK Government.

Cook, G. (1994) 'Repetition and Learning by Heart: An Aspect of Intimate Discourse and its Implications'. *ELT Journal*, 48/2: 133–41.

Cook, G. (1998) 'The Uses of Reality: A Reply to Ronald Carter'. *ELT Journal*, 52/1: 57–63.

Cook, G. (2003) *Applied Linguistics*. Oxford: OUP.

Cook, G. (2008). 'Plenary: An Unmarked Improvement: Using Translation in ELT', in B. Beaven (ed.) *IATEFL 2007 Aberdeen Conference Selections*. Canterbury: IATEFL, 76–85.

Cook, G. (2010) *Translation in Language Teaching*. Oxford: OUP.

Cook, V. (2001) 'Using the First Language in the Classroom'. *Canadian Modern Language Review*, 57/3: 402–23.

Cook, V. (2016) *Second Language Learning and Language Teaching*. 5th edition. London: Hodder Education.

Coombe, C., McCloskey, M., Stephenson, L., and Anderson, N. (eds) (2008) *Leadership in English Language Teaching and Learning*. Ann Arbor, MI: University of Michigan Press.

Corbridge-Pataniowska, M. (1948/1992) *Teach Yourself Polish*. London: Hodder & Stoughton.

Corder, S. (1967) 'The Significance of Learners' Errors'. *International Review of Applied Linguistics*, 5: 161–70.

Corder, S. (1973) *Introducing Applied Linguistics*. Harmondsworth: Penguin.

Corder, S. (1981) *Error Analysis and Interlanguage*. Oxford: OUP.

Cortazzi, M. and Jin, L. (1996) 'Cultures of Learning: Language Classrooms in China', in H. Coleman (ed.) *Society and the Language Classroom*. Cambridge: CUP, 169–206.

Cotterall, S. (2008) 'Autonomy and Good Language Learners', in C. Griffiths (ed.) *Lessons from Good Language Learners*. Cambridge: CUP, 110–20.

Coyle, D., Hood, P. and Marsh, D. (2010) *CLIL: Content and Integrated Language Learning*. Cambridge: CUP.

Crandall, J. (2012) 'Content-Based Instruction and Content and Language Integrated Learning', in A. Burns and J. Richards (eds) *The Cambridge Guide to Pedagogy and Practice in Second Language Teaching*. Cambridge: CUP, 149–60.

Crookes, G. (2003) *A Practicum in TESOL: Professional Development through Language Teaching*. Cambridge: CUP.

Crookes, G. (2009) *Values, Philosophies, and Beliefs in TESOL: Making a Statement*. Cambridge: CUP.

Crookes, G. (2016) 'Educational perspectives on ELT: society and the individual; traditional, progressive and transformative', in G. Hall (ed.) *The Routledge Handbook of English Language Teaching*. London: Routledge, 64–76.

Crookes, G. and Schmidt, R. (1991) 'Motivation: Reopening the Research Agenda'. *Language Learning*, 41/4: 469–512.

Crystal, D. (2000) *Language Death*. Cambridge: CUP.

Crystal, D. (2012) 'A Global Language', in P. Seargeant and J. Swann (eds) *English in the world: History, diversity, change*. Abingdon: Routledge, 151–77.

Cullen, R. (2002) 'Supportive Teacher Talk: The Importance of the F-move'. *ELT Journal*, 56/2: 117–27.

Curran, C. (1972) *Counseling-Learning: A Whole Person Model for Education*. New York: Grune & Stratton.

Dalton-Puffer, C., Llinares, A., Lorenzo, F. and Nikula, T. (2014) 'You can stand under my umbrella: Immersion, CLIL and bilingual education. A response to Cenoz, Genesee and Gorter'. *Applied Linguistics*, 35/2: 213–18.

Daniels, J. (2004) 'Acculturation', in M. Byram (ed.) *Routledge Encyclopedia of Language Teaching and Learning*. London: Routledge, 1–3.

Davies, A. (1995) 'Proficiency or the Native Speaker: What Are We Trying to Achieve in ELT?', in G. Cook and B. Seidlhofer (eds) *Principle and Practice in Applied Linguistics*. Oxford: OUP, 145–58.

Davies, A. (2003) 'Three Heresies of Language Testing Research'. *Language Testing*, 20/4: 355–68.

Davies, A. (2004) 'The Native Speaker in Applied Linguistics', in A. Davies and C. Elder (eds) *The Handbook of Applied Linguistics*. London: Blackwell, 431–50.

De Bot, K. (1996) 'The psycholinguistics of the Output Hypothesis'. *Language Learning*, 46/3: 529–55.

DeKeyser, R. (ed.) (2007) *Practice in a second language: Perspectives from applied linguistics and cognitive psychology*. Cambridge: CUP.

Dewey, J. (1909) *Moral Principles in Education*. Boston: Houghton Mifflin.

Dikilitaş, K., Wyatt, M., Hanks, J. and Bullock, D. (2016) *Teachers Engaging in Research*. Faversham: IATEFL Research Special Interest Group.

DiPietro, R. (1987) *Strategic interaction: Learning languages through scenarios*. Cambridge: CUP.

Dörnyei, Z. (2001) *Motivational Strategies in the Language Classroom*. Cambridge: CUP.

Dörnyei, Z. (2005) *The Psychology of the Language Learner*. Mahwah, NJ: Routledge.

Dörnyei, Z. (2009) *The Psychology of Second Language Acquisition*. Oxford: OUP.

Dörnyei, Z. and Csizér, K. (1998) 'Ten Commandments for Motivating Language Learners: Results of an Empirical Study'. *Language Teaching Research*, 2/3: 203–29.

Douglas, D. (2010) *Understanding Language Testing*. London: Hodder Education.

Duda, R. and Riley, P. (2004) 'Learning Styles', in M. Byram (ed.) *Routledge Encyclopedia of Language Teaching and Learning*. London: Routledge, 346–51.

Dudeney, G. and Hockly, N. (2012) 'ICT in ELT: how did we get here and where are we going?' *ELT Journal*, 66/4: 533–42.

Dudley-Evans, A. and St John, M. (1998) *Developments in English for Specific Purposes*. Cambridge: CUP.

Dulay, H. and Burt, M. (1974) 'Natural Sequences in Child Second Language Acquisition'. *Language Learning*, 24/1: 37–53.

Edge, J. (1989) *Mistakes and Correction*. London: Longman.

Edge, J. (1996) 'Cross-cultural Paradoxes in a Profession of Values'. *TESOL Quarterly*, 30/1: 9–30.

Edge, J. (ed.) (2001) *Action Research*. Alexandria, VA: TESOL, Inc.

Edge, J. (ed.) (2002) *Continuing Professional Development*. Whitstable: IATEFL.

Edge, J. and Garton, S. (2009) *From Knowledge to Experience in ELT*. Oxford: OUP.

Edwards, E. and Burns, A. (2016) 'Language teacher action research: achieving sustainability'. *ELT Journal*, 70/1: 6–15.

Ehrman, M. (1996) *Understanding Second Language Learning Difficulties*. Thousand Oaks, CA: Sage Publications.

Ehrman, M. (2008). 'Personality and Good Language Learners', in C. Griffiths (ed.) *Lessons from Good Language Learners*. Cambridge: CUP, 61–72.

Ehrman, M., Leaver, B. and Oxford, R. (2003) 'A Brief Overview of Individual Differences in Second Language Learning'. *System*, 31/3: 313–30.

Eklöf, H. (2010) 'Skill and will: Test-taking motivation and assessment quality'. *Assessment in Higher Education: Principles, Policy & Practice*, 17/4: 345–56.

Ellis, G. and Sinclair, B. (1989) *Learning to Learn English: Teacher's Book*. Cambridge: CUP.

Ellis, R. (1985) *Understanding Second Language Acquisition*. Oxford: OUP.

Ellis, R. (1992) *Second Language Acquisition and Language Pedagogy*. Clevedon: Multilingual Matters.

Ellis, R. (1994) *The Study of Second Language Acquisition*. 1st edition. Oxford: OUP.

Ellis, R. (1997) *Second Language Acquisition*. Oxford: OUP.

Ellis, R. (1998) 'Plenary: Second Language Acquisition Research – What's in it for Teachers?', in P. Grundy (ed.) *IATEFL 1998 Manchester Conference Selections*. Canterbury: IATEFL, 10–18.

Ellis, R. (1999) 'Theoretical Perspectives on Interaction and Language Learning', in R. Ellis (ed.) *Learning a Second Language Through Interaction*. Amsterdam: John Benjamins, 3–31.

Ellis, R. (2001) 'The Metaphorical Constructions of Second Language Learners', in M. Breen (ed.) *Learner Contributions to Language Learning*. Harlow: Longman, 65–85.

Ellis, R. (2003) *Task-Based Language Teaching and Learning*. Oxford: OUP.

Ellis, R. (2005) 'Principles of Instructed Language Learning'. *System*, 33/2: 209–24.

Ellis, R. (2006). 'Current Issues in the Teaching of Grammar: An SLA Perspective'. *TESOL Quarterly*, 40/1: 83–107.

Ellis, R. (2009) 'Task-based Language Teaching: Sorting out the Misunderstandings'. *International Journal of Applied Linguistics*, 19/3: 221–46.

Ellis, R. and Shintani, N. (2014) *Exploring Language Pedagogy through Second Language Acquisition Research*. London: Routledge.

English UK (2013) *Estimate of the value of ELT to the UK's towns, cities, counties and nations*. London: English UK.

Ericksen, S. (1984) *The Essence of Good Teaching*. San Francisco: Jossey-Bass.

Erikson, F. (1986) 'Qualitative Methods in Research on Teaching', in M. Wittrock (ed.) *Handbook of Research on Teaching*. Chicago: Rand McNally, 119–61.

Eysenck, H. (1965) *Fact and Fiction in Psychology*. Harmondsworth: Penguin.

Field, J. (2011) *Listening in the language classroom*. Cambridge: CUP.

Finkbeiner, C. (2008) 'Culture and Good Language Learners', in C. Griffiths (ed.) *Lessons from Good Language Learners*. Cambridge: CUP, 131–41.

Firth, A. and Wagner, J. (1997) 'On Discourse, Communication, and (Some) Fundamental Concepts in SLA Research'. *Modern Language Journal*, 81/3: 285–300.

Forey, G. and Lockwood, J. (eds) (2010) *Globalization, Communication and the Workplace*. London: Continuum.

Frankenberg-Garcia, A. (2016) 'Corpora in ELT', in G. Hall (ed.) *The Routledge Handbook of English Language Teaching*. London: Routledge, 383–98.

Freeman, D. (1996) 'Redefining the Relationship Between Research and What Teachers Should Know', in K. Bailey and D. Nunan (eds) *Voices from the Language Classroom*. Cambridge: CUP, 88–115.

Freire, P. (1970/1993) *Pedagogy of the Oppressed*. London: Penguin.

Fulcher, G. and Owen, N. (2016) 'Dealing with the demands of language testing and assessment', in G. Hall (ed.) *The Routledge Handbook of English Language Teaching*. London: Routledge, 109–20.

Gardner, R. (1985) *Social Psychology and Language Learning: The Role of Attitudes and Motivation*. London: Edward Arnold.

Garrett, N. (2009) 'Computer-assisted language learning trends and issues revisited: Integrating innovation'. *Modern Language Journal*, 93/1: 719–40.

Gass, S. and Selinker, L. (2008) *Second Language Acquisition: An Introductory Course*. 3rd edition. Oxford: Routledge.

Gass, S. and Varonis, E. (1986) 'Sex Differences in Non-native Speaker Interactions', in R. Day (ed.) *Talking to Learn: Conversation in Second Language Acquisition*. New York: Newbury House.

Georgiou, S. I. (2012) 'Reviewing the puzzle of CLIL'. *ELT Journal*, 66/4: 495–504.

Gieve, S. and Miller, I. (2006) 'What do we mean by "Quality of Classroom Life"?', in S. Gieve and I. Miller (eds) *Understanding the Language Classroom*. Basingstoke: Palgrave Macmillan, 18–46.

Goh, C. and Burns, A. (2012) *Teaching speaking: a holistic approach*. Cambridge: CUP.

Goldberg, L. and Rosolack, T. (1994) 'The Big Five factor structure as an integrative framework: an empirical comparison with Eysenck's PEN model', in C. Halverston Jr, G. Kohnstamm and R. Martin (eds) *The developing structure of temperament and personality from infancy to adulthood*. New York: Lawrence Erlbaum, 7–35.

González Davies, M. (2004) *Multiple Voices in the Translation Classroom*. Amsterdam: John Benjamins.

Graves, K. (2000) *Designing language courses: a guide for teachers*. Boston: Heinle Cengage.

Graves, K. (2008) 'The Language Curriculum: A Social Contextual Perspective'. *Language Teaching*, 41/2: 147–81.

Gray, J. (2016) 'ELT materials: claims and critiques', in G. Hall (ed.) *The Routledge Handbook of English Language Teaching*. London: Routledge, 95–108.

Greer, D. (2000) 'The eyes of hito: A Japanese cultural monitor of behavior in the communicative language classroom'. *JALT Journal*, 22/1: 183–95.

Gregersen, T. and MacIntyre, P. (2014) *Capitalizing on Learner Individuality*. Bristol: Multilingual Matters.

Griffiths, C. (2008) 'Strategies and Good Language Learners', in C. Griffiths (ed.) *Lessons from Good Language Learners*. Cambridge: CUP, 83–98.

Griffiths, C. (2015) 'What have we learnt from "good language learners"?' *ELT Journal*, 69/4: 425–33.

Griffiths, C. and Oxford, R. (2014) 'The twenty-first century landscape of language learning strategies: Introduction to this special issue'. *System*, 43: 1–10.

Gruba, P. (2004) 'Computer Assisted Language Learning', in A. Davies and C. Elder (eds) *The Handbook of Applied Linguistics*. London: Blackwell, 623–48.

Gruba, P., Hinkelman, D., and Cárdenas-Claros, M. S. (2016) 'New technologies, blended learning and the "flipped classroom" in ELT', in G. Hall (ed.) *The Routledge Handbook of English Language Teaching*. London: Routledge, 135–49.

Grundy, P. (1999) 'Comment: From Model to Muddle'. *ELT Journal*, 53/1: 54–5.

Grundy, P. (2004) 'Humanistic Language Teaching', in M. Byram (ed.) *Routledge Encyclopedia of Language Teaching and Learning*. London: Routledge, 282–5.

Gu, Y. (2002) 'Gender, Academic Major, and Vocabulary Learning Strategies of Chinese EFL Learners'. *RELC Journal*, 33/1: 35–54.

Hafernik, J., Messerschmitt, D. and Vandrick, S. (2002). *Ethical Issues for ESL Faculty*. Mahwah, NJ: Routledge.

Hall, C. (2013) 'Cognitive Contributions to Plurilithic Views of English and Other Languages'. *Applied Linguistics*, 34/2: 211–31.

Hall, G. (2016) 'Method, methods and methodology: historical trends and current debates', in G. Hall (ed.) *The Routledge Handbook of English Language Teaching*. London: Routledge, 209–23.

Hall, G. and Cook, G. (2012) 'Own-language use in language teaching and learning'. *Language Teaching*, 45/3: 271–308.

Hall, G. and Cook, G. (2013) *Own-language use in ELT: exploring global practices and attitudes in ELT*. London: British Council.

Hanks, J. (2017) *Exploratory Practice in Language Teaching: Puzzling About Principles and Practices*. Basingstoke: Palgrave Macmillan.

Hansen, D. (1993) 'From Role to Person: The Moral Layeredness of Classroom Teaching'. *American Educational Research Journal*, 30/4: 651–74.

Harmer, J. (2003) 'Popular Culture, Methods and Context'. *ELT Journal*, 57/3: 288–94.

Harmer, J. (2007) *The Practice of English Language Teaching*. 4th edition. Harlow: Longman.

Harmer, J. (2015) *The Practice of English Language Teaching*. 5th edition. Harlow: Longman.

Hartley, B. and Viney, P. (1978) *Streamline English Departures (Unit 14)*. Oxford: OUP.

Harwood, N. (ed.) (2010) *English Language Teaching Materials: Theory and Practice*. Cambridge: CUP.

Harwood, N. (ed.) (2014) *English Language Teaching Textbooks: Content, Consumption, Production*. Basingstoke: Palgrave Macmillan.

Hayes, D. (1997) 'Helping Teachers to Cope with Large Classes'. *ELT Journal*, 51/2: 106–16.

Heaton, J. (1988) *Writing English Language Tests*. Harlow: Longman.

Hendrickson, J. (1978) 'Error Correction in Foreign Language Teaching: Recent Theory, Research and Practice'. *Modern Language Journal*, 62: 387–98.

Heron, J. (1989) *The Facilitator's Handbook*. London: Kogan Page.

Hess, N. (2001) *Teaching large multilevel classes*. Cambridge: CUP.

Hockly, N. (2015) 'Developments in online learning'. *ELT Journal*, 69/3: 308–13.

Holec, H. (1981) *Autonomy and Foreign Language Learning*. Oxford: Pergamon.

Holliday, A. (1994) *Appropriate Methodology and Social Context.* Cambridge: CUP.

Holliday, A. (2003) 'Social Autonomy: Addressing the Dangers of Culturism in TESOL', in D. Palfreyman and R. Smith (eds) *Learner Autonomy Across Cultures: Language Education Perspectives.* Basingstoke: Palgrave Macmillan, 110–26.

Holliday, A. (2005) *The Struggle to Teach English as an International Language.* Oxford: OUP.

Holliday, A. (2006a) 'What Happens between People: Who We Are and What we Do', in S. Gieve and I. Miller (eds) *Understanding the Language Classroom.* Basingstoke: Palgrave Macmillan, 47–63.

Holliday, A. (2006b) 'Native-speakerism'. *ELT Journal,* 60/4: 385–7.

Holme, R. (2004) 'Metaphor', in M. Byram (ed.) *Routledge Encyclopedia of Language Teaching and Learning.* London: Routledge, 410–13.

Howatt, A. (1984) *A History of English Language Teaching.* 1st edition. Oxford: OUP.

Hsiao, J. (2010) 'Suggestions for using "A Very Practical Guide to the New TOEIC"'. Coursework Assignment, MA TESOL module in Materials Evaluation and Design, University of Nottingham (Malaysia).

Hubbard, P., Jones, H., Thornton, B. and Wheeler, R. (1983) *A Training Course in TEFL.* Hong Kong: OUP.

Hunter, D. and Smith, R. (2012) 'Unpackaging the past: "CLT" through ELTJ keywords'. *ELT Journal,* 66/4: 430–9.

Hutchinson, T. and Torres, E. (1994) 'The Textbook as Agent of Change'. *ELT Journal,* 48/4: 315–28.

Hutchinson, T. and Waters, A. (1987) *English for Specific Purposes.* Cambridge: CUP.

Hymes, D. (1972) 'On Communicative Competence', in J. Gumperz and D. Hymes (eds) *Directions in Sociolinguistics.* New York: Holt & Reinhardt.

Impey, G. and Underhill, N. (1994) *The ELT Manager's Handbook.* Oxford: Macmillan.

Jackson, P. (1992) 'Conceptions of Curriculum and Curriculum Specialists', in P. Jackson (ed.) *Handbook of Research on Curriculum.* New York: Macmillan.

Jacobs, G. and Farrell, T. (2003) 'Understanding and Implementing the CLT (Communicative Language Teaching) Paradigm'. *RELC Journal,* 34/1: 5–30.

Jenkins, J. (2005) *World Englishes: A Resource Book for Students.* 1st edition. London: Routledge.

Jenkins, J. (2006) 'The Spread of EIL: A Testing Time for Testers'. *ELT Journal,* 60/1: 42–50.

Jenkins, J. (2007) *English as a Lingua Franca: Attitude and Identity.* Oxford: OUP.

Jenkins, J. (2015) *Global Englishes: A Resource Book for Students.* 3rd edition. London: Routledge.

Jenkins, J., Cogo, A. and Dewey, M. (2011) 'Review of developments in research into English as a Lingua Franca'. *Language Teaching,* 44/3: 281–315.

Jiménez Raya, M., Lamb, T. and Vieira, F. (2007) *Pedagogy for autonomy in language education in Europe: towards a framework for learner and teacher development.* Dublin: Authentik.

Johns, A. (ed.) (2002) *Genre in the Classroom: Multiple Perspectives*. Mahwah, NJ: Routledge.

Johns, T., (1991) 'Should you be persuaded: Two samples of data-driven learning materials'. *English Language Research Journal*, 4: 1–16.

Johnson, R. K. (1989) 'A Decision-making Framework for the Coherent Language Curriculum', in R. K. Johnson (ed.) *The Second Language Curriculum*. Cambridge: CUP, 1–23.

Johnson, K. (1996) *Language Teaching and Skill Learning*. Oxford: Blackwell.

Johnson, K. (2008) *An Introduction to Foreign Language Learning and Teaching*. 2nd edition. Harlow: Longman.

Johnson, K. E. (1999) *Understanding Language Teaching: Reasoning in Action*. London: Heinle & Heinle.

Johnston, B. (2003) *Values in English Language Teaching*. London: Routledge.

Johnston, B., Juhász, A., Marken, J. and Rolfs Ruiz, B. (1998) 'The ESL Teacher as Moral Agent'. *Research in the Teaching of English*, 32/2: 161–81.

Kachru, B. (1985) 'Standards, Codification and Sociolinguistic Realism: The English Language in the Outer Circle', in R. Quirk and H. Widdowson (eds) *English in the World: Teaching and Learning the Language and Literatures*. Cambridge: CUP, 11–36.

Kelly, L. (1969) *25 Centuries of Language Teaching*. Rowley, MA: Newbury House.

Kennedy, C. (2010) 'Learning English in a Global Context', in S. Hunston and D. Oakey (eds) *Introducing Applied Linguistics: Concepts and Skills*. London: Routledge, 87–93.

Kern, R. (2006) 'Perspectives on Technology in Learning and Teaching Languages'. *TESOL Quarterly*, 40/1: 183–210.

Kern, R., Ware, P. and Warschauer, M. (2016) 'Computer-mediated communication and language learning', in G. Hall (ed.) *The Routledge Handbook of English Language Teaching*. London: Routledge, 542–55.

Kerr, P. (2016) 'Questioning English-only classrooms: own-language use in ELT', in G. Hall (ed.) *The Routledge Handbook of English Language Teaching*. London: Routledge, 513–26.

Kirkpatrick, A. (2007) *World Englishes*. Cambridge: CUP.

Kramsch, C. (1987) 'Interactive Discourse in Small and Large Groups', in W. Rivers (ed.) *Interactive Language Teaching*. Cambridge: CUP, 17–30.

Kramsch, C. (2003) 'Metaphor and the Subjective Construction of Belief', in P. Kalaja and A. M. Barcelos (eds) *New Approaches to Research on Beliefs about SLA*. New York: Springer, 109–28.

Krashen, S. (1977) 'Some Issues Relating to the Monitor Model', in H. Brown, C. Yorio and R. Crymes (eds) *On TESOL '77: Teaching and Learning English as a Second Language: Trends in Research and Practice*. Washington: TESOL, Inc., 144–58.

Krashen, S. (1982) *Principles and Practice in Second Language Acquisition*. Oxford: Pergamon.

Krashen, S. (1985) *The Input Hypothesis: Issues and Implications*. Harlow: Longman.

Krashen, S. and Terrell, T. (1983) *The Natural Approach: Language Acquisition in the Classroom*. Oxford: Pergamon.

Kuhn, T. (1970/1996) *The Structure of Scientifics Revolutions*. 3rd edition. Chicago: University of Chicago Press.

Kukulska-Hulme, A., Sharples, M., Milrad, M., Arnedillo-Sánchez, I. and Vavoula, G. (2009) 'Will mobile learning change language learning?' *ReCALL*, 21/1: 157–65.

Kumaravadivelu, B. (1993) 'The Name of the Task and the Task of Naming: Methodological Aspects of Task-Based Pedagogy', in G. Crookes and S. Gass (eds) *Tasks in Pedagogical Context*. Clevedon: Multilingual Matters, 69–96.

Kumaravadivelu, B. (1994) 'The Postmethod Condition: (E)merging Strategies for Second/Foreign Language Teaching'. *TESOL Quarterly*, 28/1: 27–48.

Kumaravadivelu, B. (2003) *Beyond Methods: Macrostrategies for Language Teaching*. New Haven, CT: Yale University Press.

Kumaravadivelu, B. (2006) *Understanding Language Teaching: From Method to Postmethod*. Mahwah, NJ: Routledge.

Kumaravadivelu, B. (2012) *Language Teacher Education for a Global Society*. London: Routledge.

Lakoff, G. and Johnson, M. (1980) *Metaphors We Live By*. Chicago/London: Chicago University Press.

Lamb, M. (2016) 'Motivation', in G. Hall (ed.) *The Routledge Handbook of English Language Teaching*. London: Routledge, 324–38.

Lantolf, J. and Pavlenko, A. (2001) '(S)econd (L)anguage (A)ctivity Theory: Understanding Second Language Learners as People', in M. Breen (ed.) *Learner Contributions to Language Learning*. Harlow: Longman, 141–58.

Larsen-Freeman, D. (2001) 'Individual Cognitive/Affective Learner Contributions and Differential Success in Second Language Acquisition', in M. Breen (ed.) *Learner Contributions to Language Learning*. Harlow: Longman, 12–24.

Larsen-Freeman, D. and Anderson, M. (2011) *Techniques and Principles in Language Teaching*. 3rd edition. Oxford: OUP.

Larsen-Freeman, D. and Cameron, L. (2008) *Complex Systems and Applied Linguistics*. Oxford: OUP.

Larsen-Freeman, D. and Long, M. (1991). *An Introduction to Second Language Acquisition Research*. Harlow: Longman.

Lave, J. (1988) *The Culture of Acquisition and the Practices of Understanding*. IRL Report 88-00087. Palo Alto, CA: Institute for Research on Learning.

Lewis, G. (2009) *Bringing Technology into the Classroom*. Oxford: OUP.

Li, L. (2011) 'Obstacles and opportunities for developing thinking through interaction in language classrooms'. *Thinking Skills and Creativity*, 6/3: 146–58.

Lightbown, P. (1983) 'Exploring Relationships Between Developmental Instructional Sequences in L2 Acquisition', in H. Seliger and M. Long (eds) *Classroom Oriented Research in Second Language Acquisition*. Rowley, MA: Newbury House, 217–43.

Lightbown, P. and Spada, N. (2013) *How Languages are Learned*. 4th edition. Oxford: OUP.

Lima, C. (2009) 'ELT and the Challenges of the Times'. *ELT Journal*, 63/3: 272–4.

Lima, C. (2010) 'The Classroom and the Coral Garden'. *IATEFL Voices*, 212: 6–7.

Little, D. (1999) 'Learner Autonomy is More Than a Western Cultural Construct', in S. Cotterall and D. Crabbe (eds) *Learner Autonomy in Language Learning: Defining the Field and Effecting Change*. Frankfurt am Main: Peter Lang, 69–77.

Little, D. (2004a) 'Strategies of Language Learning', in M. Byram (ed.) *Routledge Encyclopedia of Language Teaching and Learning*. London: Routledge, 579–81.

Little, D. (2004b) 'Autonomy and Autonomous Learners', in M. Byram (ed.) *Routledge Encyclopedia of Language Teaching and Learning*. London: Routledge, 69–72.

Littlejohn, A. (1992) *Why Are ELT Materials the Way they Are?* Unpublished Ph.D. thesis, Lancaster University. Online at: www.andrewlittlejohn.net/website/art/arthome.html

Littlewood, W. (1998) *Foreign and Second Language Learning*. Cambridge: CUP.

Long, M. (1983a) 'Does Second Language Instruction Make a Difference? A Review of Research'. *TESOL Quarterly*, 17/3: 359–82.

Long, M. (1983b). 'Inside the "Black Box"', in H. Seliger and M. Long (eds) *Classroom Oriented Research in Second Language Acquisition*. Rowley, MA: Newbury House, 3–36.

Long, M. (1983c) 'Native-speaker/Non-native speaker Conversation and the Negotiation of Comprehensible Input'. *Applied Linguistics*, 4/2: 126–41.

Long, M. (1985) 'Input and Second Language Acquisition Theory', in S. Gass and C. Madden (eds) *Input in Second Language Acquisition*. Rowley, MA: Newbury House, 377–9.

Long, M. (1988) 'Instructed Interlanguage Development', in L. Beebe (ed.) *Issues in Second Language Acquisition: Multiple Perspectives*. New York: Newbury House.

Long, M. (1996) 'The role of the linguistic environment in second language acqusition', in W. Ritchie and T. Bhatia (eds) *Handbook of Second Language Acquisition*. San Diego: Academic Press, 413–68.

Long, M. (2004) 'Acquisition and Teaching', in M. Byram (ed.) *Routledge Encyclopedia of Language Teaching and Learning*. London: Routledge, 4–5.

Long, M. (2007) *Problems in SLA*. New York: Routledge.

Long, M. and Porter, P. (1985) 'Group Work, Interlanguage Talk, and Second Language Acquisition'. *TESOL Quarterly*, 19/2: 207–28.

Lortie, D. (1975) *Schoolteacher: A Sociological Study*. London: University of Chicago Press.

Louden, W. (1991) 'Collegiality, Curriculum and Educational Change'. *Curriculum Journal*, 2/3: 361–73.

Lozanov, G. (1978) *Suggestology and Outlines of Suggestopedy*. New York: Gordon & Breach.

Lynch, T. (1996) *Communication in the Language Classroom*. Oxford: OUP.

Lynch, T. (1997) 'Nudge, Nudge: Teacher Interventions in Task-based Learner Talk'. *ELT Journal*, 51/4: 317–25.

Lyster, R. and Ranta, L. (1997) 'Corrective feedback and uptake'. *Studies in Second Language Acquisition*, 19/1: 37–66.

MacIntyre, P. and Gardner, R. (1994) 'The Subtle Effects of Language Anxiety on Cognitive Processing in Native and Second Languages'. *Language Learning*, 41: 283–305.

MacIntyre, P., Gregersen, T. and Clément, R. (2016) 'Individual Differences', in G. Hall (ed.) *The Routledge Handbook of English Language Teaching.* London: Routledge: 310–23.

Mackey, A., Park, H-I, and Tagarelli, K. (2016) 'Errors, corrective feedback and repair: variations and learning outcomes', in G. Hall (ed.) *The Routledge Handbook of English Language Teaching.* London: Routledge, 499–512.

Mackey, W. (1970) 'A Typology of Bilingual Education'. *Foreign Language Annals*, 3: 596–608.

Malamah-Thomas, A. (1987) *Classroom Interaction.* Oxford: OUP.

Maley, A. (2003) 'A Modest Proposal: From Research to Inquiry'. *Humanising Language Teaching*, 5/6.

Malinowski, B. (1935/2002) *Coral Gardens and their Magic.* London: Routledge.

Mann, S. and Walsh, S. (2017) *Reflective Practice in English Language Teaching: Research-Based Principles and Practices.* London: Routledge.

Martin, J. (1970) *Explaining, Understanding and Teaching.* New York: McGraw-Hill.

McGrath, I. (2013) *Teaching Materials and the Roles of EFL/ESL Teachers: Practice and Theory.* London: Bloomsbury.

McLaughlin, B. (1987) *Theories of Second Language Learning.* London: Edward Arnold.

McLaughlin, B. (1990) 'Restructuring'. *Applied Linguistics*, 11/2: 113–28.

McNamara, T. (2000) *Language Testing.* Oxford: OUP.

Meddings, L. and Thornbury, S. (2009) *Teaching Unplugged: Dogme in English Language Teaching.* Peaslake, UK: DELTA Publishing.

Medgyes, P. (1992) 'Native or Non-native: Who's Worth More?' *ELT Journal*, 46/4: 340–9.

Medgyes, P. (1994) *The Non-native Teacher.* Oxford: Macmillan.

Meerholz-Härle, B. and Tschirner, E. (2004) 'Classroom Language', in M. Byram (ed.) *Routledge Encyclopedia of Language Teaching and Learning.* London: Routledge, 110–13.

Mehisto, P., Marsh, D. and Frigols, M. (2008) *Uncovering CLIL: Content and Language Integrated Learning in Bilingual and Multilingual Education.* Oxford: Macmillan.

Menard-Warwick, J., Mori, M., Reznik, A. and Moglen, D. (2016) 'Values in the ELT classroom', in G. Hall (ed.) *The Routledge Handbook of English Language Teaching.* London: Routledge, 556–70.

Mercer, N. (2001) 'Language for Teaching a Language', in C. Candlin and N. Mercer (eds) *English Language Teaching in its Social Context.* London: Routledge, 243–57.

Mercer, S. (2016) 'Complexity and language teaching', in G. Hall (ed.) *The Routledge Handbook of English Language Teaching.* London: Routledge, 473–85.

Mitchell, R., Myles, F. and Marsden, E. (2013) *Second Language Learning Theories.* 3rd edition. London: Hodder Education.

Morton, T. (2016) 'Content and language integrated learning', in G. Hall (ed.) *The Routledge Handbook of English Language Teaching*. London: Routledge, 252–64.

Moskowitz, G. (1978) *Caring and Sharing in the Foreign Language Class*. Rowley, MA: Newbury House.

Muñoz, C. and Singleton, D. (2011) 'A critical review of age-related research on L2 ultimate attainment'. *Language Teaching*, 44/1: 1–35.

Murray, G. (ed.) (2014) *Social dimensions of autonomy in language learning*. Basingstoke: Palgrave Macmillan.

Naiman, N., Fröhlich, M., Stern, H. and Todesco, A. (1978) *The Good Language Learner*. Clevedon: Multilingual Matters.

Nation, I. S. P. (2009) *Teaching ESL/EFL Reading and Writing*. London: Routledge.

Nation, I. S. P. and Macalister, J. (2010) *Language curriculum design*. London: Routledge.

Negueruela-Azarola, E. and García, P. (2016) 'Sociocultural theory and the language classroom', in G. Hall (ed.) *The Routledge Handbook of English Language Teaching*. London: Routledge, 295–309.

Nel, C. (2008) 'Learning Style and Good Language Learners', in C. Griffiths (ed.) *Lessons from Good Language Learners*. Cambridge: CUP, 49–60.

Newby, D. (2004) 'Syllabus and Curriculum Design', in M. Byram (ed.) *Routledge Encyclopedia of Language Teaching and Learning*. London: Routledge, 590–4.

Newton, J. (2016) 'Teaching Language Skills', in G. Hall (ed.) *The Routledge Handbook of English Language Teaching*. London: Routledge, 428–40.

Norton, B. (2001) 'Non-participation, Imagined Communities and the Language Classroom', in M. Breen (ed.) *Learner Contributions to Language Learning*. Harlow: Longman, 159–71.

Norton, B. and Toohey, K. (2001) 'Changing Perspectives on Good Language Learners'. *TESOL Quarterly*, 35/2: 307–22.

Norton, B. and McKinney, C. (2011) 'An Identity Approach to Second Language Acquisition', in D. Atkinson (ed.) *Alternative Approaches to Second Language Acquisition*. London: Routledge, 73–94.

Norton Pierce, B. (1995) 'Social Identity, Investment, and Language Learning'. *TESOL Quarterly*, 29/1: 9–31.

Nunan, D. (1988a) *The Learner-Centred Curriculum: A Study in Second Language Teaching*. Cambridge: CUP.

Nunan, D. (1988b) *Syllabus Design*. Oxford: OUP.

Nunan, D. (1989a) 'Toward a Collaborative Approach to Curriculum Development: A Case Study'. *TESOL Quarterly*, 23/1: 9–25.

Nunan, D. (1989b) 'Hidden Agendas: The Role of the Learner in Programme Implementation', in R. K. Johnson (ed.) *The Second Language Curriculum*. Cambridge: CUP, 176–86.

Nunan, D. (1990) 'The Teacher as Researcher', in C. Brumfit and R. Mitchell (eds) *Research in the Language Classroom (ELT Documents 133)*. London: MEP in association with the British Council, 16–32.

Nunan, D. (1991) *Language Teaching Methodology*. New York: Prentice Hall.

Nunan, D. (2004) *Task-Based Language Teaching*. Cambridge: CUP.

Nunan, D. and Lamb, C. (1996) *The Self-Directed Teacher*. Cambridge: CUP.

Nunn, R. (1999) 'The Purpose of Language Teachers' Questions'. *International Review of Applied Linguistics*, 37: 23–42.

Nyikos, M. (2008) 'Gender and Good Language Learners', in C. Griffiths (ed.) *Lessons from Good Language Learners*. Cambridge: CUP, 73–82.

O'Keefe, A., McCarthy, M. and Carter, R. (2007) *From Corpus to Classroom: Language Use and Language Teaching*. Cambridge: CUP.

O'Malley, J. and Chamot, A. (1990) *Learning Strategies in Second Language Acquisition*. Cambridge: CUP.

O'Neill, R. (1991) 'The Plausible Myth of Learner-centredness: Or the Importance of Doing Ordinary Things Well'. *ELT Journal*, 45/4: 293–304.

Ortega, L. (2009) *Understanding Second Language Acquisition*. London: Hodder Education.

Oxford, R. (1990) *Language Learning Strategies: What Every Teacher Should Know*. New York: Newbury House.

Oxford, R. (1996) 'Why is Culture Important for Language Learning Strategies?', in R. Oxford (ed.) *Language Learning Strategies Around the World: Cross-Cultural Perspectives*. Honolulu: University of Hawai'i Press, ix–xv.

Oxford, R. (1999) 'Anxiety and the Language Learner: New Insights', in J. Arnold (ed.) *Affect in Language Learning*. Cambridge: CUP, 58–67.

Oxford, R. and Lee, K. (2008) 'The Learners' Landscape and Journey: A Summary', in C. Griffiths (ed.) *Lessons from Good Language Learners*. Cambridge: CUP, 306–17.

Oxford, R., Tomlinson, S., Barcelos, A., Harrington, C., Lavine, R., Saleh, A. and Longhini, A. (1998) 'Clashing Metaphors About Classroom Teachers: Toward a Systematic Typology for the Language Teaching Field'. *System*, 26/1: 3–50.

Pajares, M. (1992) 'Teacher's Beliefs and Educational Research: Cleaning up a Messy Construct'. *Review of Educational Research*, 62/3: 307–22.

Palfreyman, D. (2003) 'Introduction: Culture and Learner Autonomy', in D. Palfreyman and R. Smith (eds) *Learner Autonomy Across Cultures: Language Education Perspectives*. Basingstoke: Palgrave Macmillan, 1–19.

Pang, M. (2016) 'Companion guides for lesson planning: a planning template and the lesson plan pro forma'. *ELT Journal*, 70/4: 444–54.

Pawlak, M. (2008) 'Form-focused Instruction and the Acquisition of the Present Perfect', in B. Beaven (ed.) *IATEFL 2007 Aberdeen Conference Selections*. Canterbury: IATEFL, 193–6.

Pennycook, A. (1989) 'The Concept of Method, Interested Knowledge, and the Politics of Language Teaching'. *TESOL Quarterly*, 23/4: 589–618.

Pennycook, A. (1990) 'Critical Pedagogy and Second Language Education'. *System*, 18/3: 303–14.

Pennycook, A. (1994) *The Cultural Politics of English as an International Language*. Harlow: Longman.

Pennycook, A. (1997) 'Vulgar Pragmatism, Critical Pragmatism and EAP'. *English for Specific Purposes*, 16/4: 253–69.

Pennycook, A. (2000) 'The Social Politics and the Cultural Politics of Language Classrooms', in J. K. Hall and W. G. Eggington (eds) *The Sociopolitics of English Language Teaching*. Clevedon: Multilingual Matters, 89–103.

Pennycook, A. (2004) 'History: After 1945', in M. Byram (ed.) *Routledge Encyclopedia of Language Teaching and Learning*. London: Routledge, 275–82.

Pennycook, A. (2016) 'Politics, power relationships and ELT', in G. Hall (ed.) *The Routledge Handbook of English Language Teaching*. London: Routledge, 26–37.

Phillipson, R. (1992) *Linguistic Imperialism*. Oxford: OUP.

Phipps, S. and Borg, S. (2009) 'Exploring Tensions Between Teachers' Grammar Teaching Beliefs and Practices'. *System*, 37/3: 380–90.

Pienemann, M. (1985) 'Learnability and Syllabus Construction', in K. Hyltenstam and M. Pienemann (eds) *Modelling and Assessing Second Language Acquisition*. Clevedon: Multilingual Matters, 23–75.

Pienemann, M. (1989) 'Is Language Teachable? Psycholinguistic Experiments and Hypotheses'. *Applied Linguistics*, 10/1: 52–79.

Pienemann, M. (2003) 'Language Processing Capacity', in C. Doughty and M. Long (eds) *The Handbook of Second Language Acquisition*. Oxford: Blackwell, 679–714.

Prabhu, N. S. (1987) *Second Language Pedagogy*. Oxford: OUP.

Prabhu, N. S. (1990) 'There is No Best Method – Why?' *TESOL Quarterly* 24/2: 161–76.

Prodromou, L. (1996) 'Correspondence'. *ELT Journal*, 50/4: 371–3.

Quirk, R. (1990) 'Language Varieties and Standard Language'. *English Today*, 21: 3–10.

Rampton, B. (1990) 'Displacing the "Native Speaker": Expertise, Affiliation and Inheritance'. *ELT Journal*, 44/2: 97–101.

Ranta, L. (2008) 'Aptitude and Good Language Learners', in C. Griffiths (ed.) *Lessons from Good Language Learners*. Cambridge: CUP, 142–55.

Reid, J. (1987) 'The Learning Style Preferences of ESL Students'. *TESOL Quarterly*, 21/1: 87–111.

Reinders, H. and White, C. (2016) '20 Years of Autonomy and Technology: How far have we come and where to next?' *Language Learning & Technology*, 20/2: 143–54.

Révész, A. (2012) 'Working memory and the observed effectiveness of recasts on different L2 outcome measures'. *Language Learning*, 62/1: 93–132.

Richards, J. (1984) 'The Secret Life of Methods'. *TESOL Quarterly*, 18/1: 7–23.

Richards, J. (1998) *Beyond Training*. Cambridge: CUP.

Richards, J. (2001) *Curriculum Development in Language Teaching*. Cambridge: CUP.

Richards, J. (2013) 'Curriculum approaches in language teaching; Forward, central and backwards design'. *RELC Journal*, 44/1: 5–33.

Richards, J. and Farrell, T. (2005) *Professional Development for Language Teachers*. Cambridge: CUP.

Richards, J. and Rodgers, T. (2014) *Approaches and Methods in Language Teaching*. 3rd edition. Oxford: OUP.

Richards, J., Platt, T. and Weber, H. (1985) *A Dictionary of Applied Linguistics*. Harlow: Longman.

Richmond, I. (1999) 'Is Your CALL Connected? Dedicated Software vs. Integrated CALL', in K. Cameron (ed.) *CALL: Media, Design and Applications*. Lisse: Swets & Zeitlinger, 295–314.

Rivers, W. (1964) *The Psychologist and the Foreign Language Teacher*. Chicago: University of Chicago Press.

Rivers, W. (1981) *Teaching Foreign Language Skills*. 2nd edition. Chicago: University of Chicago Press.

Rivers, W. (1987) 'Interaction as the Key to Teaching Language for Communication', in W. Rivers (ed.) *Interactive Language Teaching*. Cambridge: CUP, 3–16.

Robinson, P. (2004) 'Languages for Specific Purposes', in M. Byram (ed.) *Routledge Encyclopedia of Language Teaching and Learning*. London: Routledge, 337–42.

Robinson, P. (2007) 'Aptitudes, abilities, contexts, and practice', in R. DeKeyser (ed.) *Practice in second language*. Cambridge: CUP, 256–86.

Rogers, J. (1982) '"The World for Sick Proper"'. *ELT Journal*, 36/3: 144–51.

Rosenshine, B. and Furst, N. (1973) 'The Use of Direct Observation to Study Teaching', in R. Travers (ed.) *Second Handbook on Research on Teaching*. Chicago: Rand McNally, 122–83.

Rowlinson, W. (1994) 'The Historical Ball and Chain', in A. Swarbrick (ed.) *Teaching Modern Languages*. London: The Open University, 7–17.

Rubin, J. (1975) 'What the "Good Language Learner" Can Teach Us'. *TESOL Quarterly*, 9/1: 41–51.

Savignon, S. (2001) 'Communicative language teaching for the twenty-first century', in M. Celce-Murcia (ed.) *Teaching English as a second or foreign language*. 3rd edition. Boston: Heinle Cengage Learning, 13–28.

Savignon, S. (2004) 'Communicative Language Teaching', in M. Byram (ed.) *Routledge Encyclopedia of Language Teaching and Learning*. London: Routledge, 124–9.

Scheidecker, D. and Freeman, W. (1999) *Bringing out the Best in Students: How Legendary Teachers Motivate Kids*. Thousand Oaks, CA: Corwin Press.

Schmidt, R. (1990) 'The Role of Consciousness in Second Language Learning'. *Applied Linguistics*, 11/1: 17–46.

Schmidt, R. and Frota, S. (1986) 'Developing Basic Conversational Ability in a Second Language: A Case-study of an Adult Learner of Portugese', in R. Day (ed.) *Talking to Learn: Conversation in Second Language Acquisition*. Rowley, MA: Newbury House, 237–326.

Schumann, J. (1978) *The Pidginization Process: A Model for Second Language Acquisition*. Rowley, MA: Newbury House.

Schumann, J. (1983) 'Art and Science in Second Language Acquisition Research'. *Language Learning*, 33/5: 49–75.

Schön, D. (1983) *The Reflective Practitioner: How Professionals Think in Action*. New York: Basic Books.

Scovel, T. (1979) 'Review of "Suggestology and Outlines of Suggestopedy"'. *TESOL Quarterly*, 13/2: 255–66.

Scovel, T. (2001) *Learning New Languages*. London: Heinle & Heinle.

Seargeant, P. (2012) *Exploring World Englishes: Language in Action*. London: Routledge.

Seargeant, P. (2016) 'World Englishes and ELF', in G. Hall (ed.) *The Routledge Handbook of English Language Teaching*. London: Routledge, 13–25.

Seedhouse, P. (1997) 'The Case of the Missing "No": The Relationship Between Pedagogy and Interaction'. *Language Learning*, 47: 547–83.

Seedhouse, P. (1999) 'Task-Based Interaction'. *ELT Journal*, 53/3: 149–56.

Seedhouse, P. (2004) *The Interactional Architecture of the Language Classroom: A Conversational Analysis Perspective*. Oxford: Blackwell.

Seidlhofer, B. (2003) *Controversies in Applied Linguistics*. Oxford: OUP.

Seidlhofer, B. (2011) *Understanding English as a Lingua Franca*. Oxford: OUP.

Selinker, L. (1972) 'Interlanguage'. *International Review of Applied Linguistics*. 10/3: 209–31.

Senior, R. (2006) *The Experience of Language Teaching*. Cambridge: CUP.

Sercu, L. (2004) 'Materials and Media', in M. Byram (ed.) *Routledge Encyclopedia of Language Teaching and Learning*. London: Routledge, 394–8.

Shamim, F. (1996) 'In or Out of the Action Zone: Location as a Feature of Interaction in Large ESL Classes in Pakistan', in K. Bailey and D. Nunan (eds) *Voices from the Language Classroom*. Cambridge: CUP, 123–44.

Shamim, F. (2012) 'Teaching large classes', in A. Burns and J. Richards (eds) *The Cambridge Guide to Pedagogy and Practice in Second Language Teaching*. Cambridge: CUP, 95–102.

Shamim, F. and Kuchah, K. (2016) 'Teaching large classes in difficult circumstances', in G. Hall (ed.) *The Routledge Handbook of English Language Teaching*. London: Routledge, 527–41.

Sharwood Smith, M. (2008) 'Plenary: You Can Take a Horse to Water but You Can't Make it Drink', in B. Beaven (ed.) *IATEFL 2007 Aberdeen Conference Selections*. Canterbury: IATEFL, 187–93.

Sheen, R. (2003). 'Focus on Form – a Myth in the Making?' *ELT Journal*, 57/3: 225–33.

Shehadeh, A. (2001) 'Self- and Other-initiated Modified Output During Task-based Interaction'. *TESOL Quarterly*, 35/4: 422–57.

Shohamy, E. (2001) *The Power of Tests*. Harlow: Longman.

Sinclair, J. (1997) 'Corpus Evidence in Language Description', in A. Wichmann, S. Fligelstone, T. McEnery and G. Knowles (eds) *Teaching and Language Corpora*. Harlow: Longman.

Sinclair, J. (editor in chief) (2005) *Collins COBUILD English Grammar*. 2nd edition. Glasgow: HarperCollins.

Sinclair, J. and Coulthard, M. (1975) *Towards an Analysis of Discourse*. Oxford: OUP.

Skehan, P. (1989) *Individual Differences in Second Language Learning*. London: Arnold.

Skehan, P. (1998) *A Cognitive Approach to Language Learning*. Oxford: OUP.

Skehan, P. (2016) 'Foreign language aptitude, acquisitional sequences, and psycholinguistic processes', in G. Granena, D. Jackson and Y. Yilmaz (eds) *Cognitive individual differences in L2 processing and acquisition*. Amsterdam: John Benjamins, 15–38.

Skinner, B. (1957) *Verbal Behaviour*. New York: Appleton.

Smyth, J. (1991) *Teachers as Collaborative Learners*. Milton Keynes: Open University Press.

Sowden, C. (2007) 'Culture and the "Good Teacher" in the English Language Classroom'. *ELT Journal*, 61/4: 304–10.

Sowden, C. (2008) 'There's More to Life than Politics'. *ELT Journal*, 62/3: 284–91.

Spolsky, B. (1989) *Conditions for Second Language Learning.* Oxford: OUP.

Spolsky, B., Green, J. and Read, J. (1974). *A Model for the Description, Analysis, and Perhaps Evaluation of Bilingual Education.* Navajo Reading Study Progress Report No. 23. Alberquerque, NM: University of New Mexico.

Starfield, S. (2016) 'English for Specific Purposes', in G. Hall (ed.) *The Routledge Handbook of English Language Teaching.* London: Routledge, 150–63.

Stern, H. (1983) *Fundamental Concepts of Language Teaching.* Oxford: OUP.

Stevick, E. (1976) 'English as an Alien Language', in J. Fanselow and R. Crymes (eds) *On TESOL 76.* Washington, DC: TESOL, Inc.

Stevick, E. (1980) *Teaching Languages: A Way and Ways.* Rowley, MA: Newbury House.

Strevens, P. (1980) 'The Paradox of Individualized Instruction: It Takes Better Teachers to Focus on the Learner', in H. Altman and C. James (eds) *Foreign Language Teaching: Meeting Individual Needs.* Oxford: Pergamon, 17–29.

Sunderland, J. (2004) 'Gender and Language Learning', in M. Byram (ed.) *Routledge Encyclopedia of Language Teaching and Learning.* London: Routledge, 229–32.

Swain, M. (1985) 'Communicative Competence: Some Roles of Comprehensible Input and Comprehensible Output in its Development', in S. Gass and C. Madden (eds) *Input and Second Language Acquisition.* Rowley, MA: Newbury House, 235–56.

Swain, M. (1995) 'Three Functions of Output in Second Language Learning', in G. Cook and B. Seidlhofer (eds) *Principle and Practice in Applied Linguistics.* Oxford: OUP, 125–44.

Swain, M. (2000) 'The Output Hypothesis and Beyond: Mediating Acquisition Through Collaborative Dialogue', in J. Lantolf (ed.) *Sociocultural Theory and Second Language Learning.* Oxford: OUP, 97–114.

Swan, M. (1992) 'The Textbook: Bridge or Wall?' *Applied Linguistics and Language Teaching,* 2/1: 32–5.

Swan, M. (1994) 'Design criteria for pedagogic language rules', in M. Bygate, A. Tonkyn and E. Williams (eds) *Grammar and the Language Teacher.* New York: Prentice Hall, 45–55.

Taylor, L. (2005) 'Washback and Impact'. *ELT Journal,* 59/2: 154–5.

Taylor, P. (1970) *How Teachers Plan their Courses.* Slough: National Federation for Educational Research in England and Wales.

Thornbury, S. (1991) 'Metaphors We Work by: EFL and its Metaphors'. *ELT Journal,* 45/3: 193–200.

Thornbury, S. (1999) *How to Teach Grammar.* London: Longman.

Thornbury, S. (2000) 'A Dogma for EFL'. *IATEFL Issues,* 153/2.

Thornbury, S. (2006) *An A-Z of ELT.* Oxford: Macmillan.

Thornbury, S. (2008) 'What Good is Second Language Acquisition Theory?' *English Teaching Professional,* 55: 4–6.

Thornbury, S. (2011) 'Language teaching methodology', in J. Simpson (ed.) *The Routledge Handbook of Applied Linguistics.* London: Routledge, 185–99.

Timmis, I. (2002) 'Native-speaker Norms and International English: A Class-room View'. *ELT Journal*, 56/3: 240–9.

Tollefson, J. (1995) *Power and Inequality in Language Education*. Cambridge: CUP.

Tomita, Y. and Spada, N. (2013) 'Form-focused instruction and learner invest-ment in L2 communication'. *Modern Language Journal*, 97/3: 591–610.

Tomlinson, B. (ed.) (1998) *Materials Development in Language Teaching*. Cambridge: CUP.

Toohey, K. (1998) 'Breaking Them up, Taking Them Away: ESL Students in Grade 1'. *TESOL Quarterly*, 32/1: 61–84.

Tsui, A. (1995) *Introducing Classroom Interaction*. London: Penguin.

Tudor, I. (1996) *Learner-centredness as Language Education*. Cambridge: CUP.

Tudor, I. (2001) *The Dynamics of the Language Classroom*. Cambridge: CUP.

Ur, P. (1996) *A Course in Language Teaching: Practice and Theory*. 1st edition. Cambridge: CUP.

Ur, P. (2012) *A Course in Language Teaching: Practice and Theory*. 2nd edition. Cambridge: CUP.

Van den Branden, K. (ed.) (2006) *Task-based language education: From theory to practice*. Cambridge: CUP.

Van den Branden, K. (2016) 'Task-based language teaching', in G. Hall (ed.) *The Routledge Handbook of English Language Teaching*. London: Routledge, 238–51.

van Lier, L. (1988a) *The Classroom and the Language Learner*. Harlow: Longman.

van Lier, L. (1988b) 'What's Wrong with Classroom Talk?' *Prospect*, 3: 267–83.

van Lier, L. (1996) *Interaction in the Language Curriculum*. London: Longman.

van Lier, L. (1997) 'Approaches to Observation in Classroom Research: Observation from an Ecological Perspective'. *TESOL Quarterly*, 31/4: 783–7.

van Lier, L. (2000) 'From Input to Affordance: Social-interactive Learning from an Ecological Perspective', in J. Lantolf (ed.) *Socio-cultural Theory and Second Language Learning*. Oxford: OUP, 245–60.

van Lier, L. (2001) 'Constraints and Resources in Classroom Talk: Issues of Equality and Symmetry', in C. Candlin and N. Mercer (eds) *English Teaching in its Social Context*. London: Routledge, 90–107.

Vygotsky, L. (1978) *Mind in Society: The Development of Higher Psych-ological Processes*. Cambridge, MA: Harvard University Press.

Wallace, M. (1998) *Action Research for Language Teachers*. Cambridge: CUP.

Walsh, S. (2006a) *Investigating Classroom Discourse*. London: Routledge.

Walsh, S. (2006b) 'Talking the Talk of the TESOL Classroom'. *ELT Journal*, 60/2: 133–41.

Walsh, S. (2011) *Exploring Classroom Discourse: Language in Action*. London: Routledge.

Walsh, S. and Li, L. (2016) 'Classroom talk, interaction and collaboration', in G. Hall (ed.) *The Routledge Handbook of English Language Teaching*. London: Routledge, 486–98.

Waters, A. (2007) 'ELT and "The Spirit of the Times"'. *ELT Journal*, 61/4: 353–9.

Waters, A. (2009) 'A Guide to Methodologia: Past, Present and Future'. *ELT Journal*, 63/2: 108–15.

Weihua, Y. (2004a) 'Grammar-translation Method', in M. Byram (ed.) *Routledge Encyclopedia of Language Teaching and Learning*. London: Routledge, 250–2.

Weihua, Y. (2004b) 'Direct Method', in M. Byram (ed.) *Routledge Encyclopedia of Language Teaching and Learning*. London: Routledge, 176–8.

Wen, Z. (2012) 'Foreign language aptitude'. *ELT Journal*, 66/2: 233–5.

Wen, Z., Biedroń, A. and Skehan, P. (2017) 'Foreign language aptitude theory: Yesterday, today and tomorrow'. *Language Teaching*, 50/1: 1–31.

Wenden, A. and Rubin, J. (eds) (1987) *Learner Strategies for Language Learning*. Englewood Cliffs, NJ: Prentice Hall.

Wenden, A. (1999) 'An Introduction to Metacognitive Knowledge and Beliefs in Language Learning: Beyond the Basics'. *System*, 27/4: 435–41.

Wenger, E. (1998) *Communities of Practice: Learning, Meaning and Identity*. Cambridge: CUP.

West, M. (1960) *Teaching English in difficult circumstances*. London: Longmans, Green. Reissued in R. C. Smith (ed.) *Teaching English as a Foreign Language*, 1936–1961, Vol. VI. London: Routledge.

White, C. (2008) 'Beliefs and Good Language Learners', in C. Griffiths (ed.) *Lessons from Good Language Learners*. Cambridge: CUP, 121–30.

White, L. (2003) *Second Language Acquisition and Universal Grammar*. Cambridge: CUP.

White, R. (1988) *The ELT Curriculum: Design, Innovation and Management*. Oxford: Blackwell.

White, R., Hockley, A., van der Horst Jansen, J. and Laughner, M. (2008) *From Teacher to Manager: Managing Language Teaching Organisations*. Cambridge: CUP.

Widdowson, H. (1987) 'The Roles of Teacher and Learner'. *ELT Journal*, 41/2: 83–8.

Widdowson, H. (1990) *Aspects of Language Teaching*. Oxford: OUP.

Widdowson, H. (1992) 'ELT and EL Teachers: Matters Arising'. *ELT Journal*, 46/4: 333–9.

Widdowson, H. (1998) 'Context, Community and Authentic Language'. *TESOL Quarterly*, 32/4: 705–16.

Widdowson, H. (2003) *Defining Issues in Language Teaching*. Oxford: OUP.

Widdowson, H. (2004) 'Skills and Knowledge in Language Learning', in M. Byram (ed.) *Routledge Encyclopedia of Language Teaching and Learning*. London: Routledge, 548–3.

Wilkins, D. (1976) *Notional Syllabuses*. Oxford: OUP.

Williams, M. and Burden, R. (1997) *Psychology for Language Teachers*. Cambridge: CUP.

Williams, M., Mercer, S., and Ryan, S. (2015) *Exploring Psychology in Language Teaching and Learning*. Oxford: OUP.

Willis, D. (1990) *The Lexical Syllabus: A New Approach to Language Teaching*. London: Collins.

Willis, D. with Jenkins, J. (1999) 'From Pronunciation to Lexicogrammar'. Talk given at International House Teacher Training Conference, London, February 1999.

Willis, J. (1996) *A Framework for Task-Based Learning*. London: Longman.

Woods, P. (2006) '"The Hedgehog and the Fox": Two Approaches to English for the Military', in J. Edge (ed.) *(Re-)Locating TESOL in an Age of Empire*. Basingstoke: Palgrave Macmillan, 208–26.

Wright, T. (1987) *Roles of Teacher and Learners*. Oxford: OUP.

Wright, T. (2005) *Classroom Management in Language Education*. Basingstoke: Palgrave Macmillan.

Wright, T. (2006) 'Managing Classroom Life', in S. Gieve and I. Miller (eds) *Understanding the Language Classroom*. Basingstoke: Palgrave Macmillan, 64–87.

Wright, T. (2012) 'Managing the Classroom', in A. Burns and J. Richards (eds) *The Cambridge Guide to Pedagogy and Practice in Second Language Teaching*. Cambridge: CUP, 60–7.

Yates, G. (2000) 'Applying Learning Style Research in the Classroom: Some Cautions and the Way Ahead', in E. Riding and S. Rayner (eds) *Interpersonal Perspectives on Individual Differences (Vol. 1: Cognitive Styles)*. Stamford, CT: Ablex, 347–64.

Yazigi, R. (2001) *A Study of Sharing Time in an L2 Second Grade Classroom*. Unpublished Master's thesis, University of Newcastle upon Tyne, England.

Ylimaki, R. (2013) 'Create a comprehensive, rigorous and coherent curricular program', in R. Ylimaki (ed.) *The new instructional leadership: ISLLC standard two*. New York: Routledge, 89–103.

Yorio, C. (1986) 'Consumerism in Second Language Teaching and Learning'. *Canadian Modern Language Review*, 42/3: 668–87.

Index

Page numbers marked 'g' refer to glossary entries.